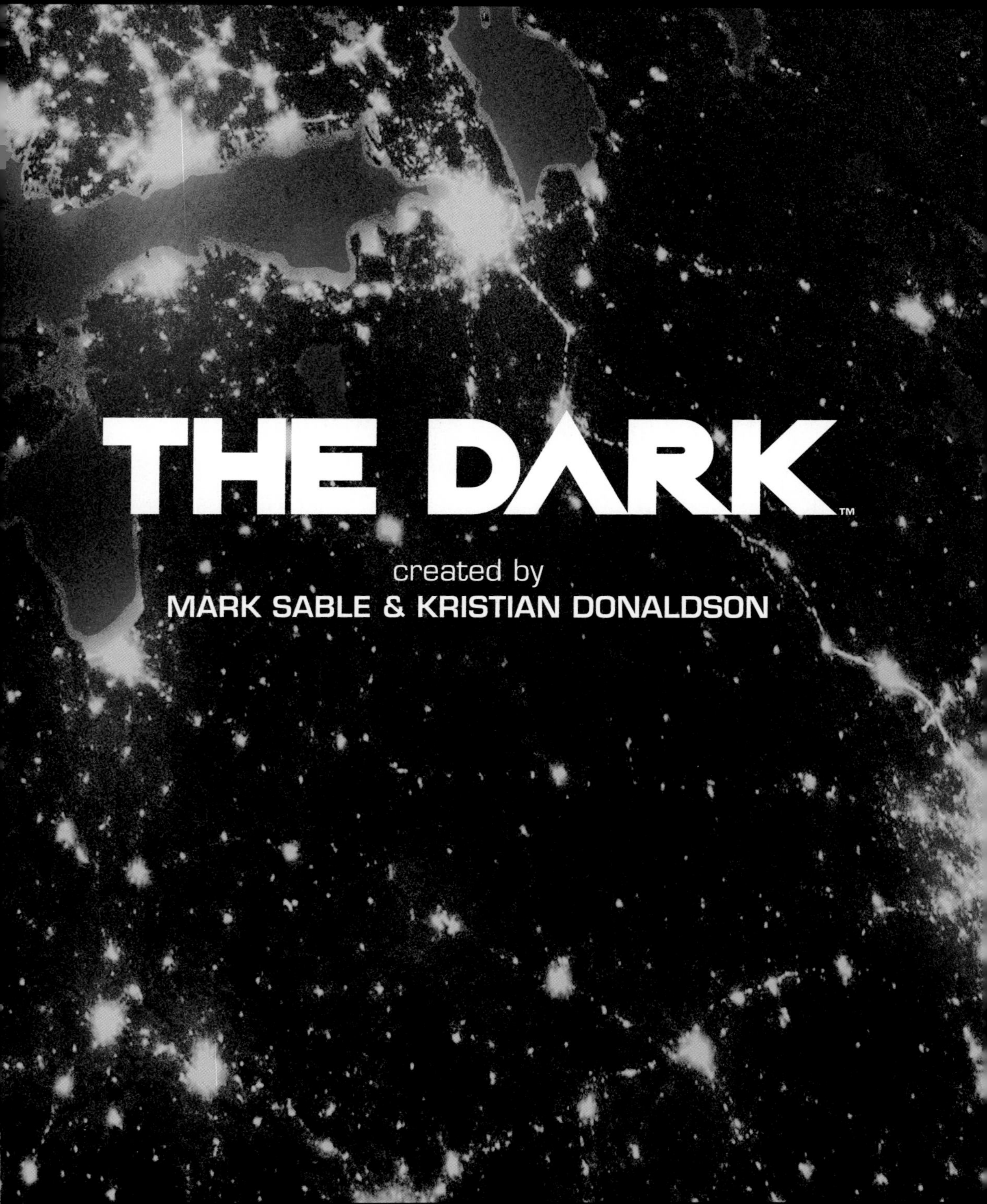

THE DARK™

created by
MARK SABLE & KRISTIAN DONALDSON

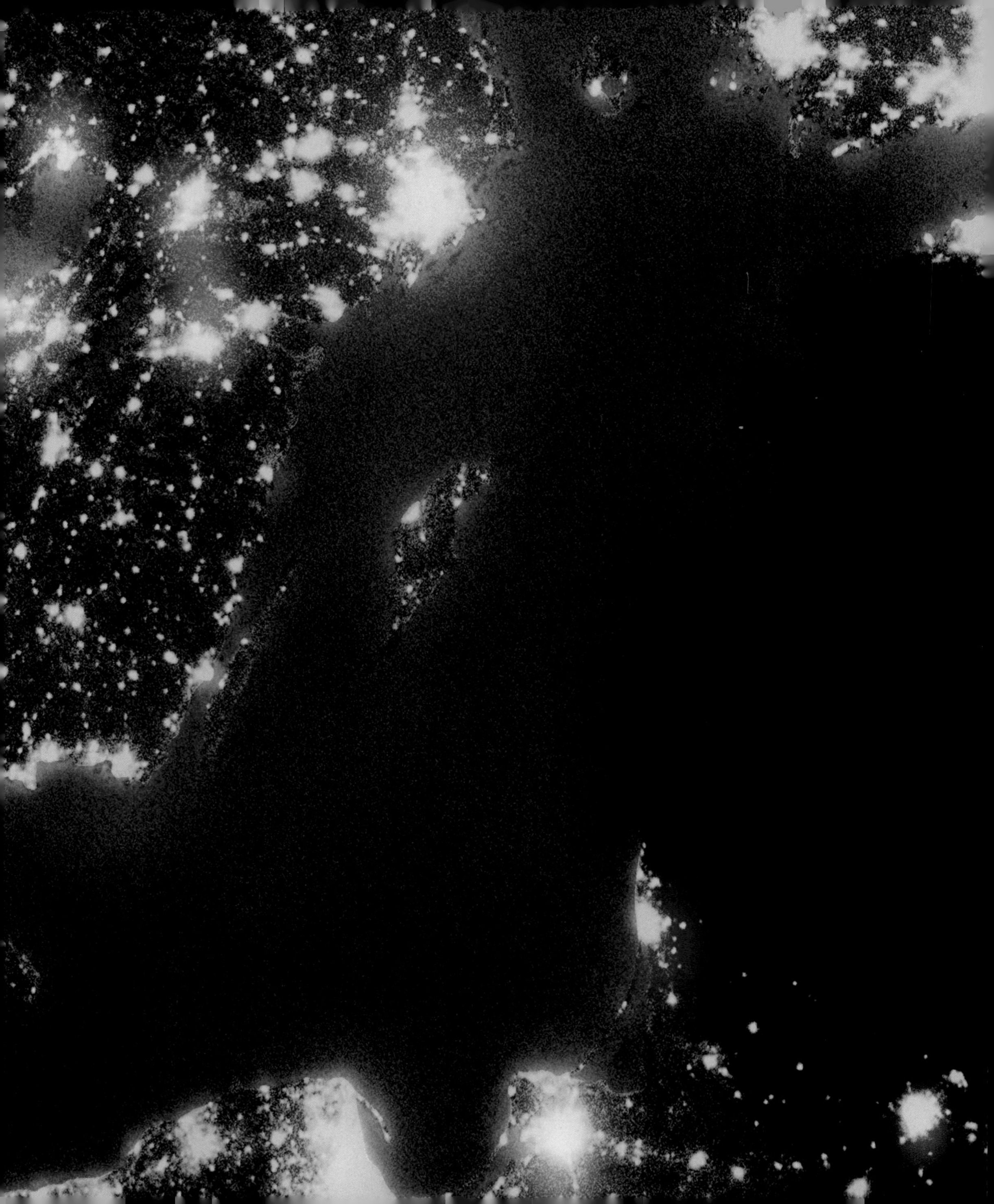

THE DARK ™

writer
MARK SABLE

artist
KRISTIAN DONALDSON

colorist
LEE LOUGHRIDGE

color assistant
DANIEL LEE

letterer & designer
THOMAS MAUER

editors
WILL DENNIS
IVAN SALAZAR

DARK HORSE BOOKS

ORIGINAL PUBLICATION TEAM
editor **Will Dennis**
editorial consultant **Mey Rude**

DARK HORSE TEAM
president and publisher **Mike Richardson**
editor **Daniel Chabon**
assistant editors **Chuck Howitt and Konner Knudsen**
designer **Brennan Thome**
digital art technician **Jason Rickerd**

Special Thanks:
Ivan Salazar
Chip Mosher
David Steinberger
August Cole

Published by Dark Horse Books
A division of Dark Horse Comics LLC
10956 SE Main Street
Milwaukie, OR 97222

First edition: December 2021
Trade paperback ISBN: 978-1-50672-459-1

1 3 5 7 9 10 8 6 4 2
Printed in China

Comic Shop Locator Service: comicshoplocator.com

The Dark™

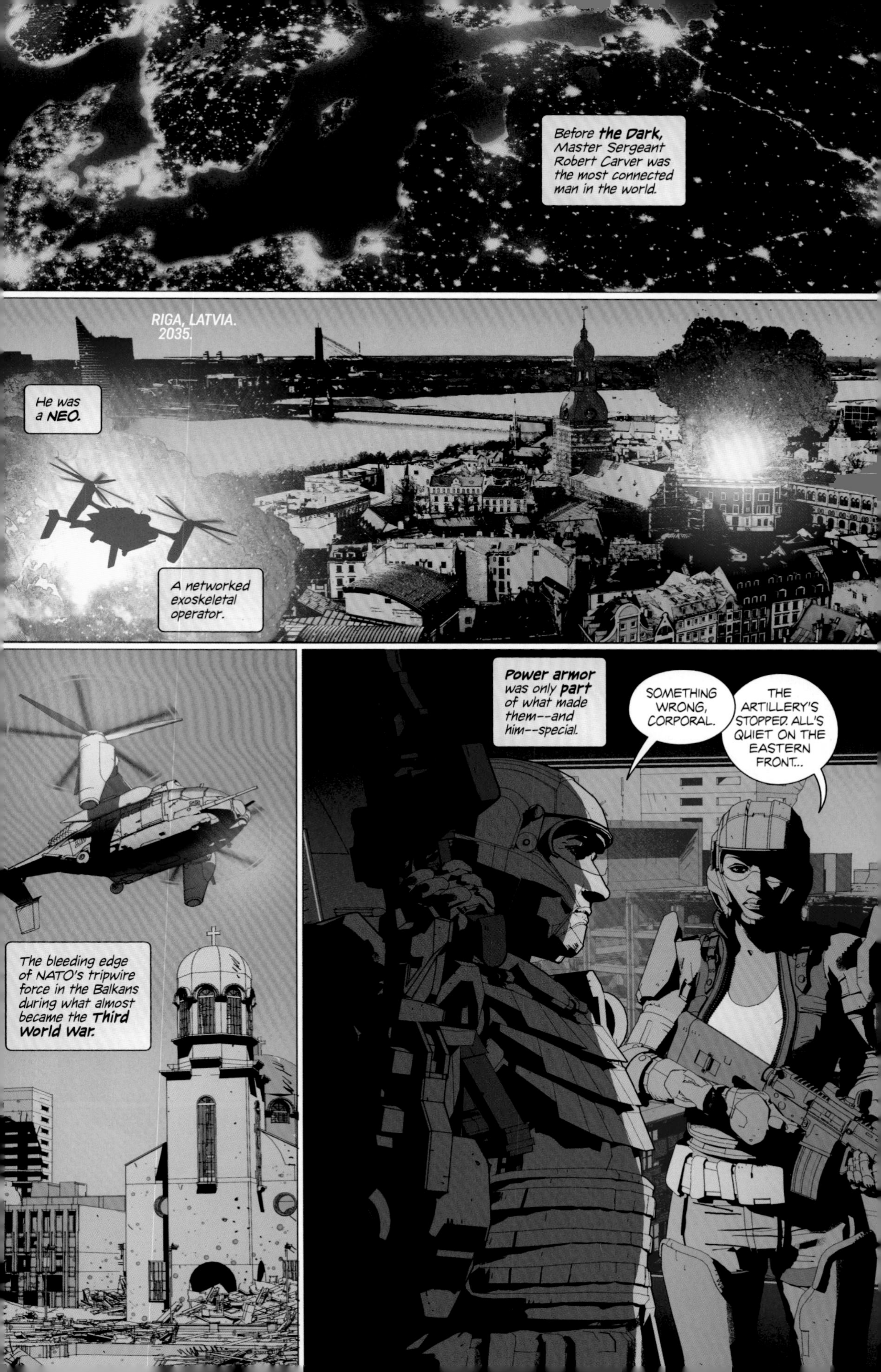

Before **the Dark,** Master Sergeant Robert Carver was the most connected man in the world.
RIGA, LATVIA. 2035.
He was a **NEO.**
A networked exoskeletal operator.
The bleeding edge of NATO's tripwire force in the Balkans during what almost became the **Third World War.**
Power armor was only **part** of what made them--and him--special.
SOMETHING WRONG, CORPORAL.
THE ARTILLERY'S STOPPED. ALL'S QUIET ON THE EASTERN FRONT...

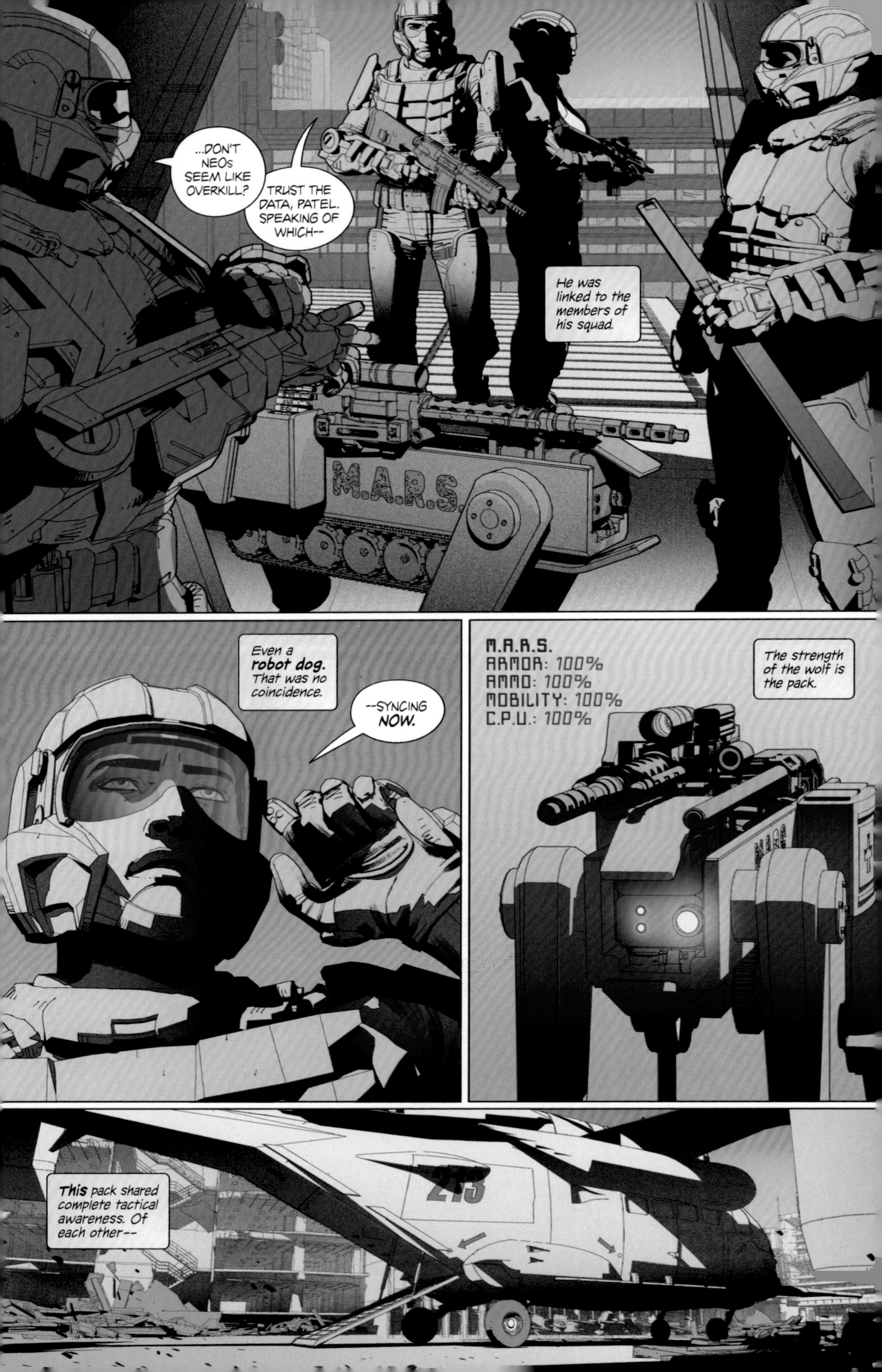

...DON'T NEOs SEEM LIKE OVERKILL?
TRUST THE DATA, PATEL. SPEAKING OF WHICH--
He was linked to the members of his squad.
M.A.R.S.
Even a **robot dog.** That was no coincidence.
--SYNCING **NOW.**
M.A.R.S.
ARMOR: 100%
AMMO: 100%
MOBILITY: 100%
C.P.U.: 100%
The strength of the wolf is the pack.
This pack shared complete tactical awareness. Of each other--

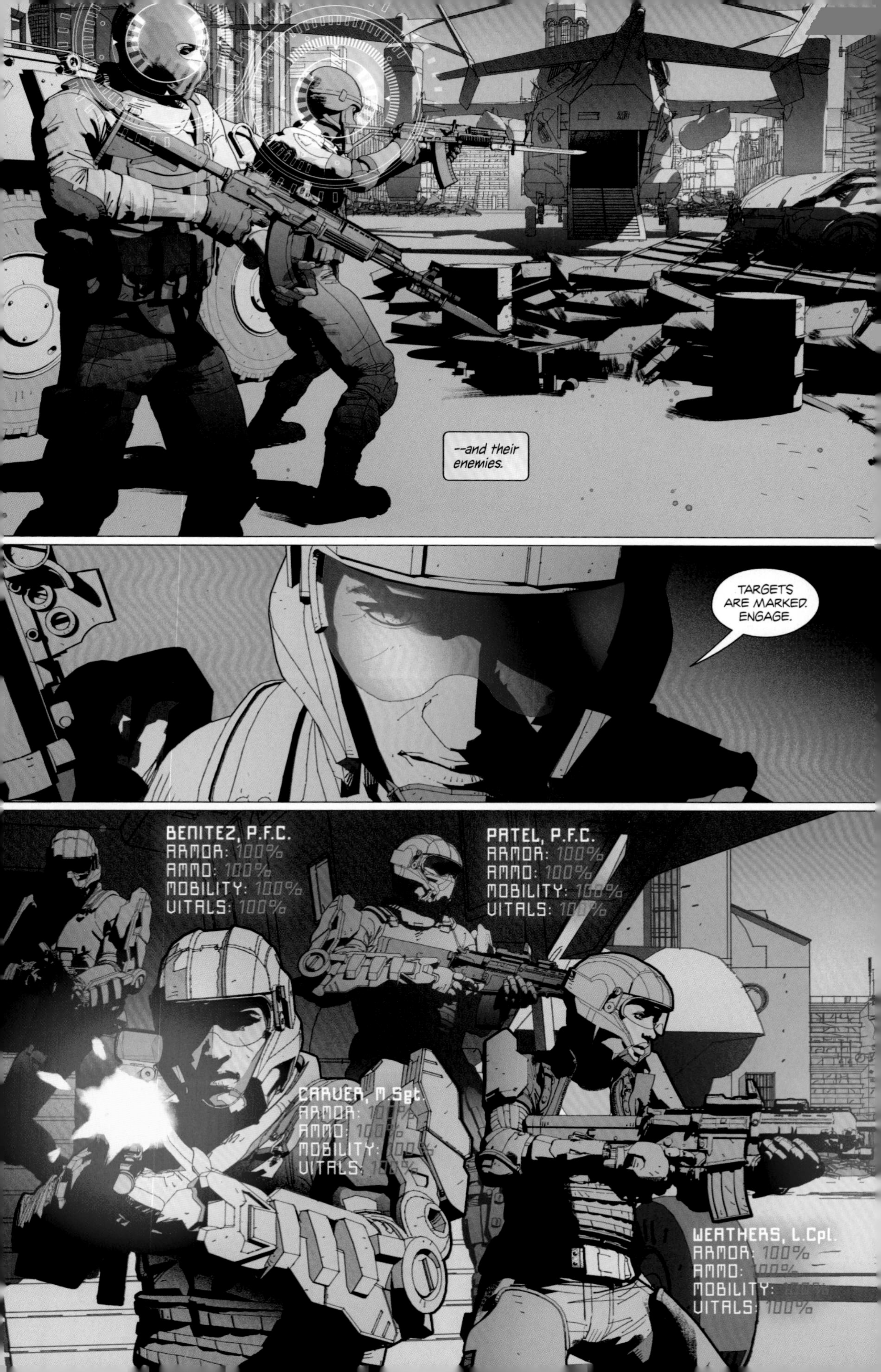
--and their enemies.
TARGETS ARE MARKED. ENGAGE.
BENITEZ, P.F.C.
ARMOR: 100%
AMMO: 100%
MOBILITY: 100%
VITALS: 100%
PATEL, P.F.C.
ARMOR: 100%
AMMO: 100%
MOBILITY: 100%
VITALS: 100%
CARVER, M.Sgt.
ARMOR: 100%
AMMO: 100%
MOBILITY: 100%
VITALS: 100%
WEATHERS, L.Cpl.
ARMOR: 100%
AMMO: 100%
MOBILITY: 100%
VITALS: 100%

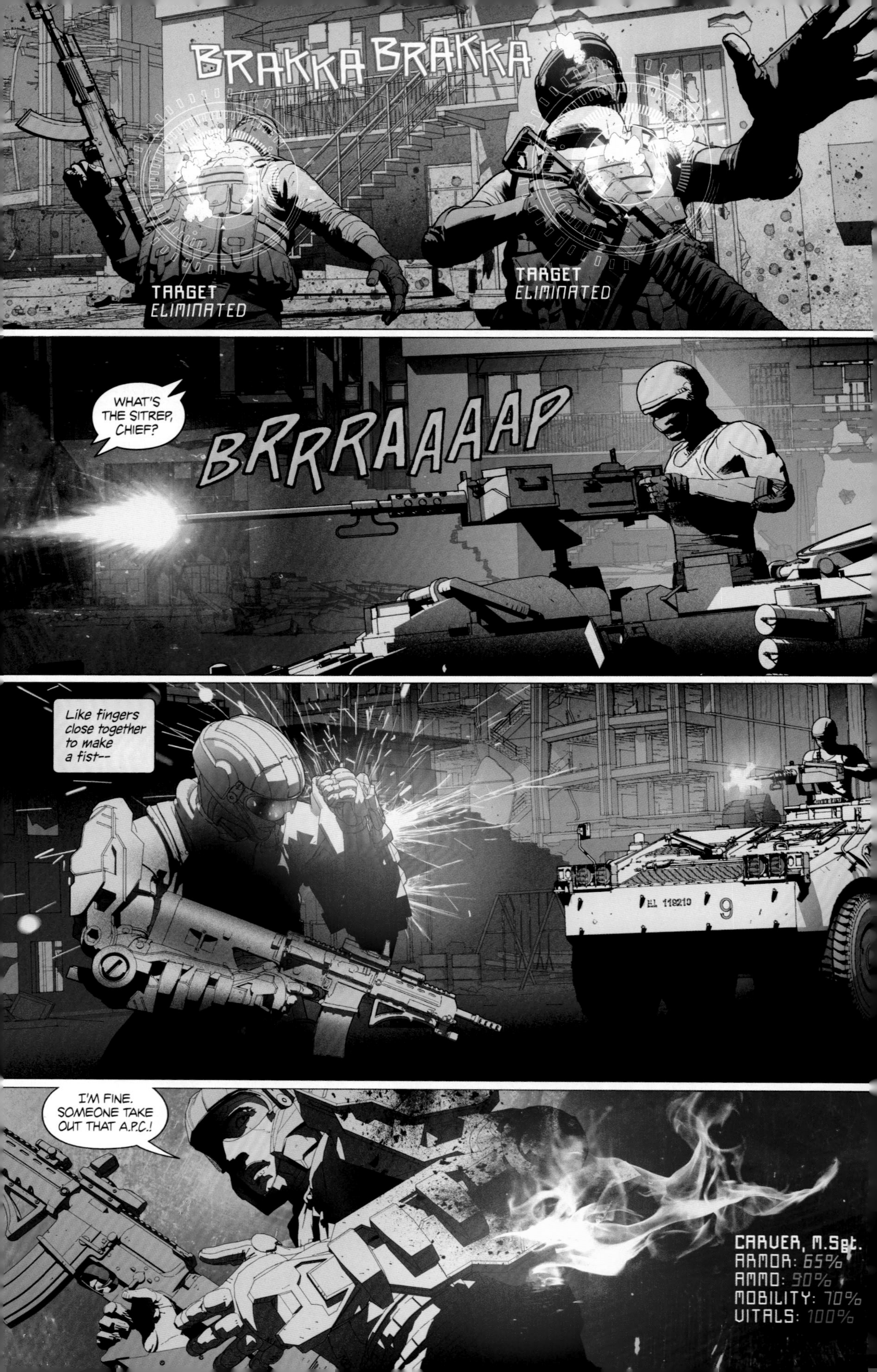
BRAKKA BRAKKA
TARGET ELIMINATED
TARGET ELIMINATED
WHAT'S THE SITREP, CHIEF?
BRRRAAAAP
Like fingers close together to make a fist--
EL 118210
9
I'M FINE. SOMEONE TAKE OUT THAT A.P.C.!
CARVER, M.Sgt.
ARMOR: 65%
AMMO: 90%
MOBILITY: 70%
VITALS: 100%

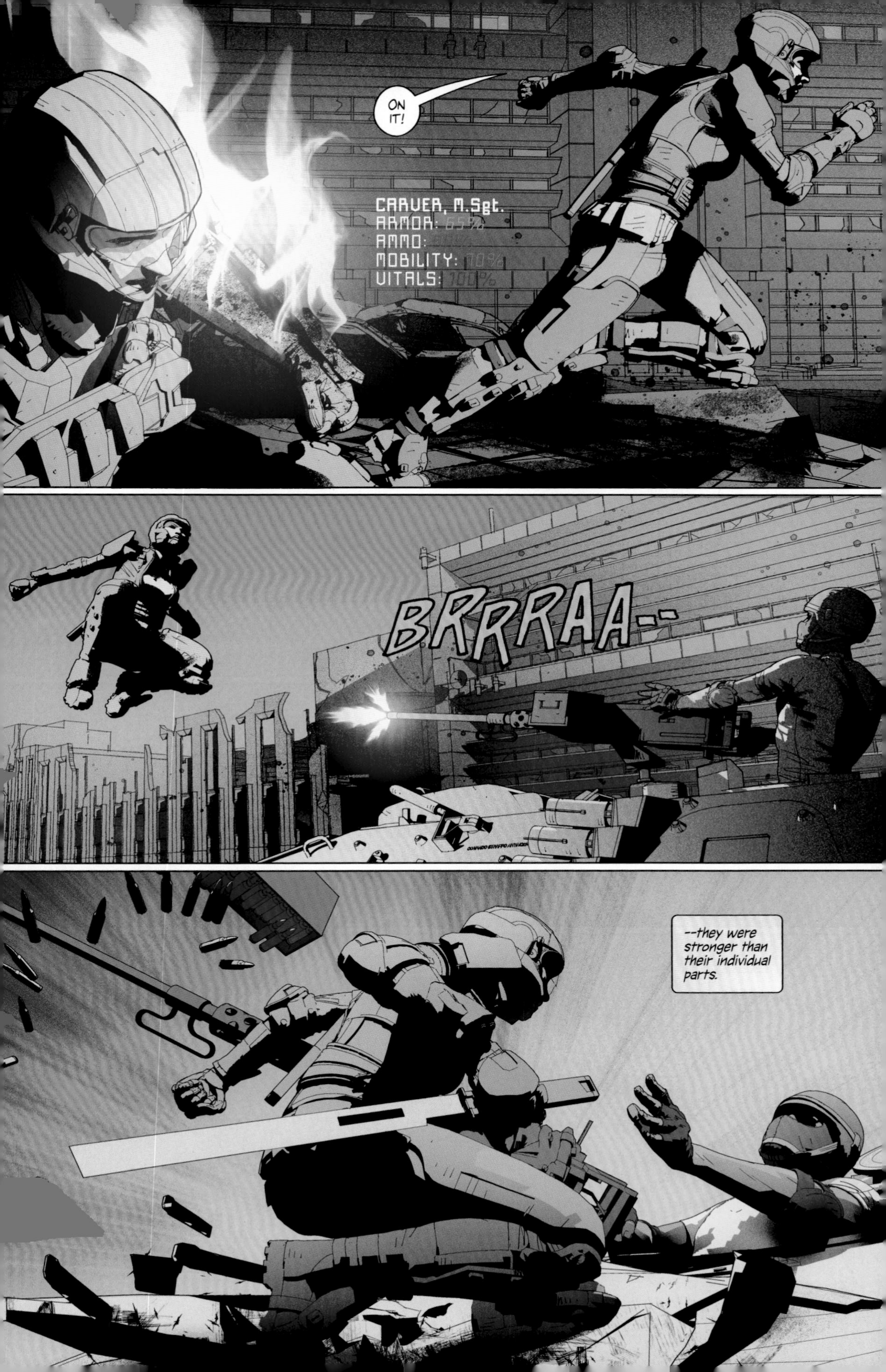
ON IT!
CARVER, M.Sgt.
ARMOR: 65%
AMMO:
MOBILITY:
VITALS: 100%
BRRRAA--
--they were stronger than their individual parts.

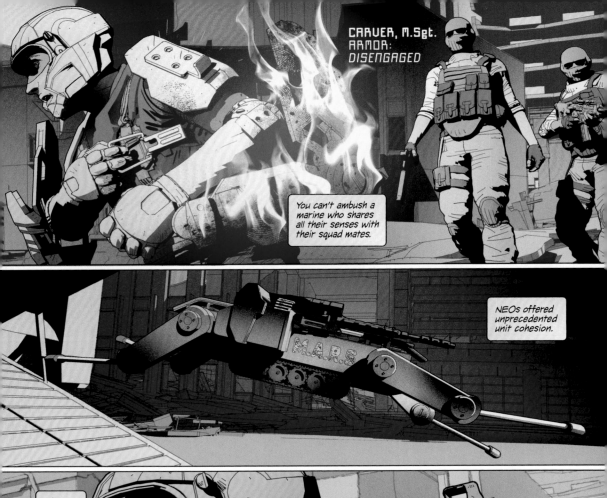

CARVER, M.Sgt.
ARMOR:
DISENGAGED

You can't ambush a marine who shares all their senses with their squad mates.

NEOs offered unprecedented unit cohesion.

They had each other's backs.

Literally.

BRRRAAAAP

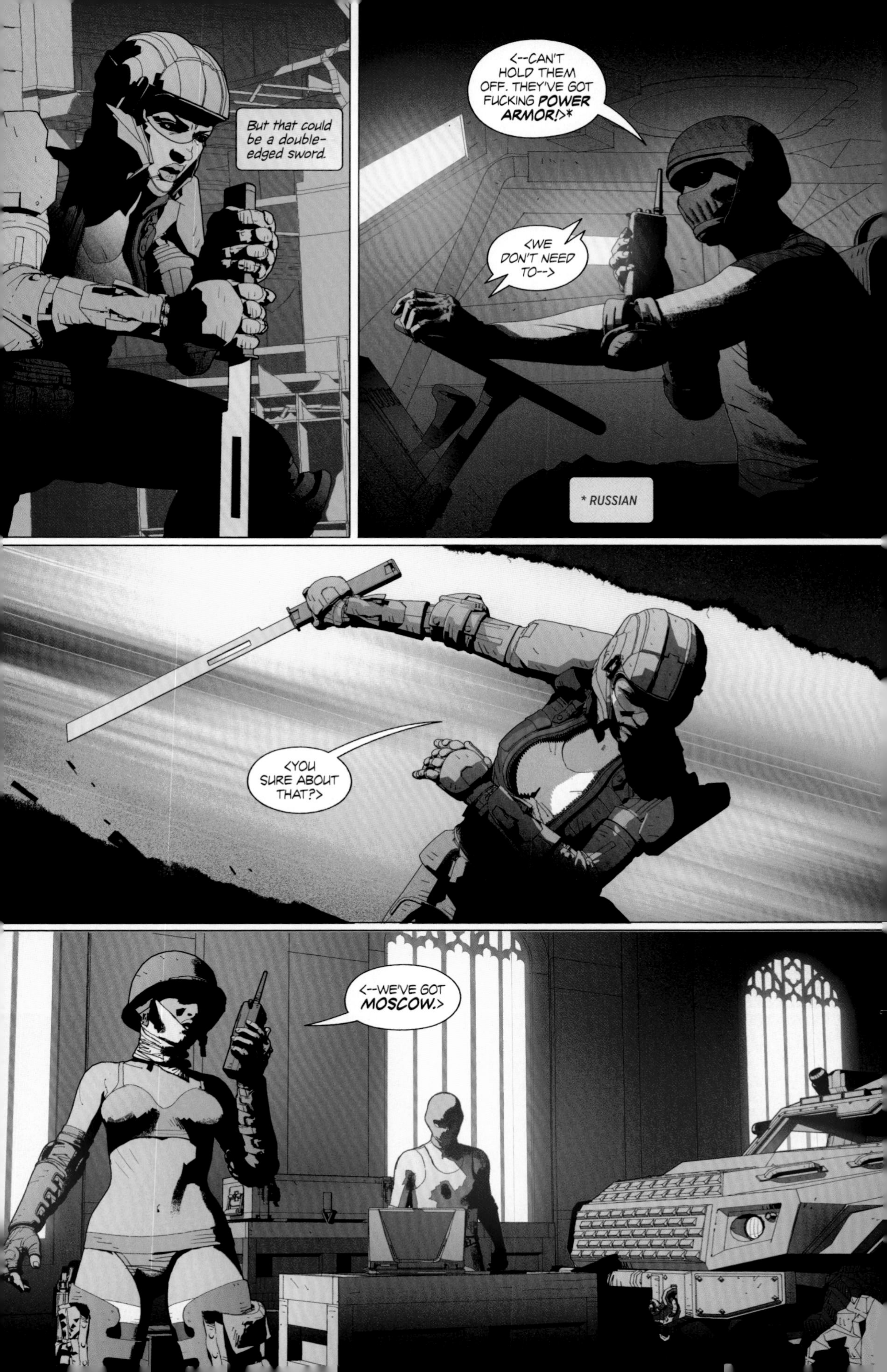
But that could be a double-edged sword.
<--CAN'T HOLD THEM OFF. THEY'VE GOT FUCKING **POWER ARMOR!**>*
<WE DON'T NEED TO-->
* RUSSIAN
<YOU SURE ABOUT THAT?>
<--WE'VE GOT **MOSCOW.**>

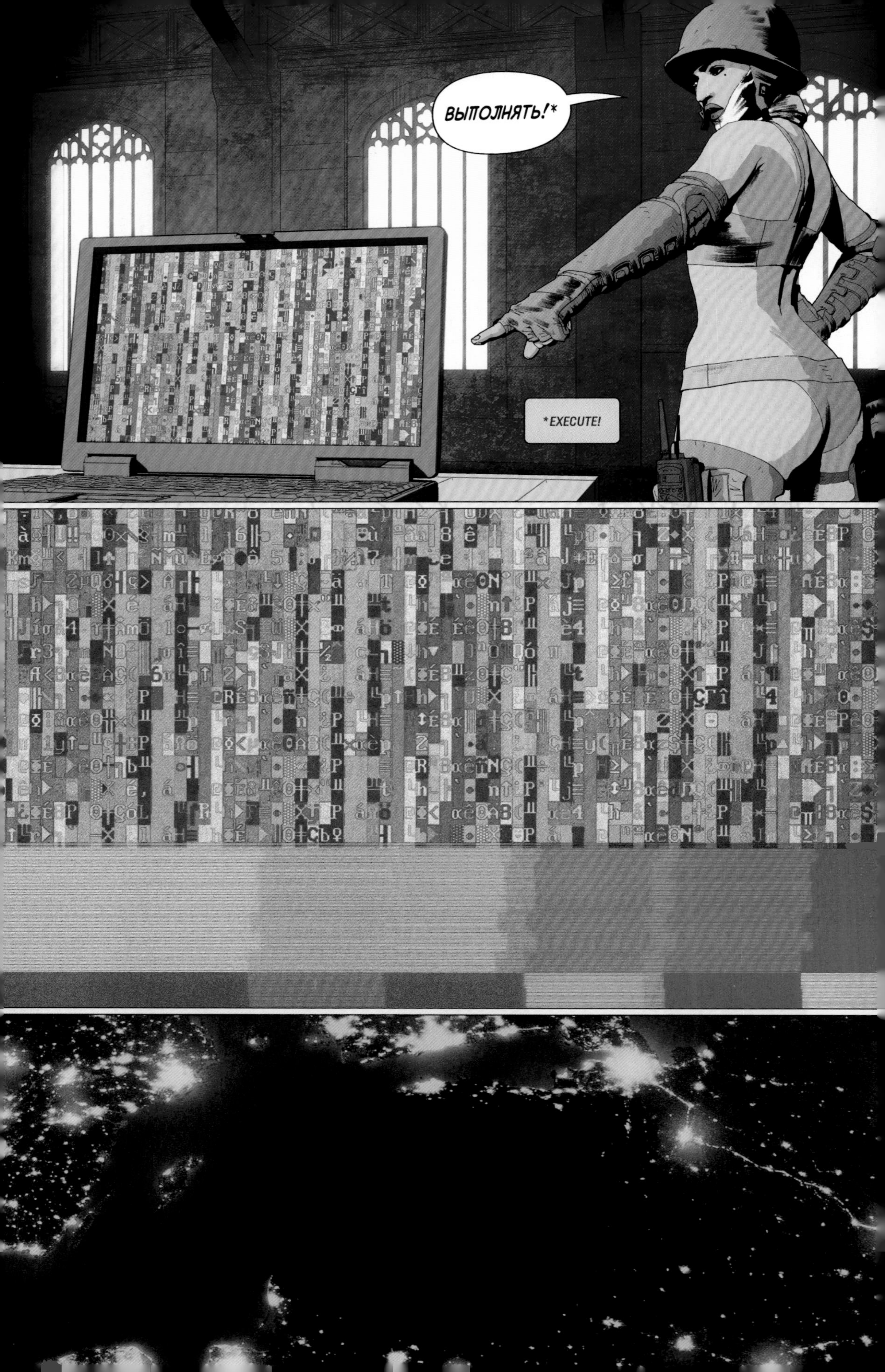
ВЫПОЛНЯТЬ!*
*EXECUTE!

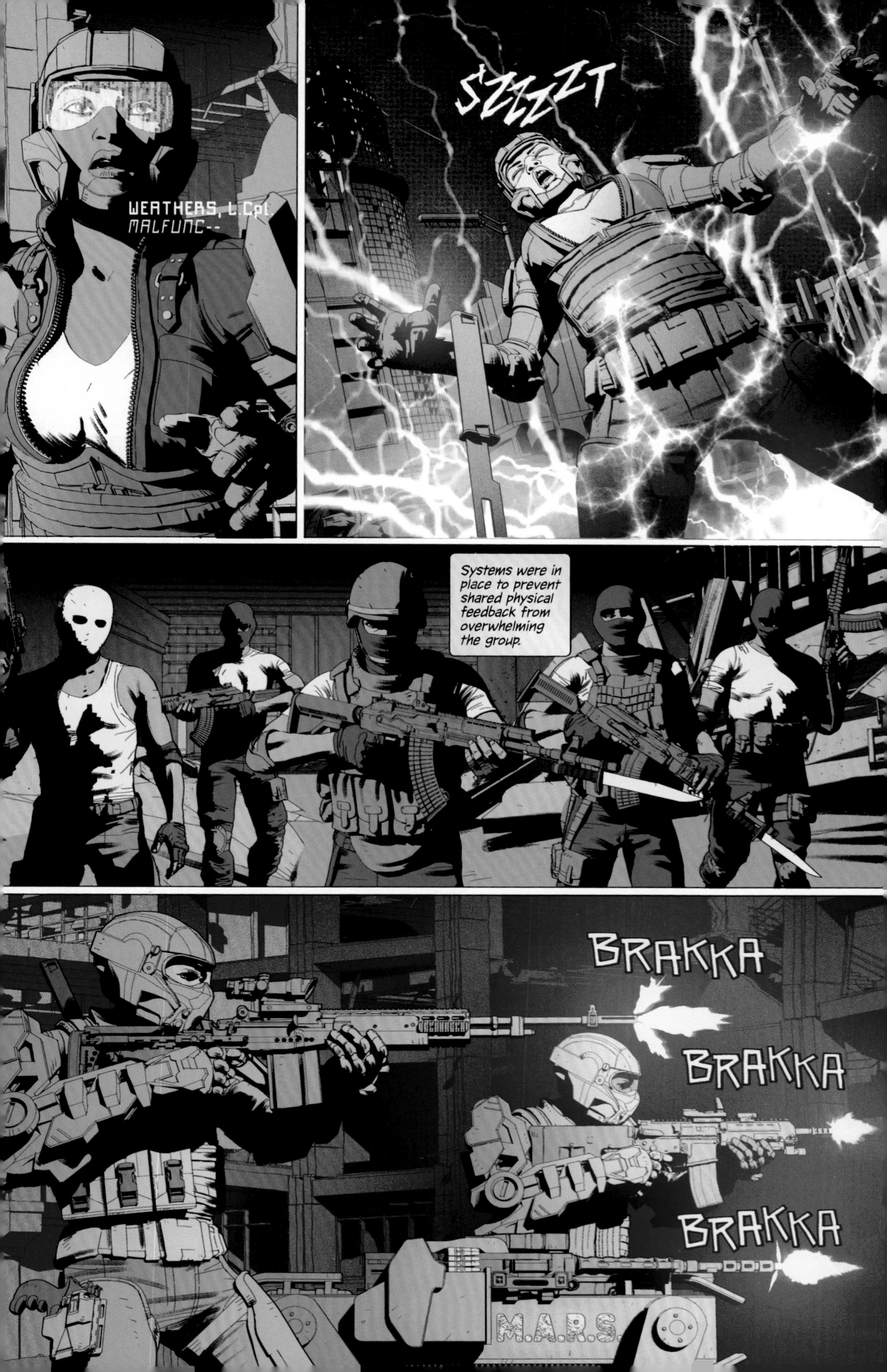
WEATHERS, L.Cpl.
MALFUNC--
SZZZZT
Systems were in place to prevent shared physical feedback from overwhelming the group.
BRAKKA
BRAKKA
BRAKKA
M.A.R.S.

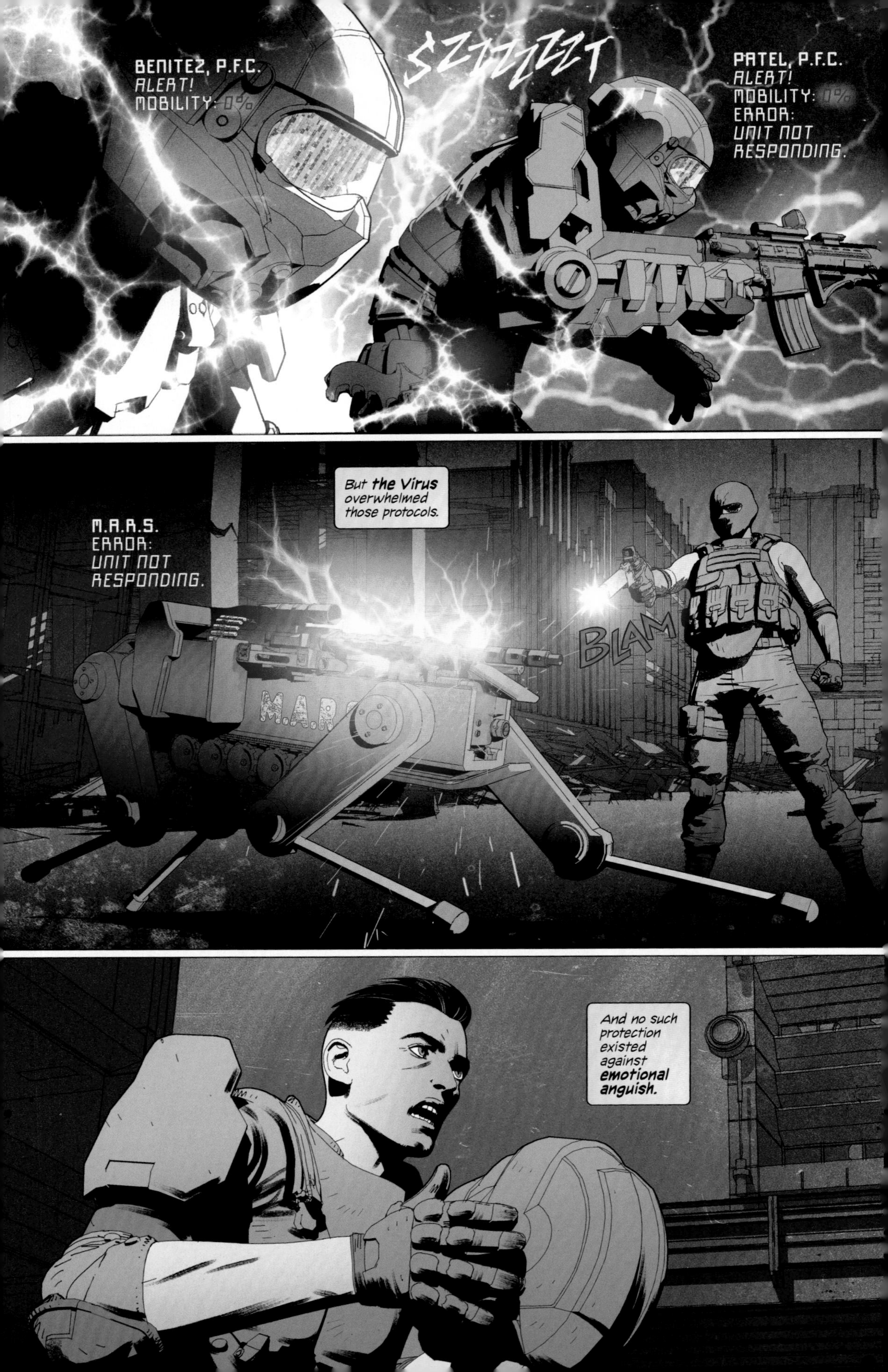
BENITEZ, P.F.C.
ALERT!
MOBILITY: 0%
SZZZZZZZT
PATEL, P.F.C.
ALERT!
MOBILITY: 0%
ERROR:
UNIT NOT
RESPONDING.
But the Virus overwhelmed those protocols.
M.A.R.S.
ERROR:
UNIT NOT
RESPONDING.
BLAM
And no such protection existed against emotional anguish.

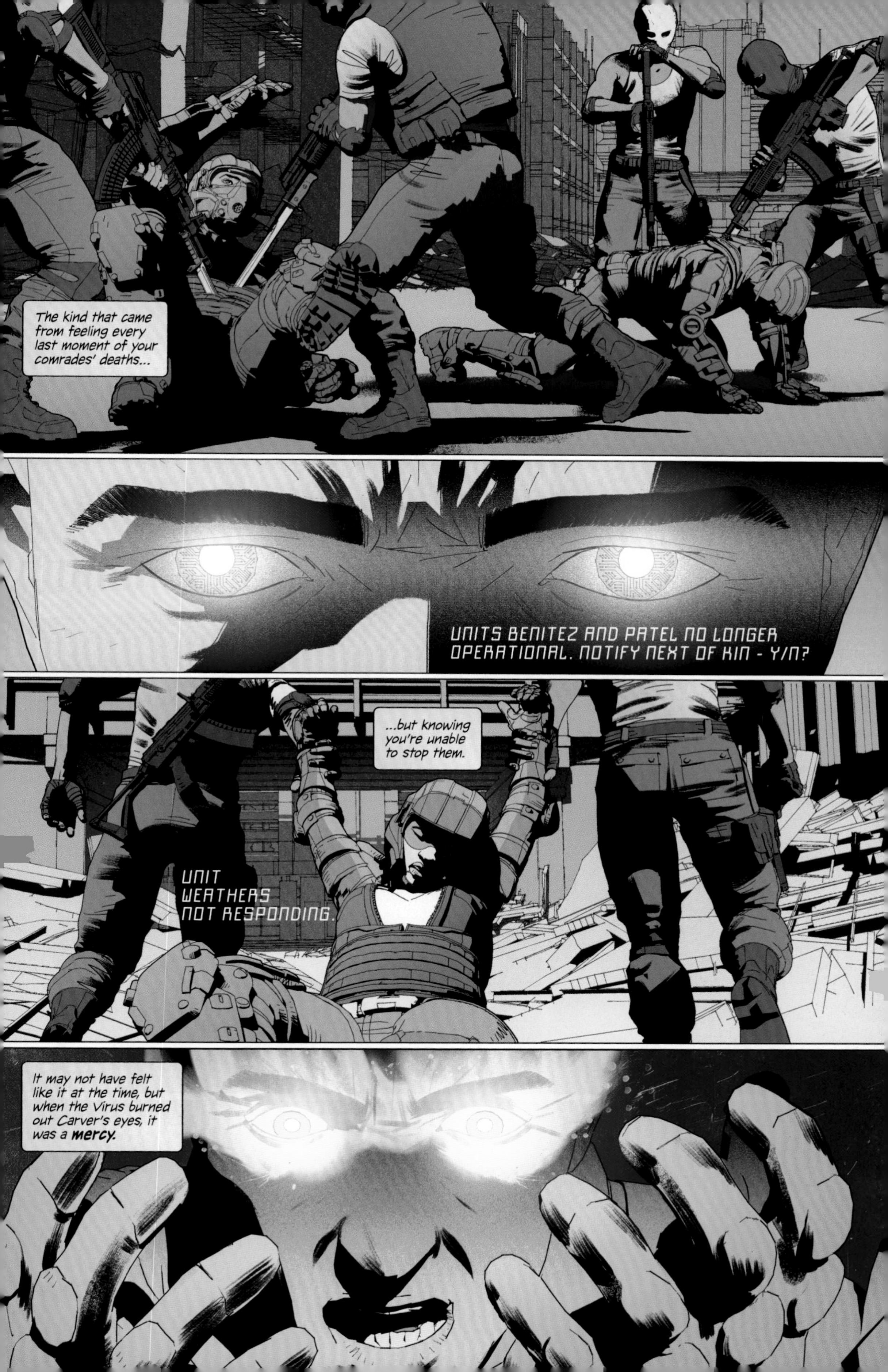
The kind that came from feeling every last moment of your comrades' deaths...
UNITS BENITEZ AND PATEL NO LONGER OPERATIONAL. NOTIFY NEXT OF KIN - Y/N?
...but knowing you're unable to stop them.
UNIT WEATHERS NOT RESPONDING.
It may not have felt like it at the time, but when the Virus burned out Carver's eyes, it was a mercy.

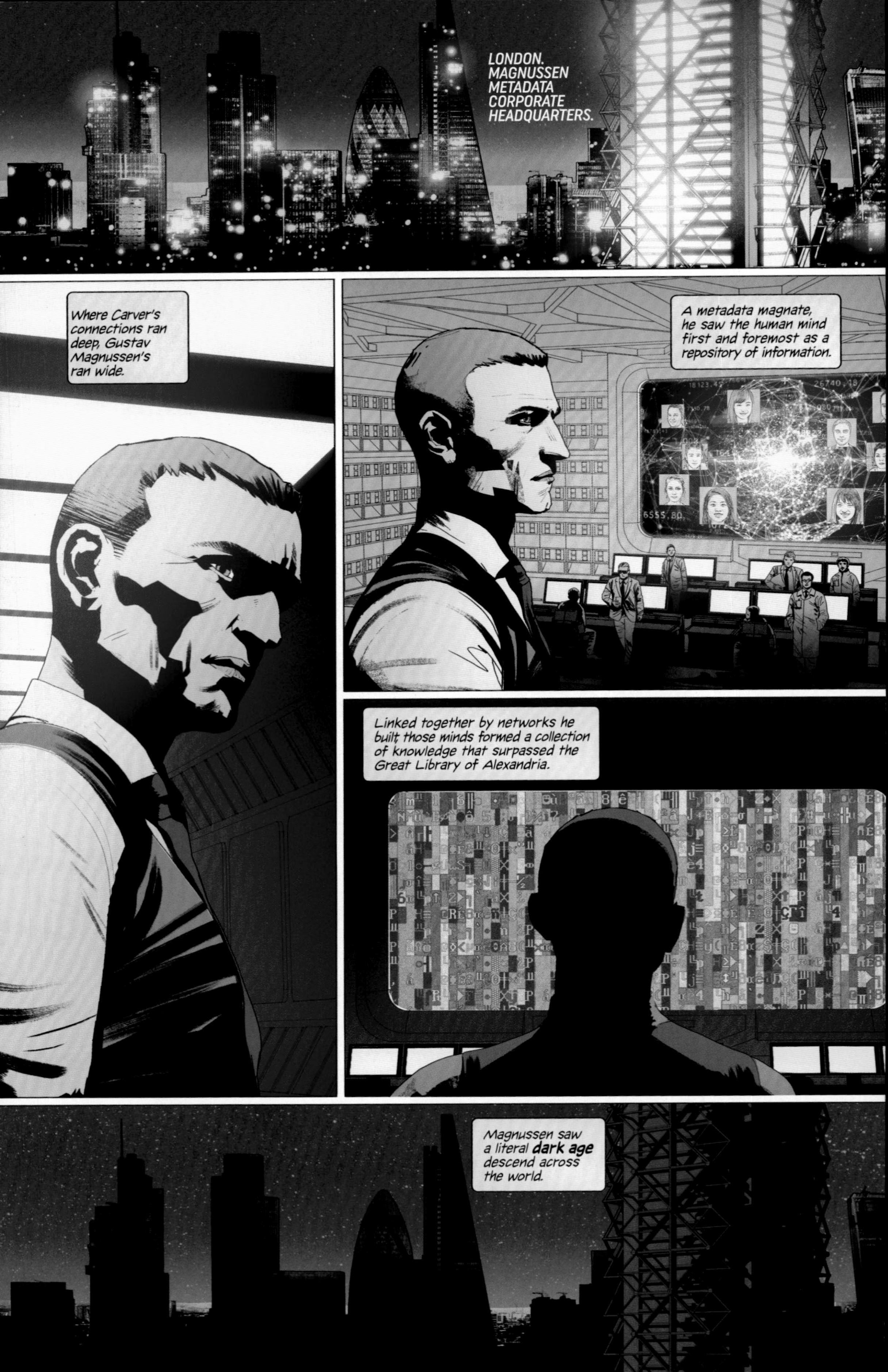
LONDON. MAGNUSSEN METADATA CORPORATE HEADQUARTERS.
Where Carver's connections ran deep, Gustav Magnussen's ran wide.
A metadata magnate, he saw the human mind first and foremost as a repository of information.
Linked together by networks he built those minds formed a collection of knowledge that surpassed the Great Library of Alexandria.
Magnussen saw a literal **dark age** descend across the world.

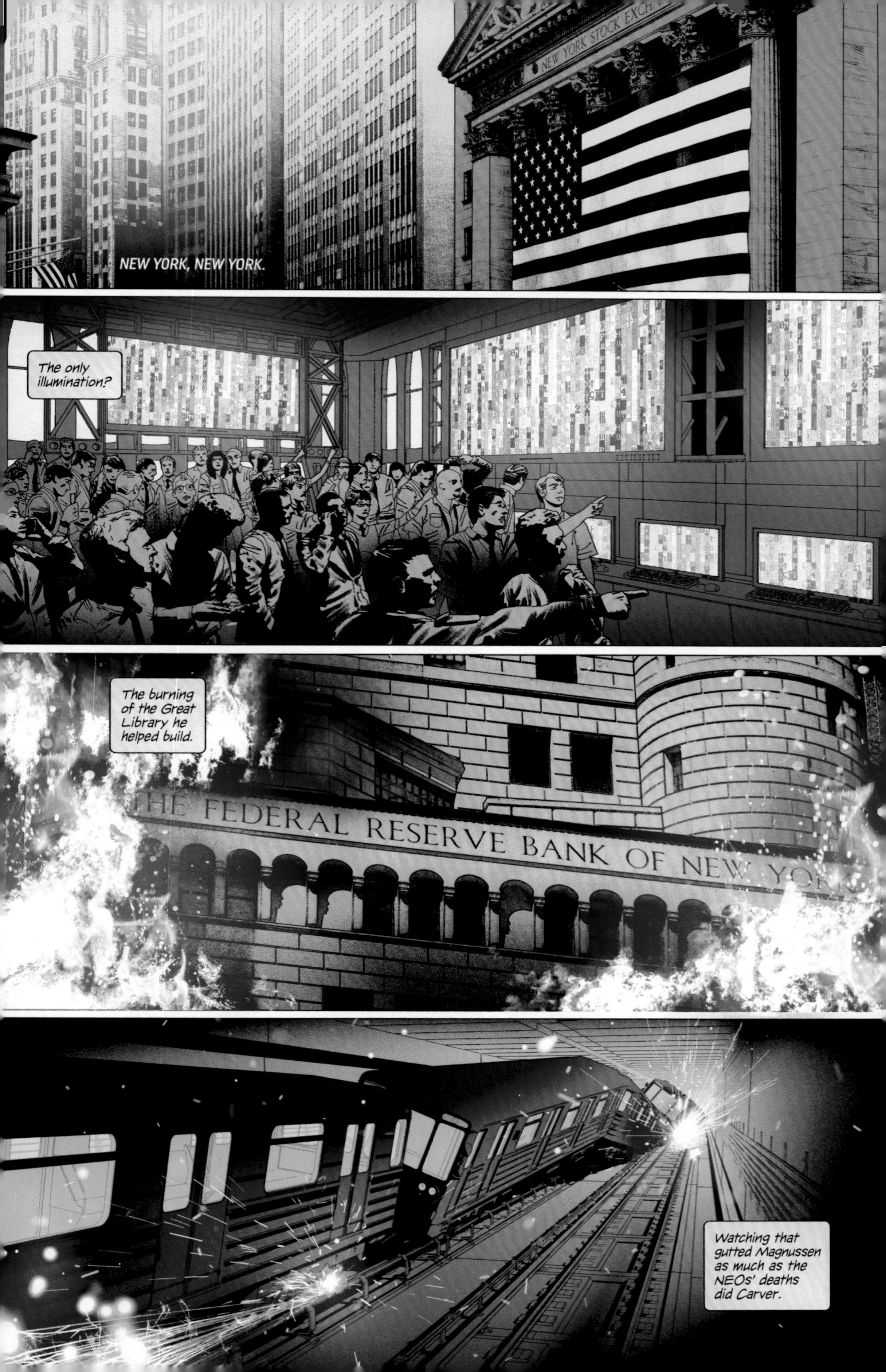
NEW YORK STOCK EXCH
NEW YORK, NEW YORK.
The only illumination?
The burning of the Great Library he helped build.
THE FEDERAL RESERVE BANK OF NEW YORK
Watching that gutted Magnussen as much as the NEOs' deaths did Carver.

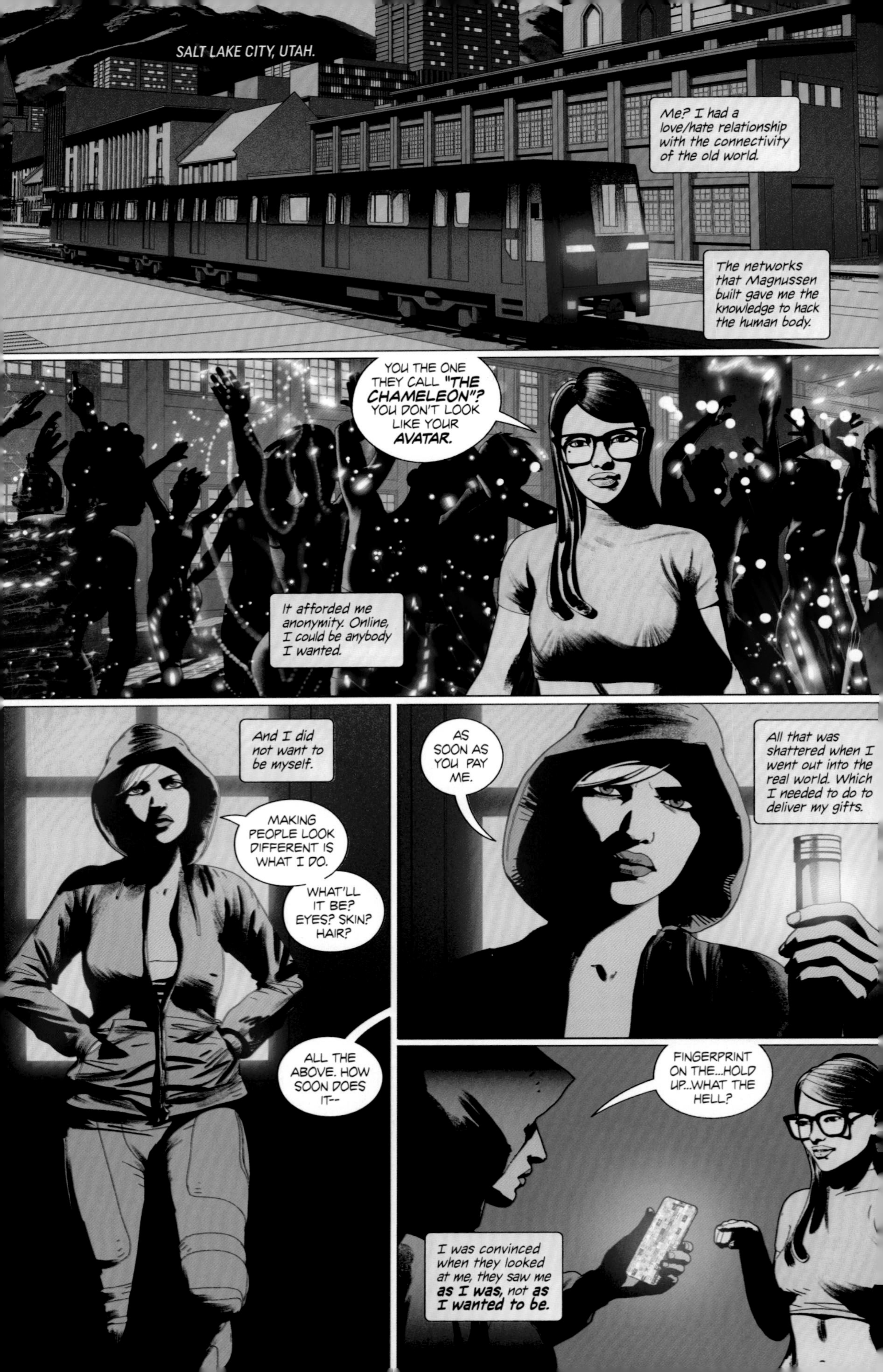
SALT LAKE CITY, UTAH.
Me? I had a love/hate relationship with the connectivity of the old world.
The networks that Magnussen built gave me the knowledge to hack the human body.
YOU THE ONE THEY CALL "THE CHAMELEON"? YOU DON'T LOOK LIKE YOUR AVATAR.
It afforded me anonymity. Online, I could be anybody I wanted.
And I did not want to be myself.
MAKING PEOPLE LOOK DIFFERENT IS WHAT I DO.
WHAT'LL IT BE? EYES? SKIN? HAIR?
ALL THE ABOVE. HOW SOON DOES IT--
AS SOON AS YOU PAY ME.
All that was shattered when I went out into the real world. Which I needed to do to deliver my gifts.
FINGERPRINT ON THE...HOLD UP...WHAT THE HELL?
I was convinced when they looked at me, they saw me as I was, not as I wanted to be.

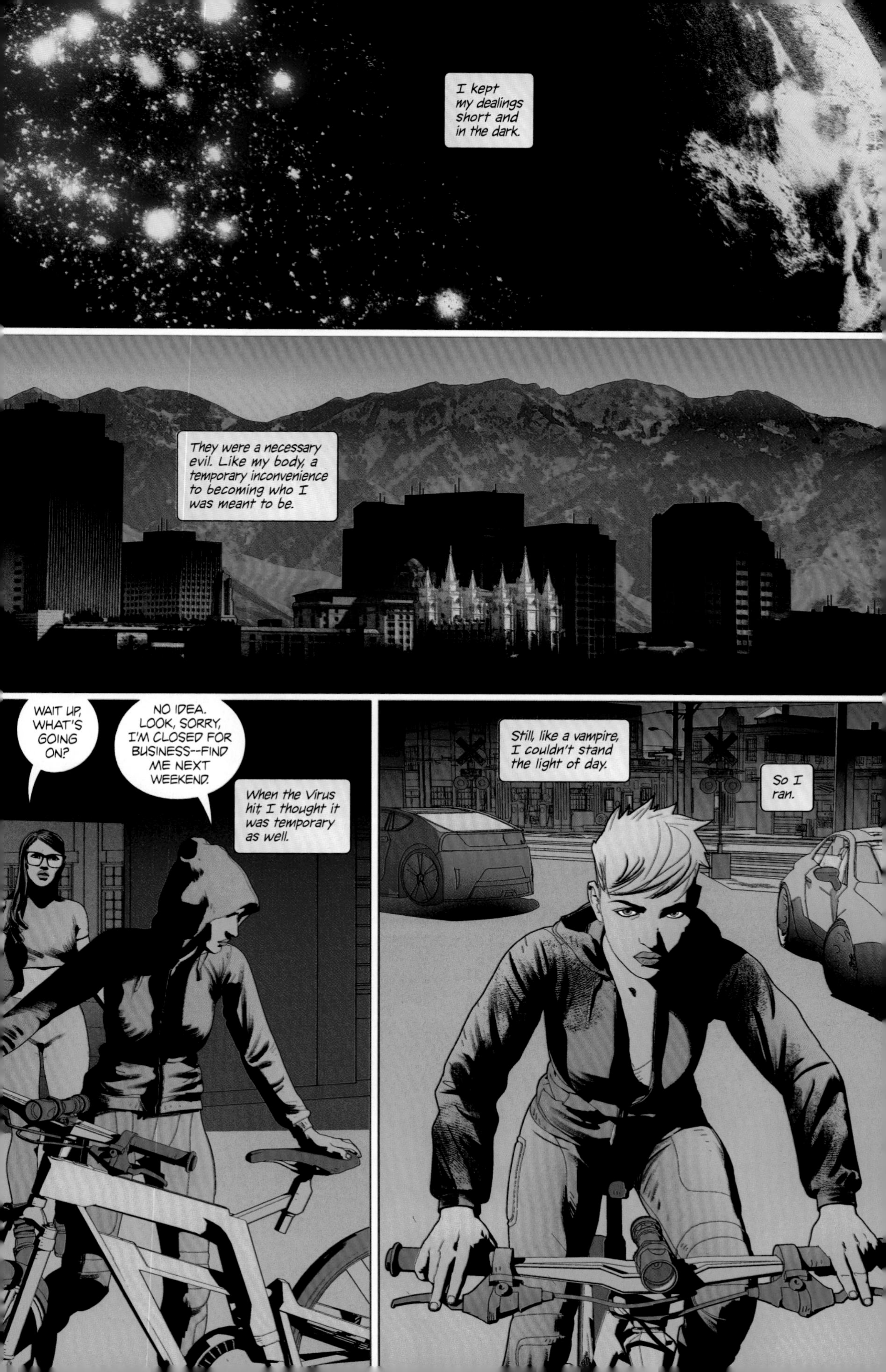
I kept my dealings short and in the dark.
They were a necessary evil. Like my body, a temporary inconvenience to becoming who I was meant to be.
WAIT UP, WHAT'S GOING ON?
NO IDEA. LOOK, SORRY, I'M CLOSED FOR BUSINESS--FIND ME NEXT WEEKEND.
When the Virus hit, I thought it was temporary as well.
Still, like a vampire, I couldn't stand the light of day.
So I ran.

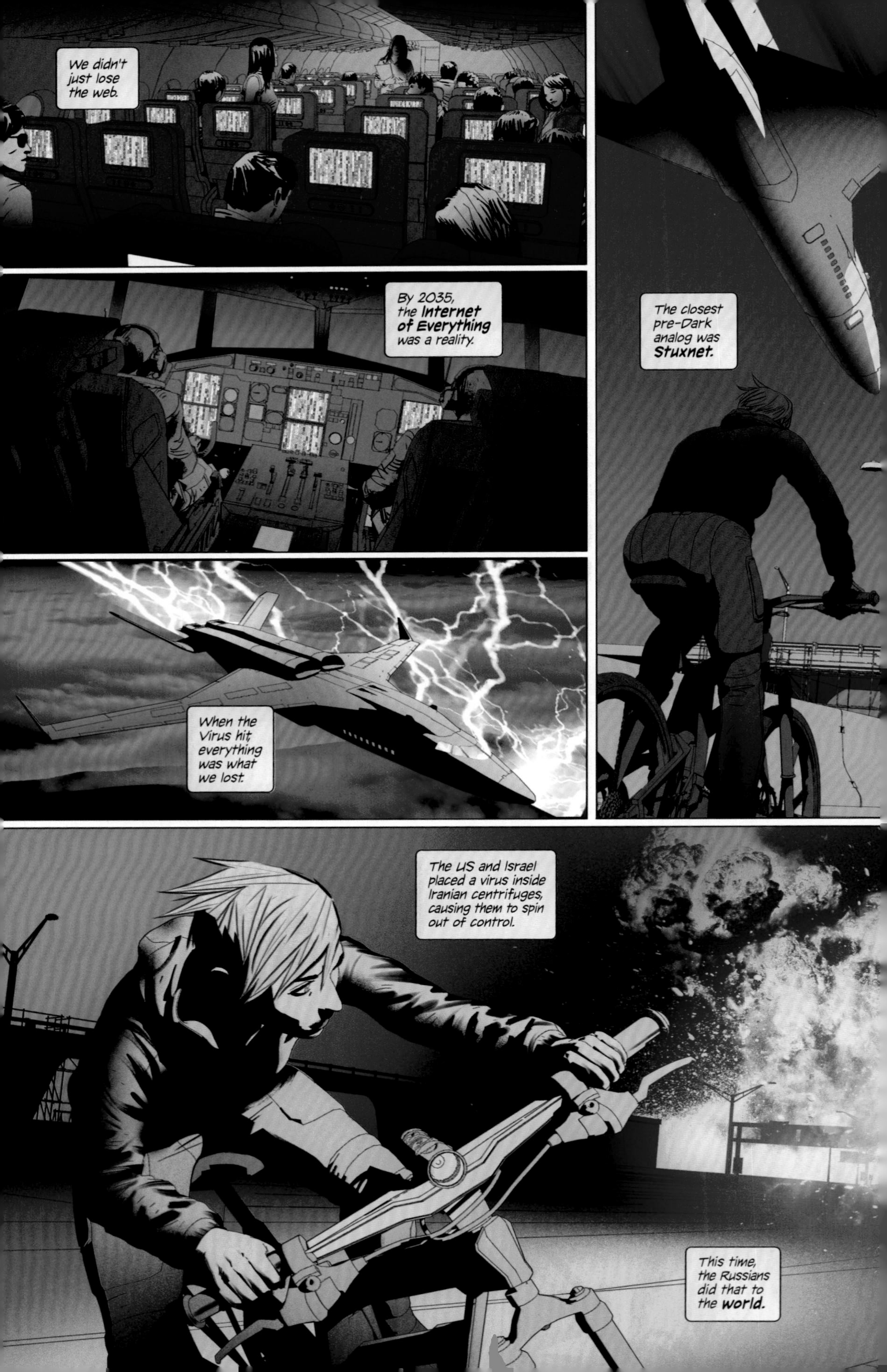
We didn't just lose the web.
By 2035, the Internet of Everything was a reality.
When the Virus hit, everything was what we lost.
The closest pre-Dark analog was Stuxnet.
The US and Israel placed a virus inside Iranian centrifuges, causing them to spin out of control.
This time, the Russians did that to the world.

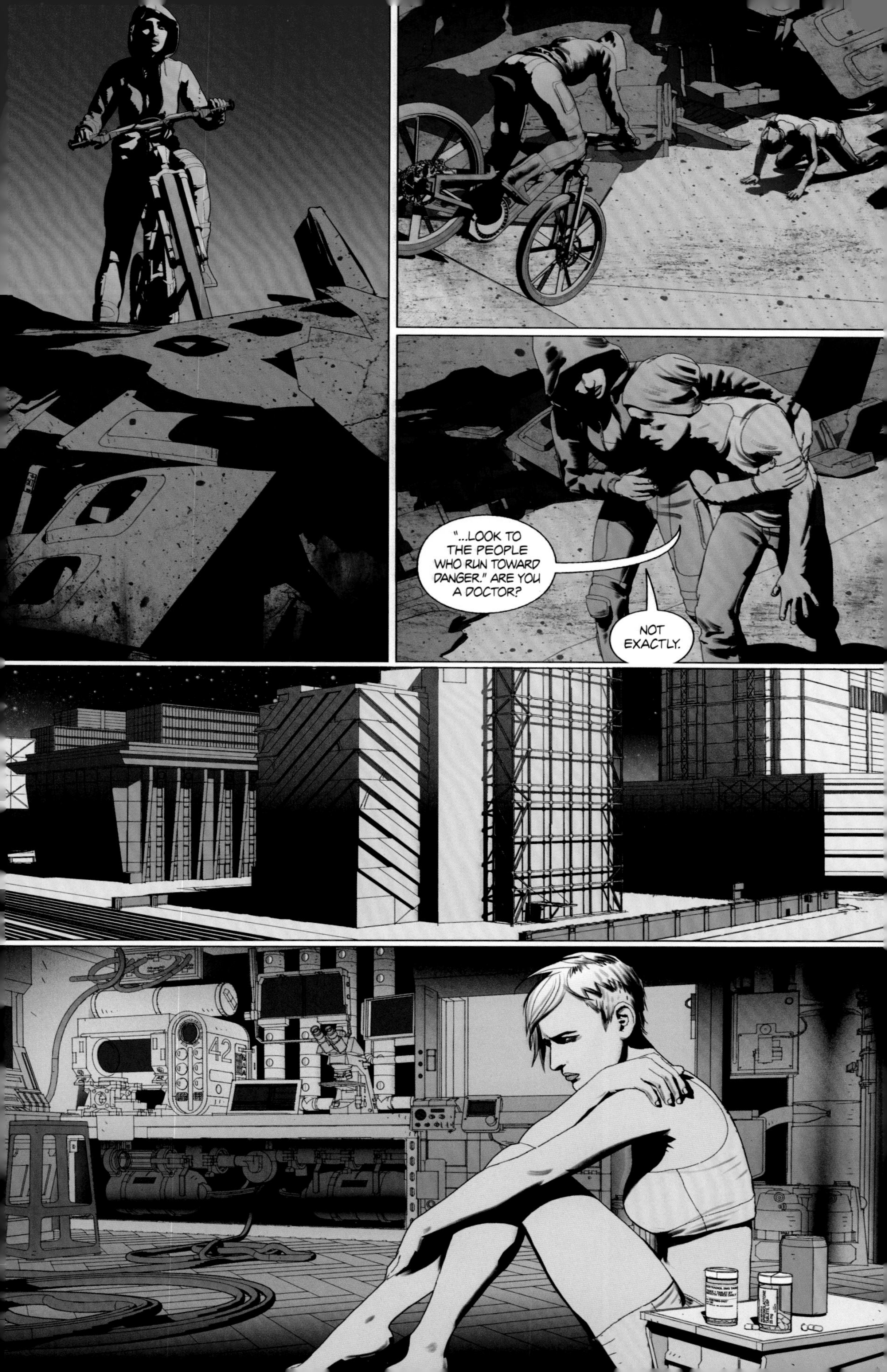
"...LOOK TO THE PEOPLE WHO RUN TOWARD DANGER." ARE YOU A DOCTOR?
NOT EXACTLY.

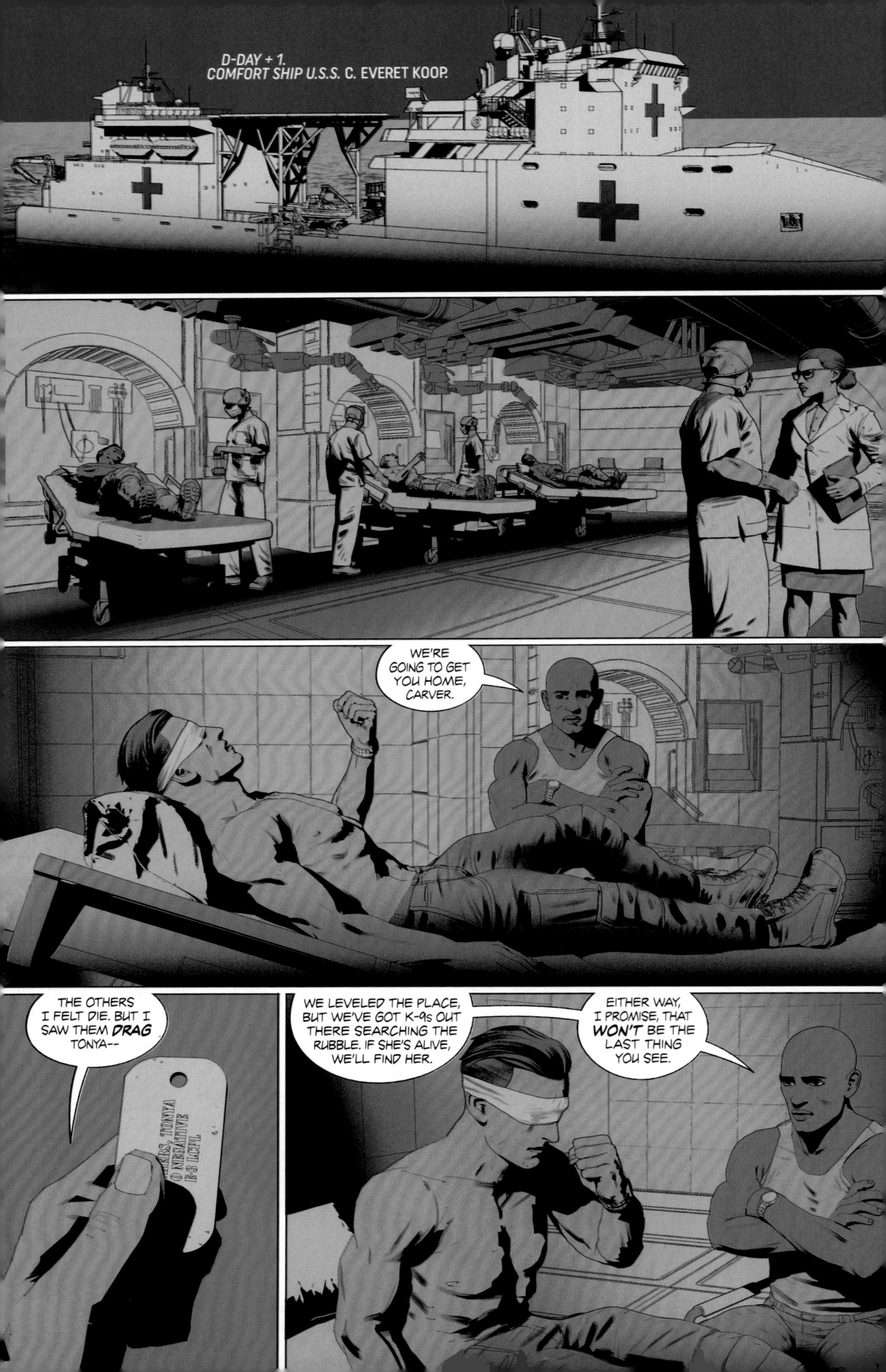
D-DAY + 1.
COMFORT SHIP U.S.S. C. EVERET KOOP.
WE'RE GOING TO GET YOU HOME, CARVER.
THE OTHERS I FELT DIE. BUT I SAW THEM *DRAG* TONYA--
...RS, TONYA
O NEGATIVE
E-3 LCPL
WE LEVELED THE PLACE, BUT WE'VE GOT K-9s OUT THERE SEARCHING THE RUBBLE. IF SHE'S ALIVE, WE'LL FIND HER.
EITHER WAY, I PROMISE, THAT *WON'T* BE THE LAST THING YOU SEE.

The colonel was true to his word.

D-DAY + 30.

New eyes with all the power of his old ones, but none of the vulnerabilities.

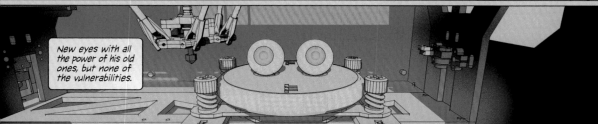

Organic, not cybernetic. Invulnerable to cyberwarfare.

But they came with a **price**.

D-DAY + 60.

A SUPPORT DOG?

HE'S... MORE THAN THAT.

HOW SO?

IT'S... CLASSIFIED.

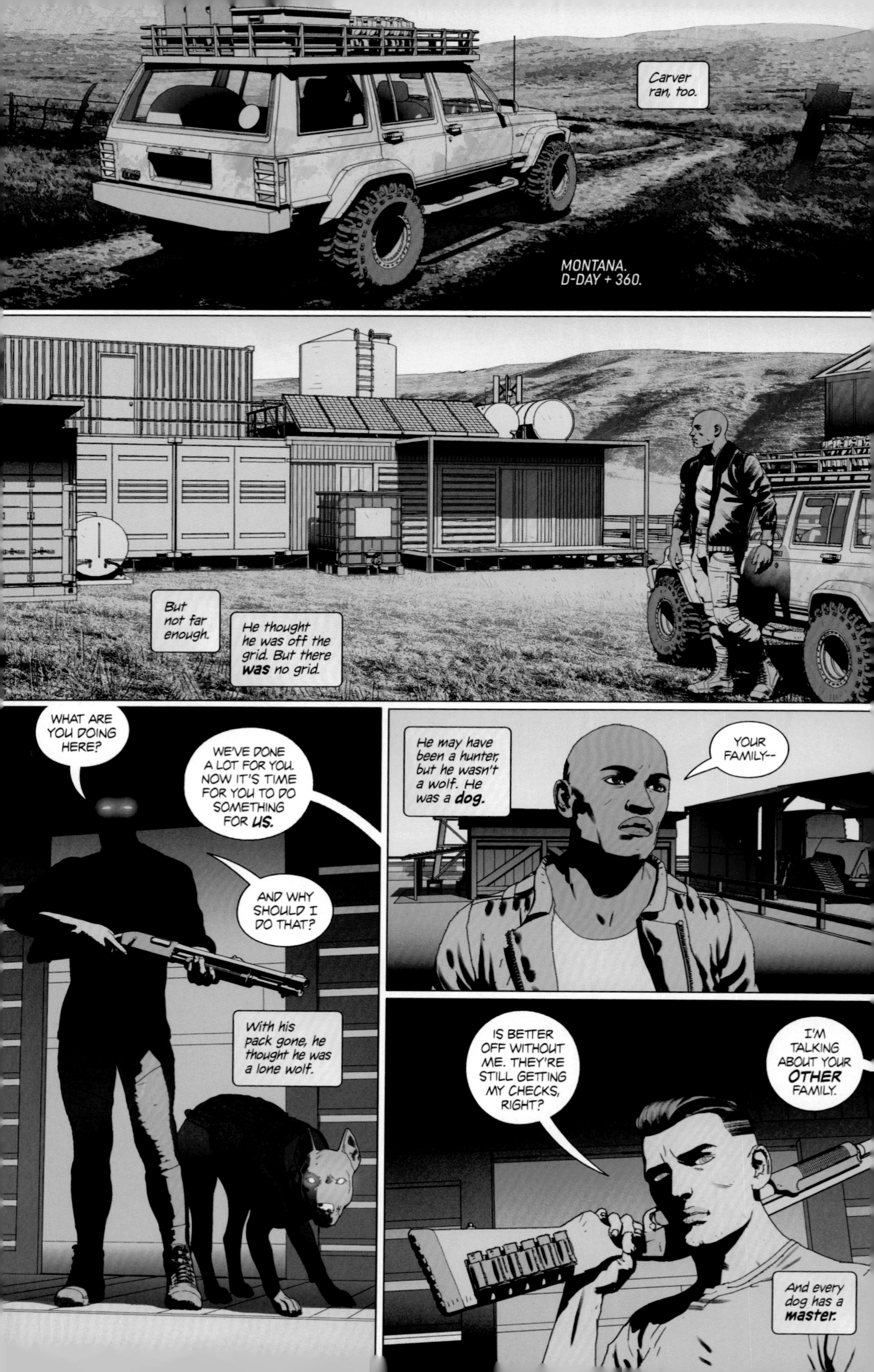

Carver ran, too.
MONTANA. D-DAY + 360.
But not far enough.
He thought he was off the grid. But there **was** no grid.
WHAT ARE YOU DOING HERE?
WE'VE DONE A LOT FOR YOU. NOW IT'S TIME FOR YOU TO DO SOMETHING FOR **US.**
AND WHY SHOULD I DO THAT?
With his pack gone, he thought he was a lone wolf.
He may have been a hunter, but he wasn't a wolf. He was a **dog.**
YOUR FAMILY--
IS BETTER OFF WITHOUT ME. THEY'RE STILL GETTING MY CHECKS, RIGHT?
I'M TALKING ABOUT YOUR **OTHER** FAMILY.
And every dog has a **master.**

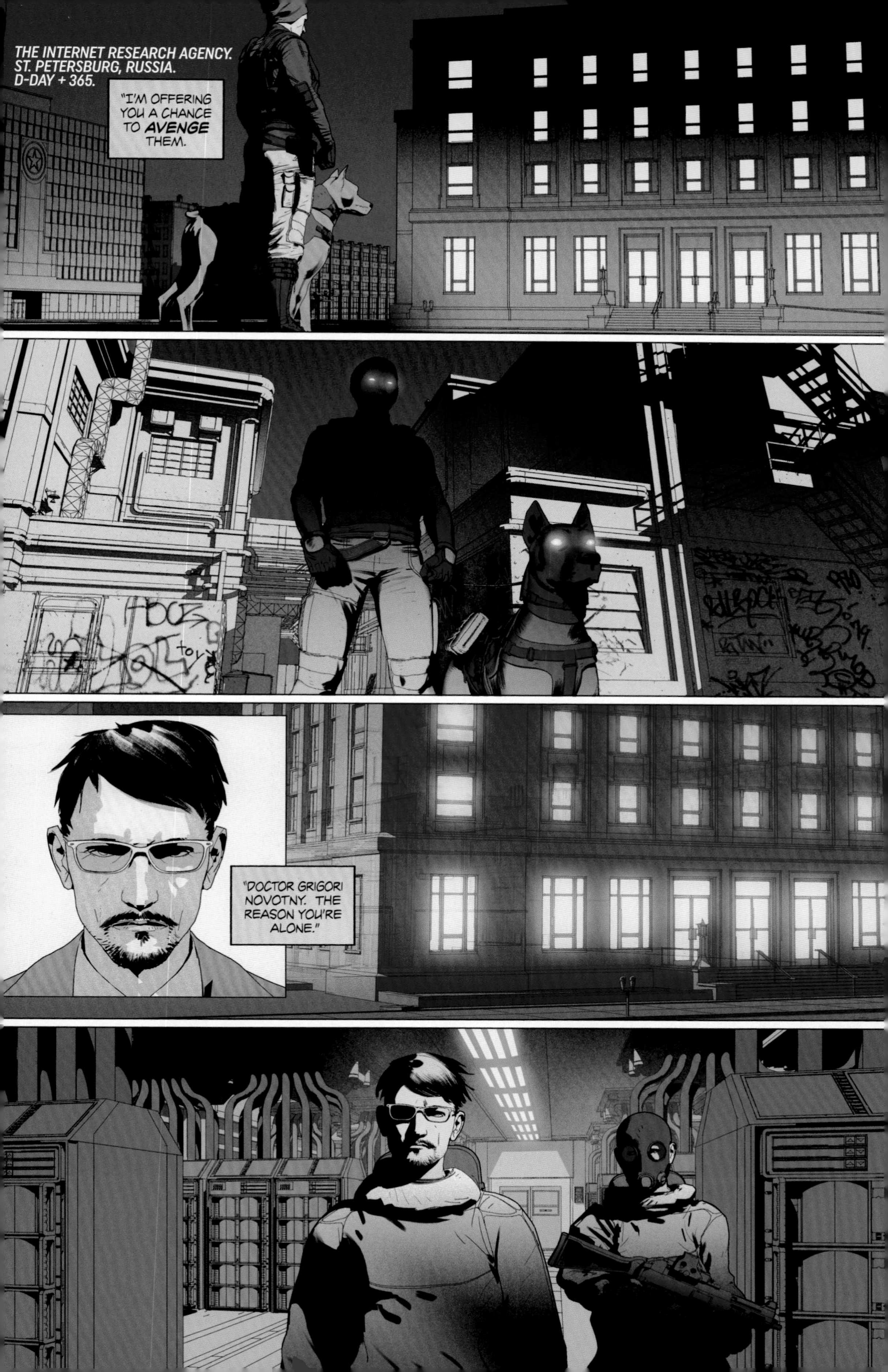
THE INTERNET RESEARCH AGENCY.
ST. PETERSBURG, RUSSIA.
D-DAY + 365.
"I'M OFFERING YOU A CHANCE TO AVENGE THEM.
"DOCTOR GRIGORI NOVOTNY. THE REASON YOU'RE ALONE."

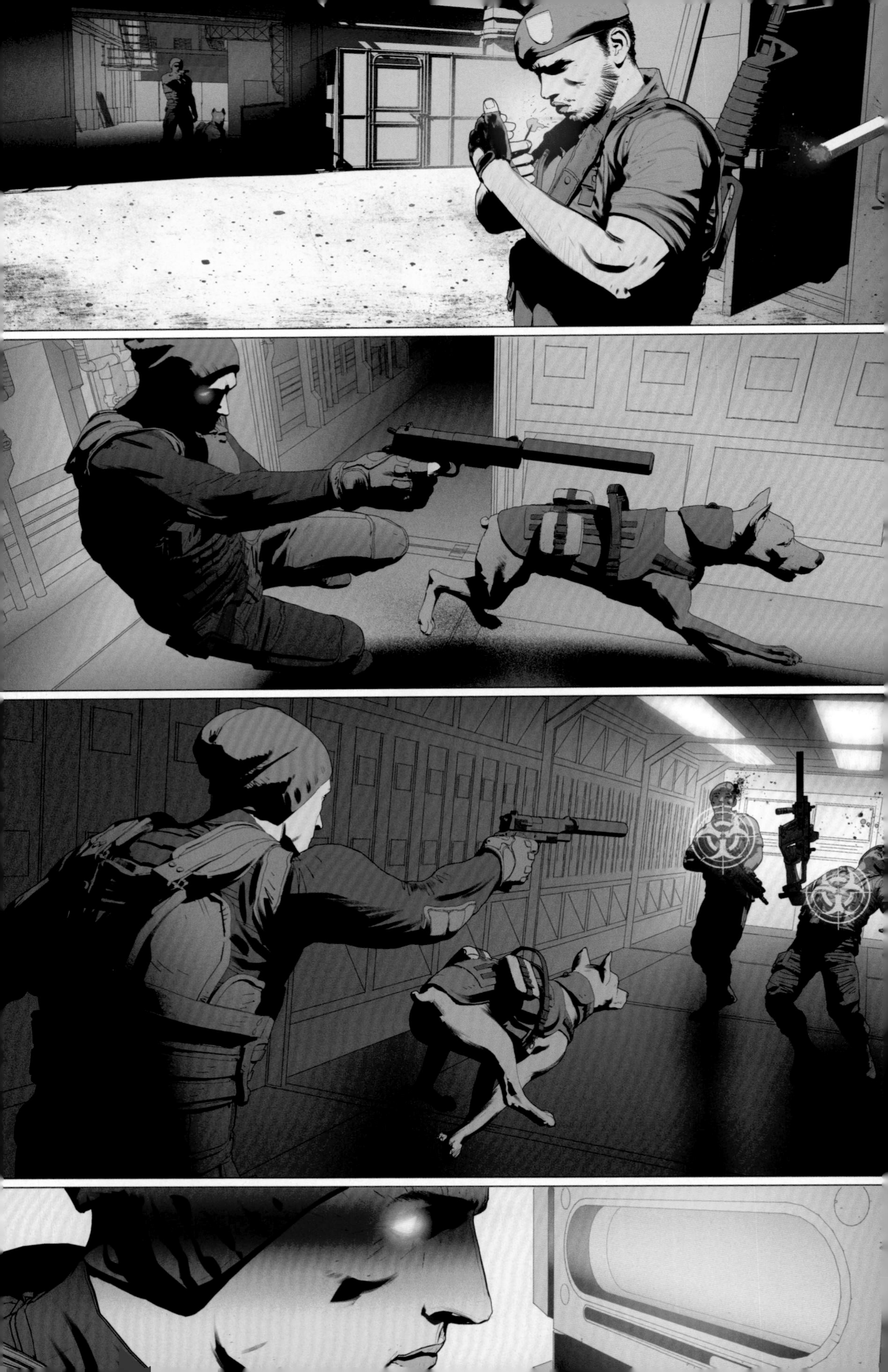

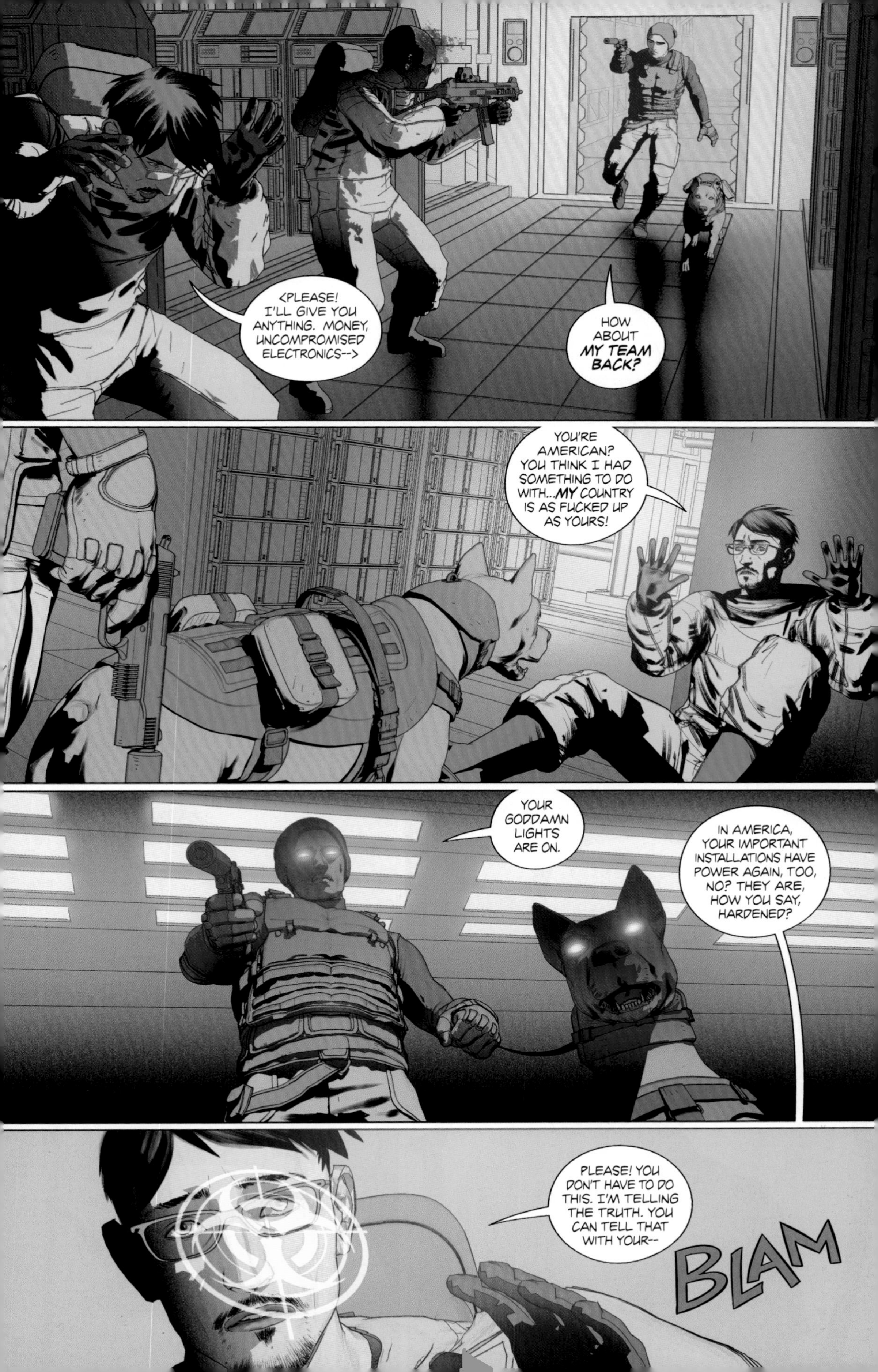
<PLEASE! I'LL GIVE YOU ANYTHING. MONEY, UNCOMPROMISED ELECTRONICS-->
HOW ABOUT MY TEAM BACK?
YOU'RE AMERICAN? YOU THINK I HAD SOMETHING TO DO WITH...MY COUNTRY IS AS FUCKED UP AS YOURS!
YOUR GODDAMN LIGHTS ARE ON.
IN AMERICA, YOUR IMPORTANT INSTALLATIONS HAVE POWER AGAIN, TOO, NO? THEY ARE, HOW YOU SAY, HARDENED?
PLEASE! YOU DON'T HAVE TO DO THIS. I'M TELLING THE TRUTH. YOU CAN TELL THAT WITH YOUR--
BLAM

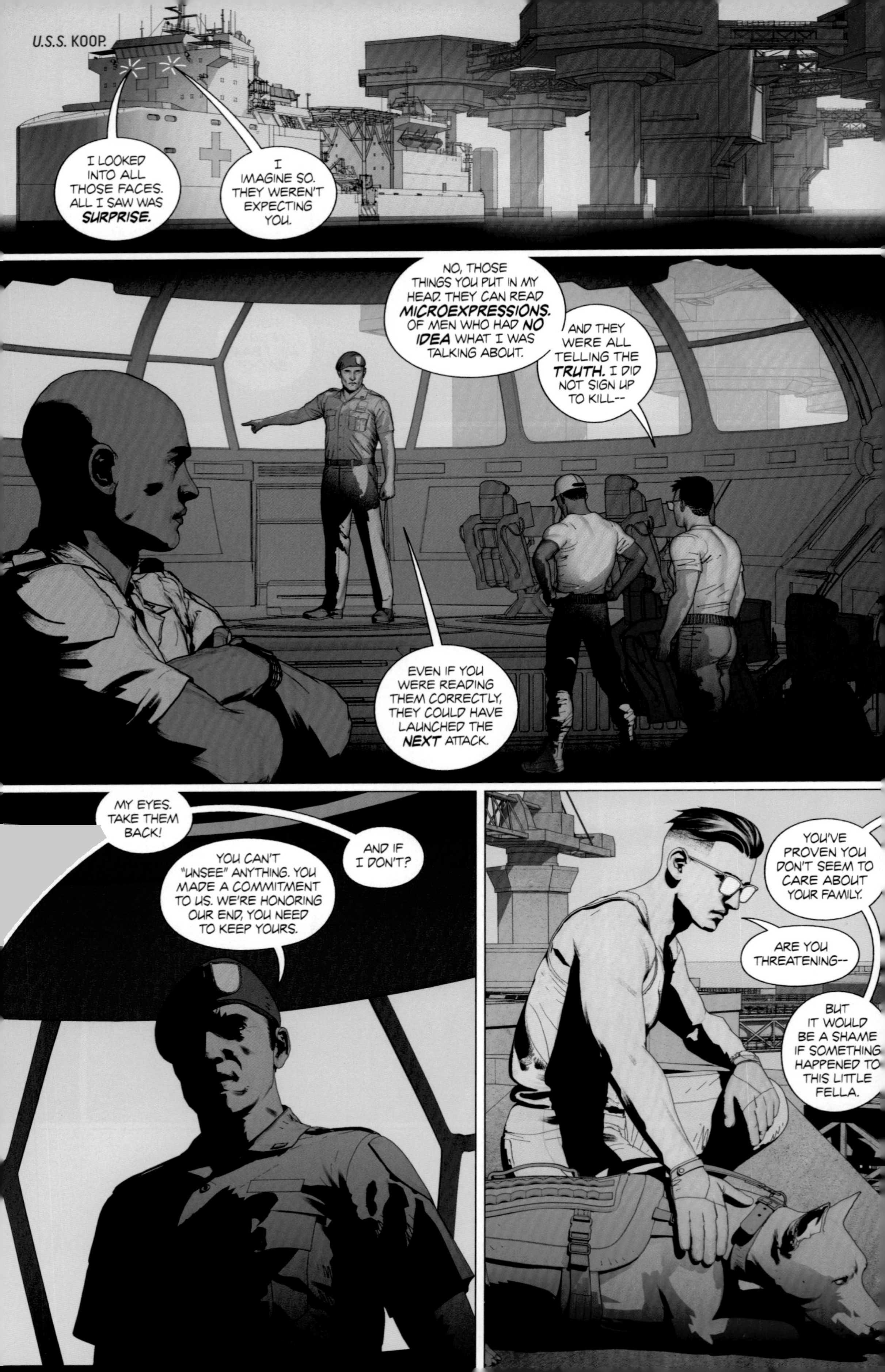
U.S.S. KOOP.
I LOOKED INTO ALL THOSE FACES. ALL I SAW WAS SURPRISE.
I IMAGINE SO. THEY WEREN'T EXPECTING YOU.
NO, THOSE THINGS YOU PUT IN MY HEAD. THEY CAN READ MICROEXPRESSIONS. OF MEN WHO HAD NO IDEA WHAT I WAS TALKING ABOUT.
AND THEY WERE ALL TELLING THE TRUTH. I DID NOT SIGN UP TO KILL--
EVEN IF YOU WERE READING THEM CORRECTLY, THEY COULD HAVE LAUNCHED THE NEXT ATTACK.
MY EYES. TAKE THEM BACK!
YOU CAN'T "UNSEE" ANYTHING. YOU MADE A COMMITMENT TO US. WE'RE HONORING OUR END, YOU NEED TO KEEP YOURS.
AND IF I DON'T?
YOU'VE PROVEN YOU DON'T SEEM TO CARE ABOUT YOUR FAMILY.
ARE YOU THREATENING--
BUT IT WOULD BE A SHAME IF SOMETHING HAPPENED TO THIS LITTLE FELLA.

TEN YEARS LATER.

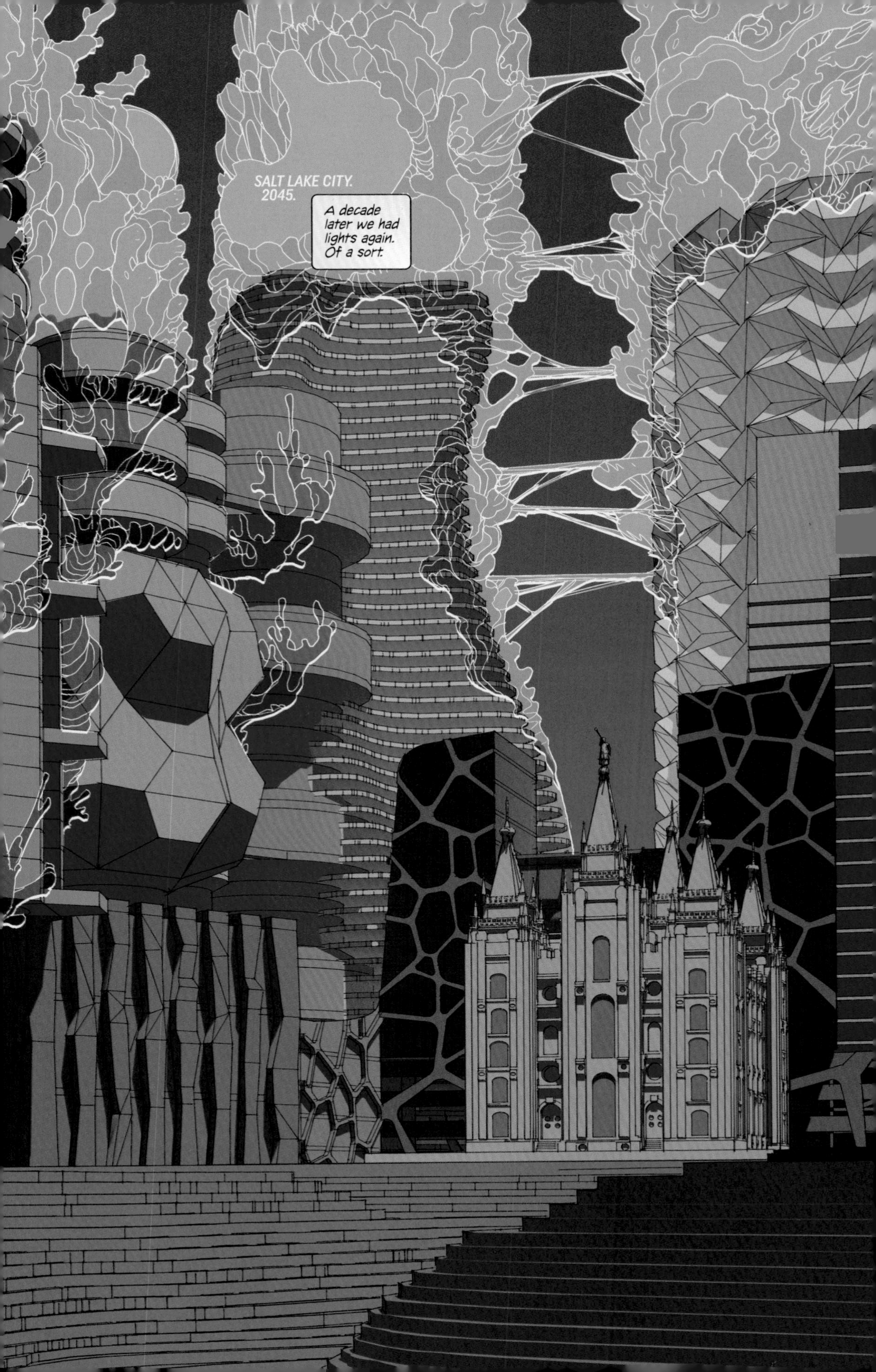
SALT LAKE CITY.
2045.
A decade later we had lights again. Of a sort.

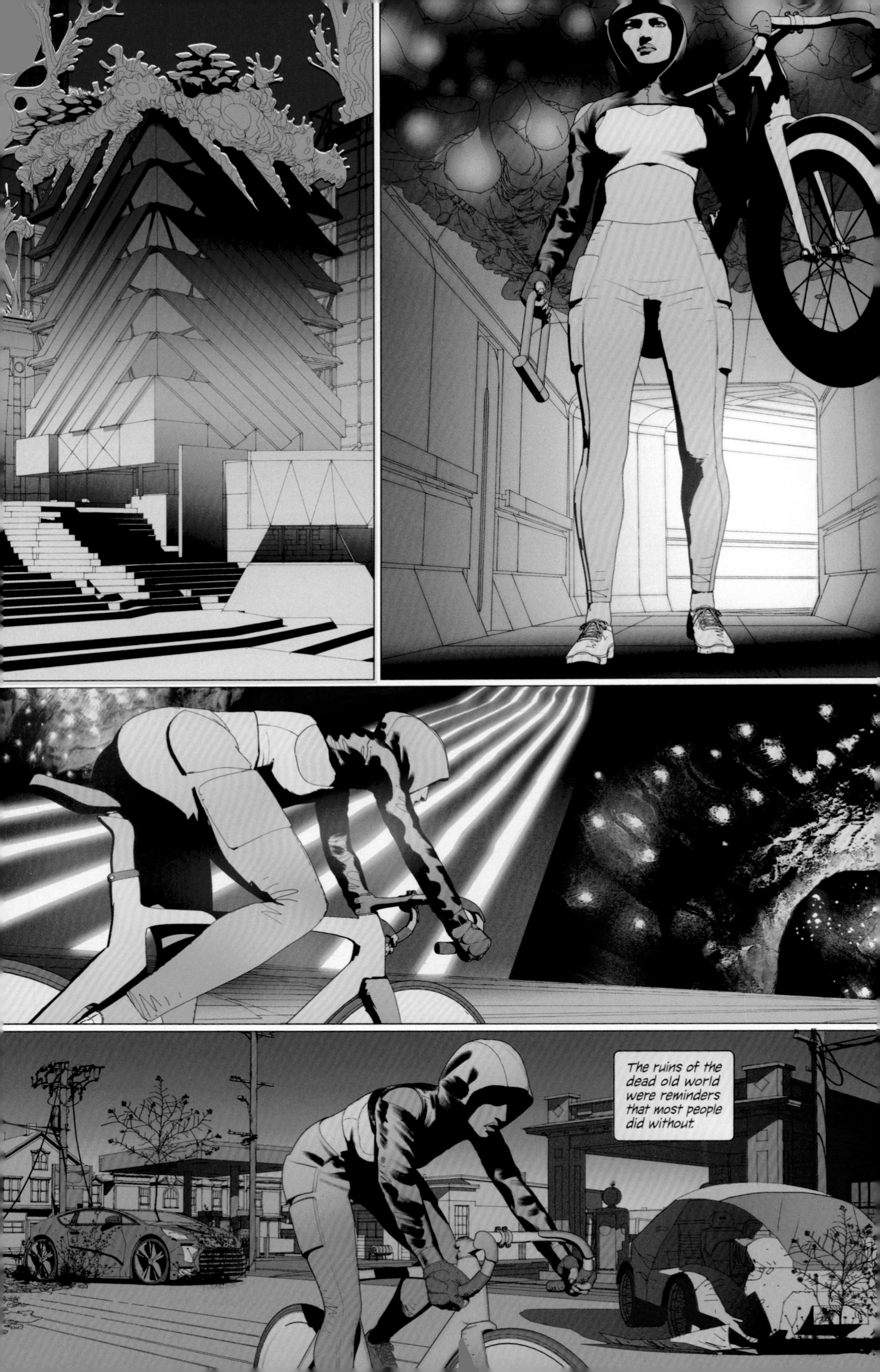
The ruins of the dead old world were reminders that most people did without.

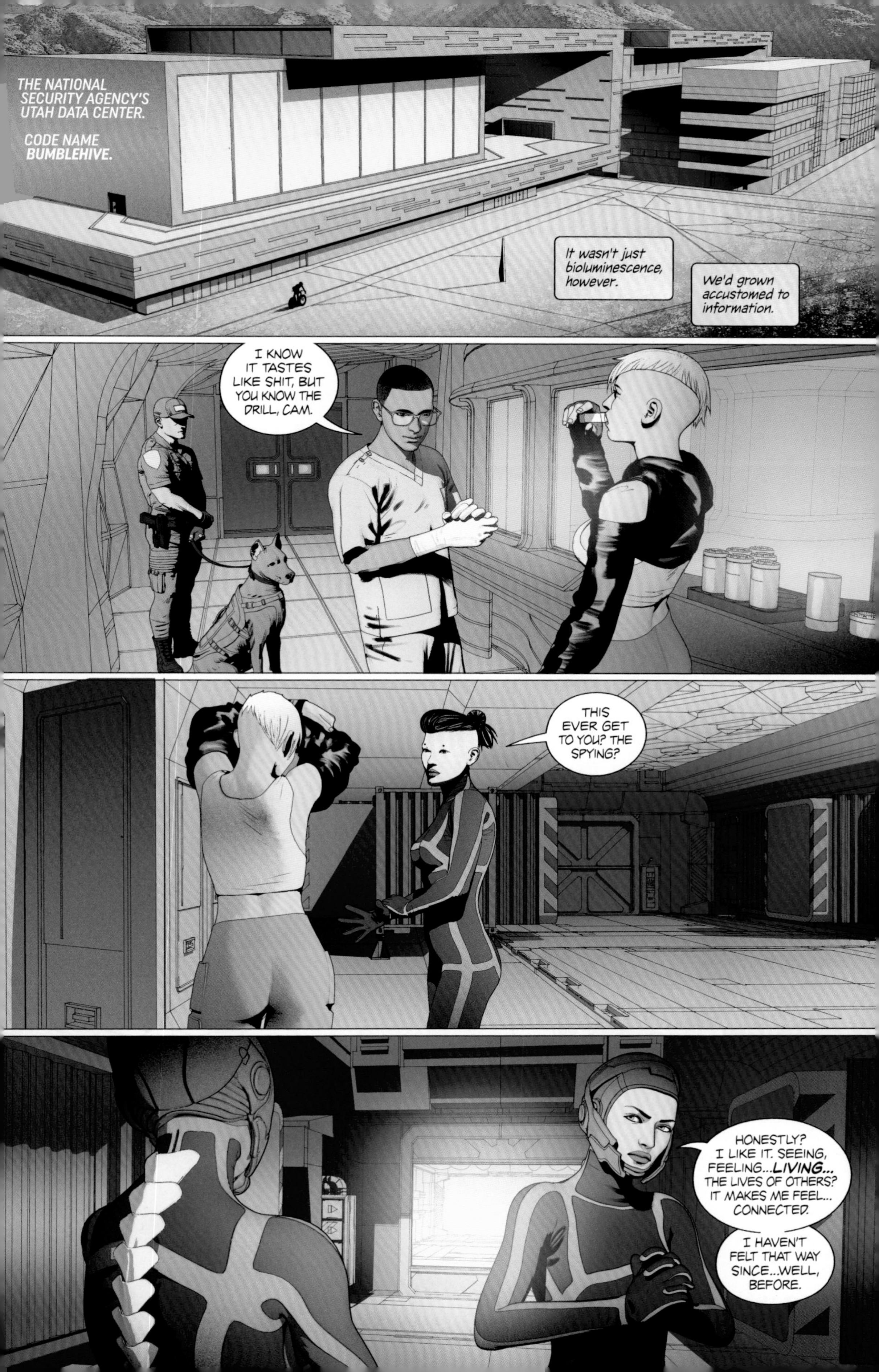
THE NATIONAL SECURITY AGENCY'S UTAH DATA CENTER.
CODE NAME **BUMBLEHIVE.**
It wasn't just bioluminescence, however.
We'd grown accustomed to information.
I KNOW IT TASTES LIKE SHIT, BUT YOU KNOW THE DRILL, CAM.
THIS EVER GET TO YOU? THE SPYING?
HONESTLY? I LIKE IT. SEEING, FEELING... **LIVING...** THE LIVES OF OTHERS? IT MAKES ME FEEL... CONNECTED.
I HAVEN'T FELT THAT WAY SINCE... WELL, BEFORE.

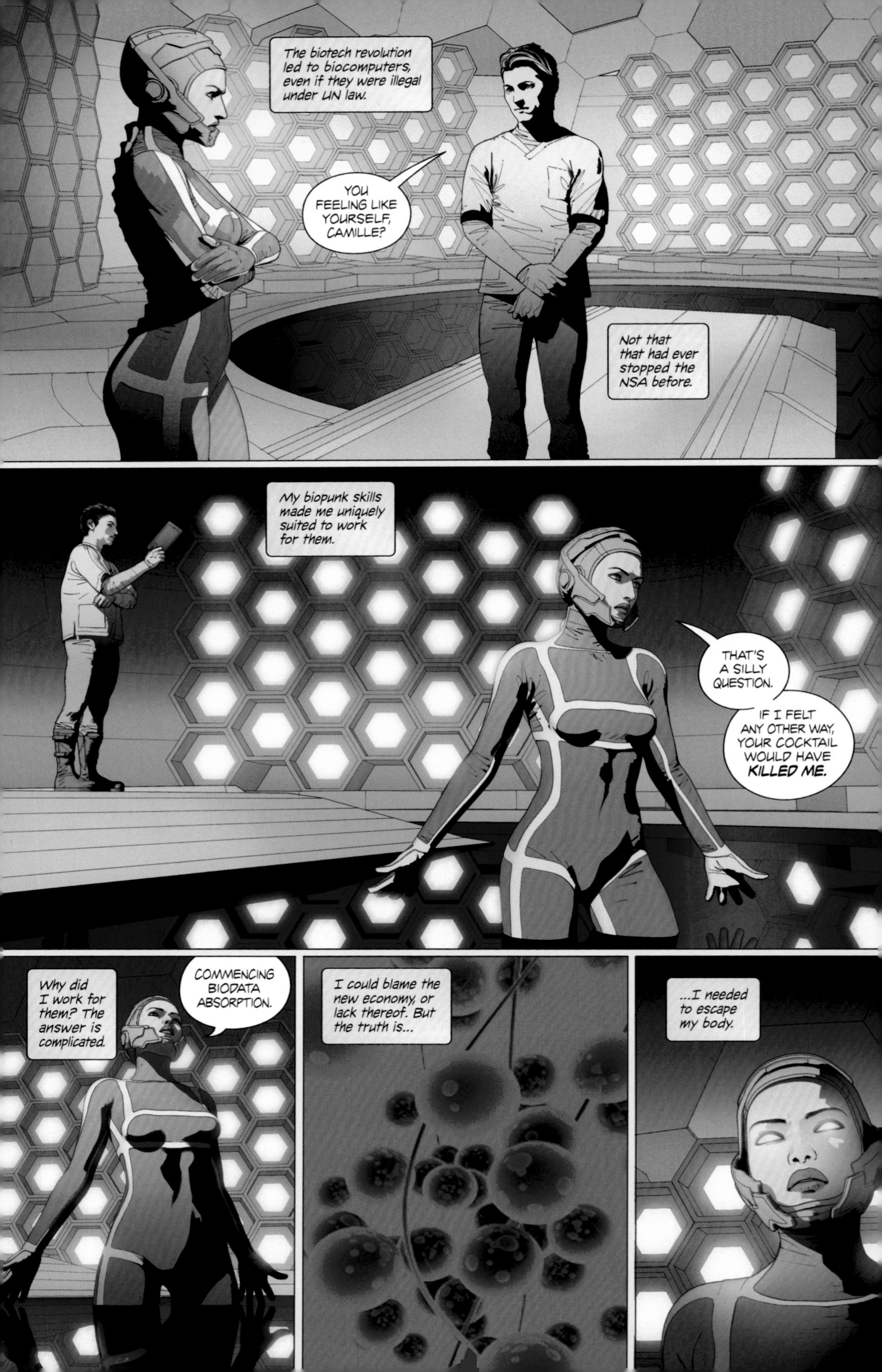
The biotech revolution led to biocomputers, even if they were illegal under UN law.
YOU FEELING LIKE YOURSELF, CAMILLE?
Not that that had ever stopped the NSA before.
My biopunk skills made me uniquely suited to work for them.
THAT'S A SILLY QUESTION.
IF I FELT ANY OTHER WAY, YOUR COCKTAIL WOULD HAVE KILLED ME.
Why did I work for them? The answer is complicated.
COMMENCING BIODATA ABSORPTION.
I could blame the new economy, or lack thereof. But the truth is...
...I needed to escape my body.

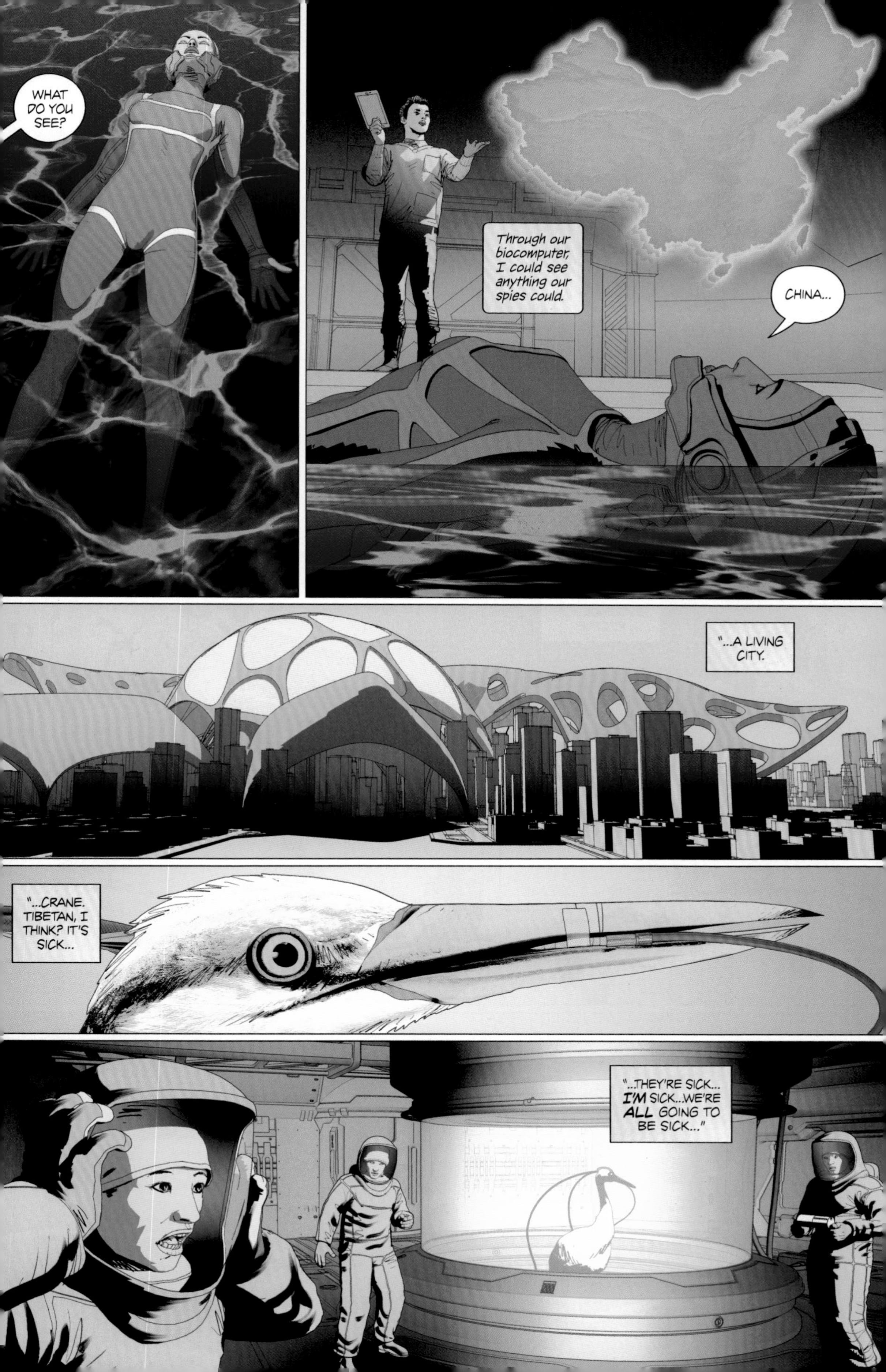
WHAT DO YOU SEE?
Through our biocomputer, I could see anything our spies could.
CHINA...
"...A LIVING CITY.
"...CRANE. TIBETAN, I THINK? IT'S SICK...
"...THEY'RE SICK... I'M SICK...WE'RE ALL GOING TO BE SICK..."

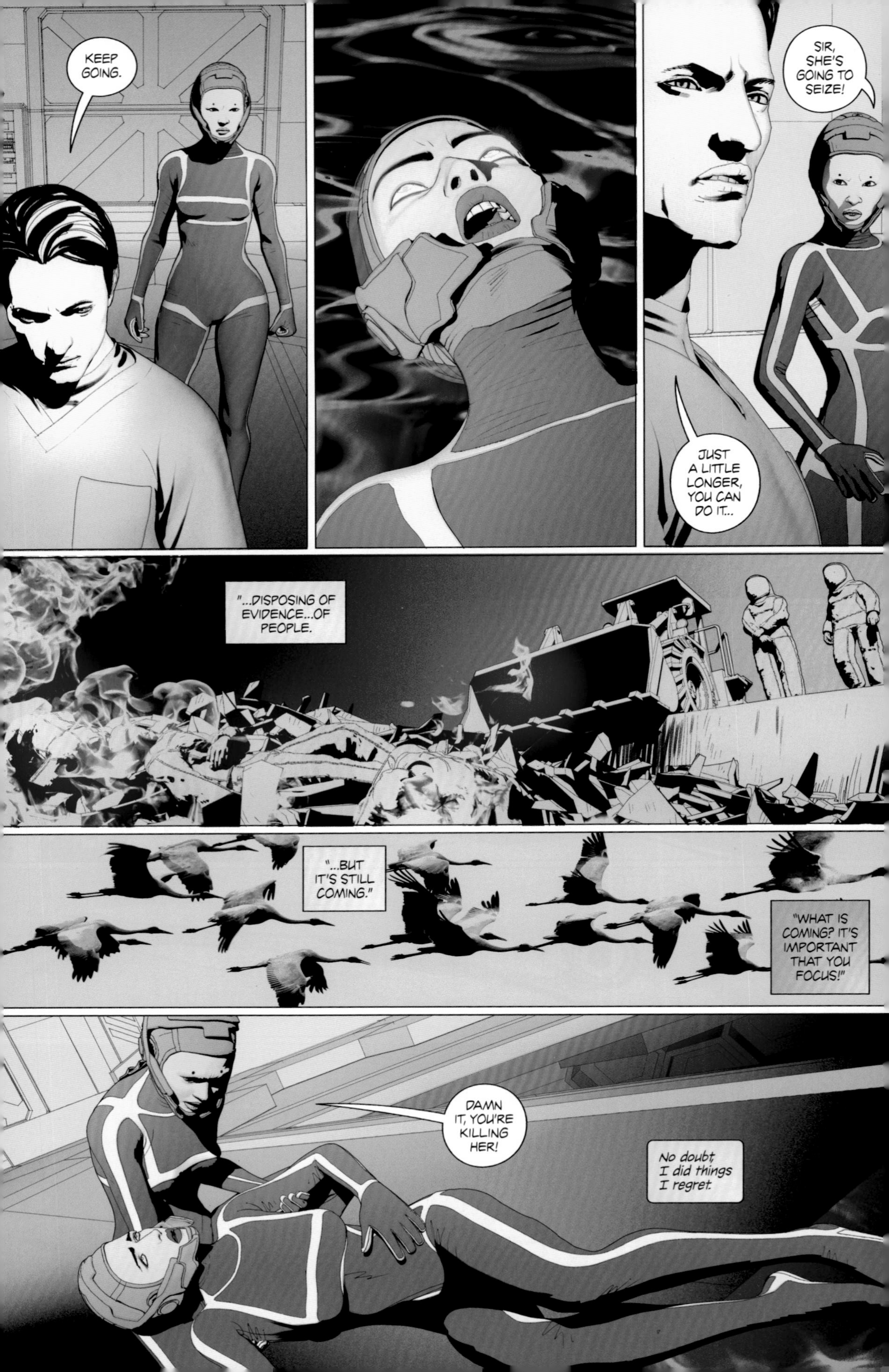
KEEP GOING.
SIR, SHE'S GOING TO SEIZE!
JUST A LITTLE LONGER, YOU CAN DO IT...
"...DISPOSING OF EVIDENCE...OF PEOPLE.
"...BUT IT'S STILL COMING."
"WHAT IS COMING? IT'S IMPORTANT THAT YOU FOCUS!"
DAMN IT, YOU'RE KILLING HER!
No doubt, I did things I regret.

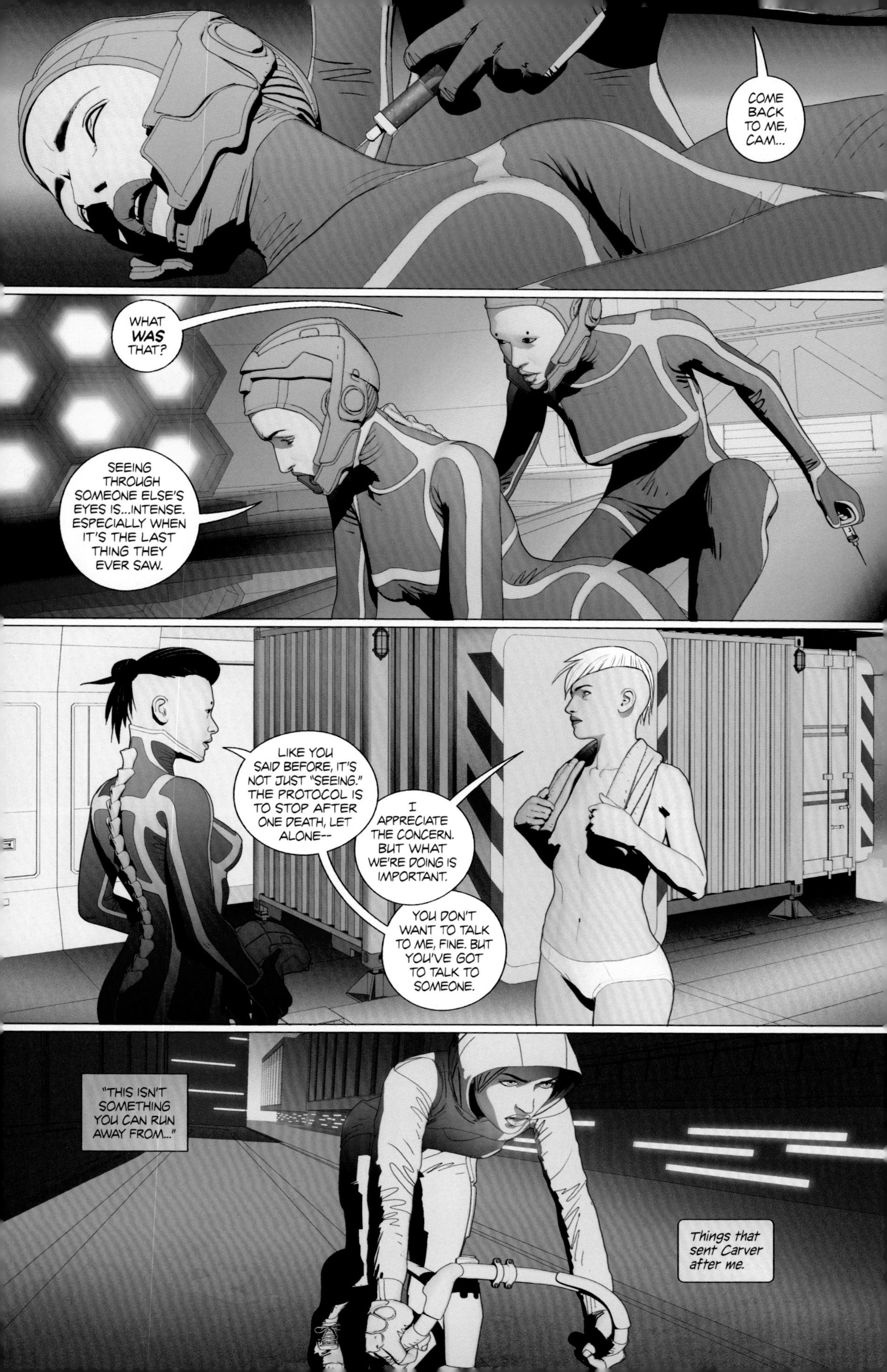
COME BACK TO ME, CAM...
WHAT **WAS** THAT?
SEEING THROUGH SOMEONE ELSE'S EYES IS...INTENSE. ESPECIALLY WHEN IT'S THE LAST THING THEY EVER SAW.
LIKE YOU SAID BEFORE, IT'S NOT JUST "SEEING." THE PROTOCOL IS TO STOP AFTER ONE DEATH, LET ALONE--
I APPRECIATE THE CONCERN. BUT WHAT WE'RE DOING IS IMPORTANT.
YOU DON'T WANT TO TALK TO ME, FINE. BUT YOU'VE GOT TO TALK TO SOMEONE.
"THIS ISN'T SOMETHING YOU CAN RUN AWAY FROM..."
Things that sent Carver after me.

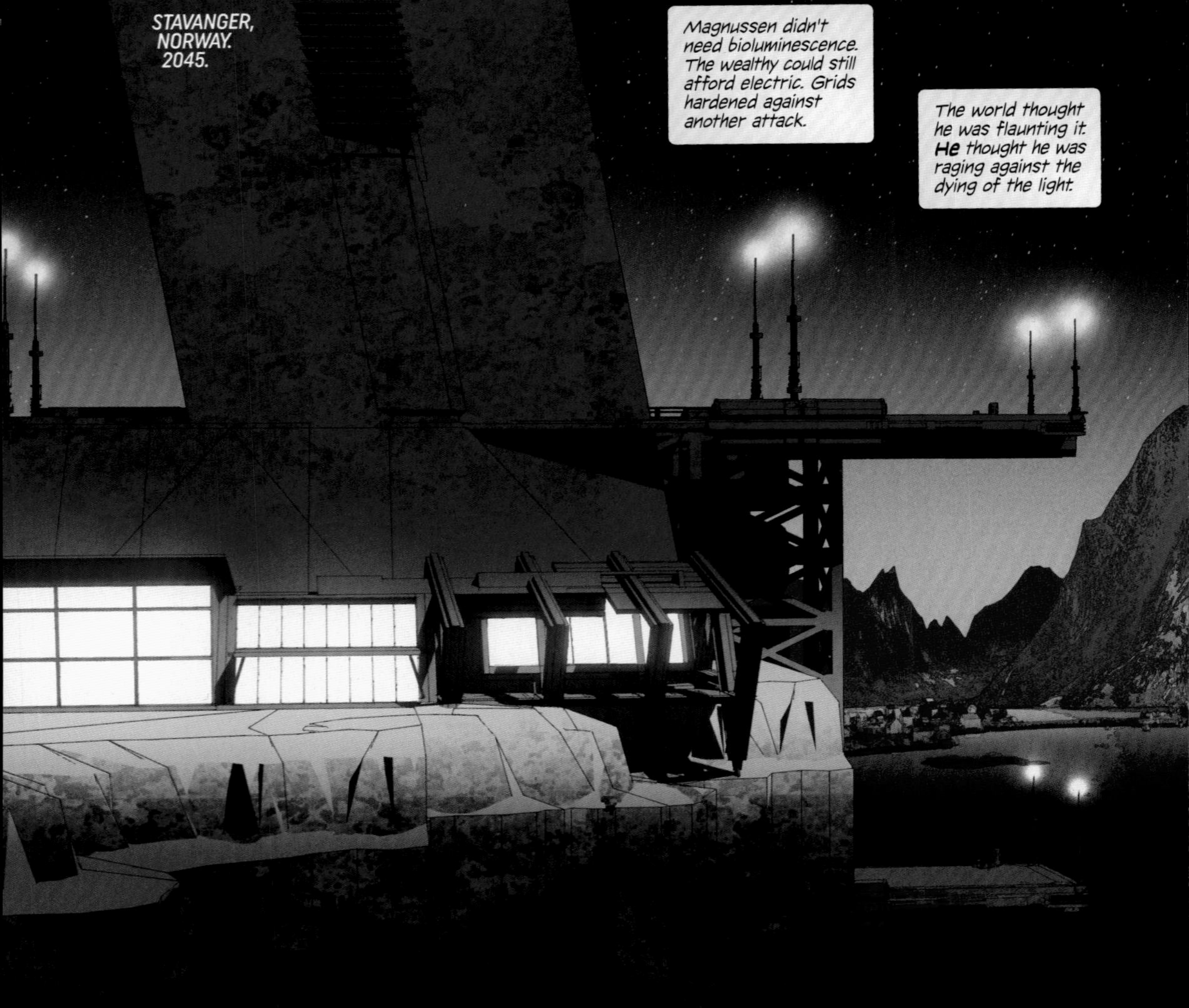
STAVANGER, NORWAY. 2045.
Magnussen didn't need bioluminescence. The wealthy could still afford electric. Grids hardened against another attack.
The world thought he was flaunting it. **He** thought he was raging against the dying of the light.

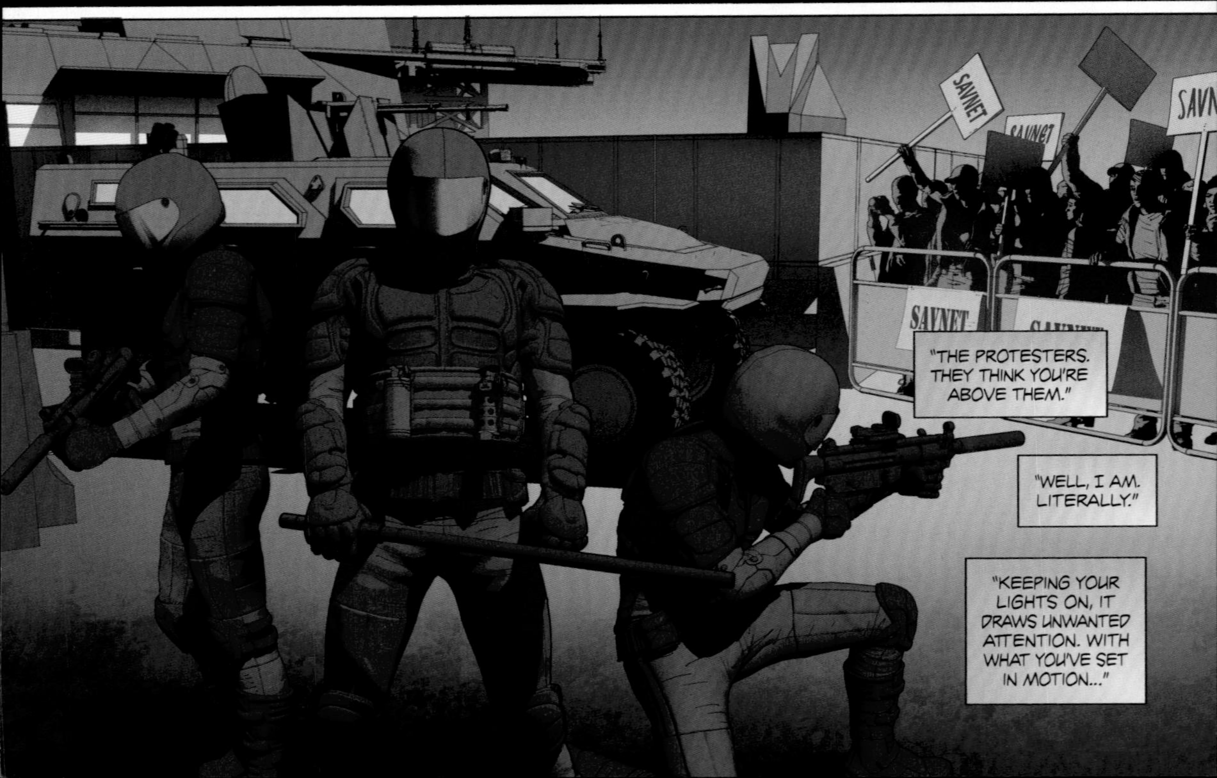
SAVNET
SAVNET
SAVNET
"THE PROTESTERS. THEY THINK YOU'RE ABOVE THEM."
"WELL, I AM. LITERALLY."
"KEEPING YOUR LIGHTS ON, IT DRAWS UNWANTED ATTENTION. WITH WHAT YOU'VE SET IN MOTION..."

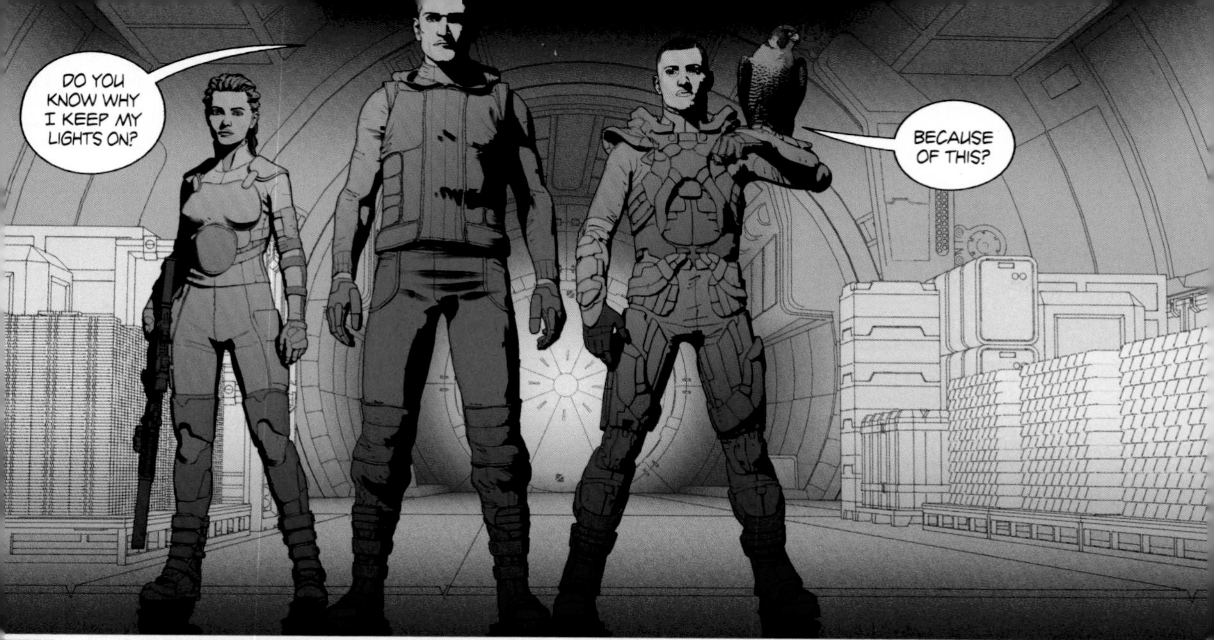
DO YOU KNOW WHY I KEEP MY LIGHTS ON?
BECAUSE OF THIS?

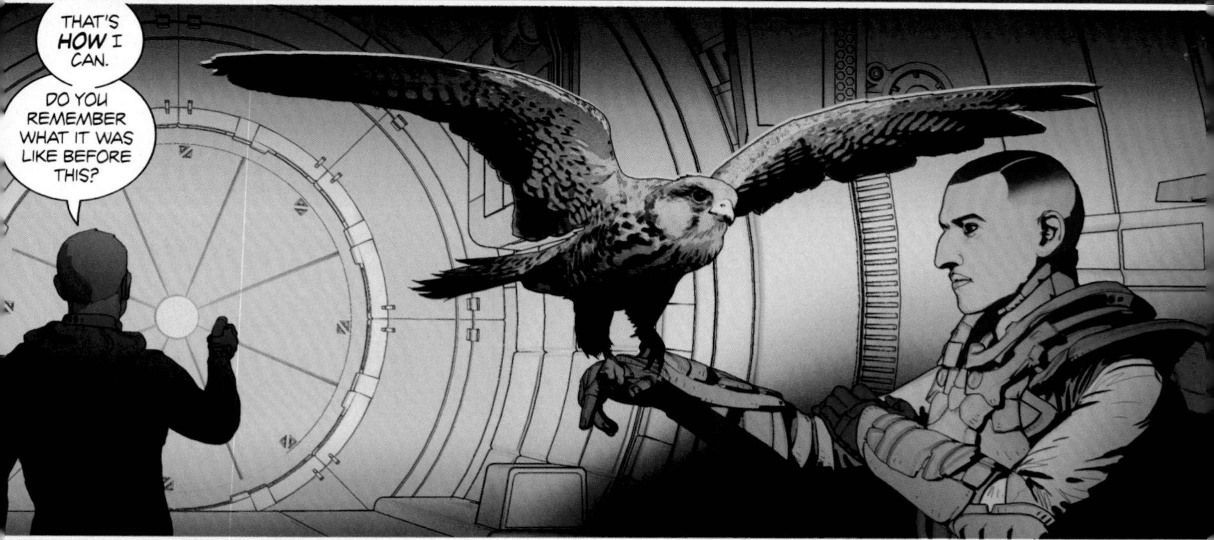
THAT'S **HOW** I CAN.
DO YOU REMEMBER WHAT IT WAS LIKE BEFORE THIS?

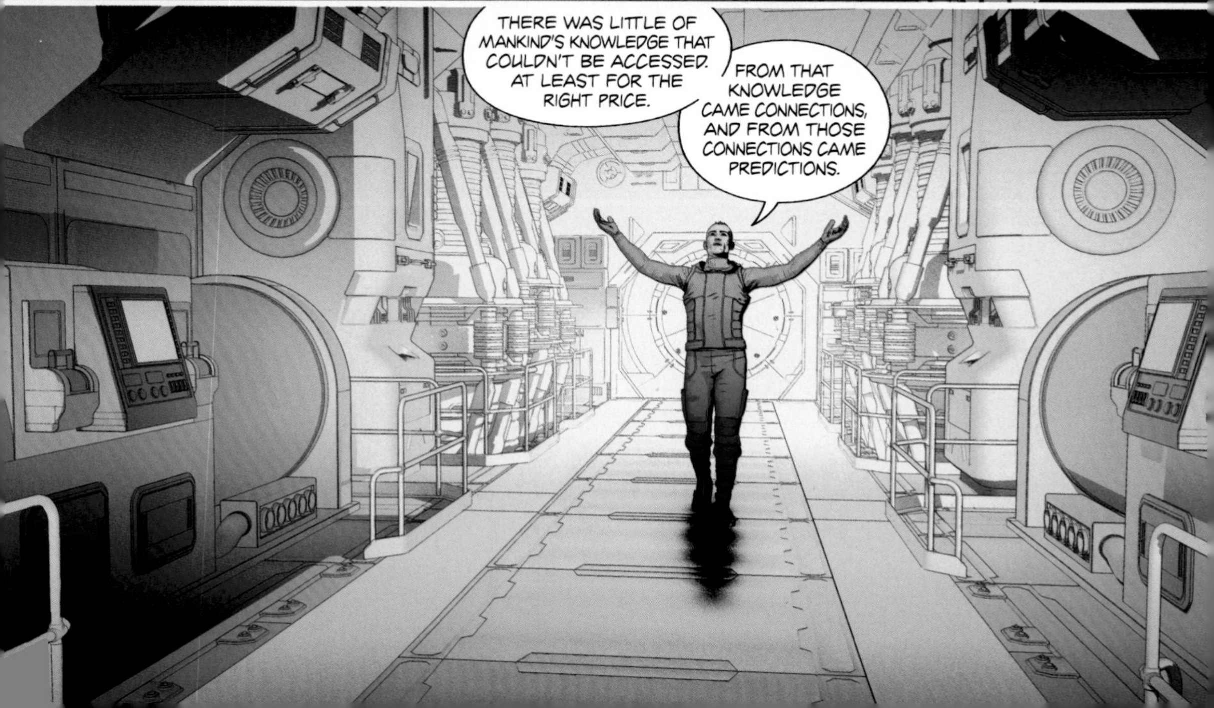
THERE WAS LITTLE OF MANKIND'S KNOWLEDGE THAT COULDN'T BE ACCESSED. AT LEAST FOR THE RIGHT PRICE.
FROM THAT KNOWLEDGE CAME CONNECTIONS, AND FROM THOSE CONNECTIONS CAME PREDICTIONS.

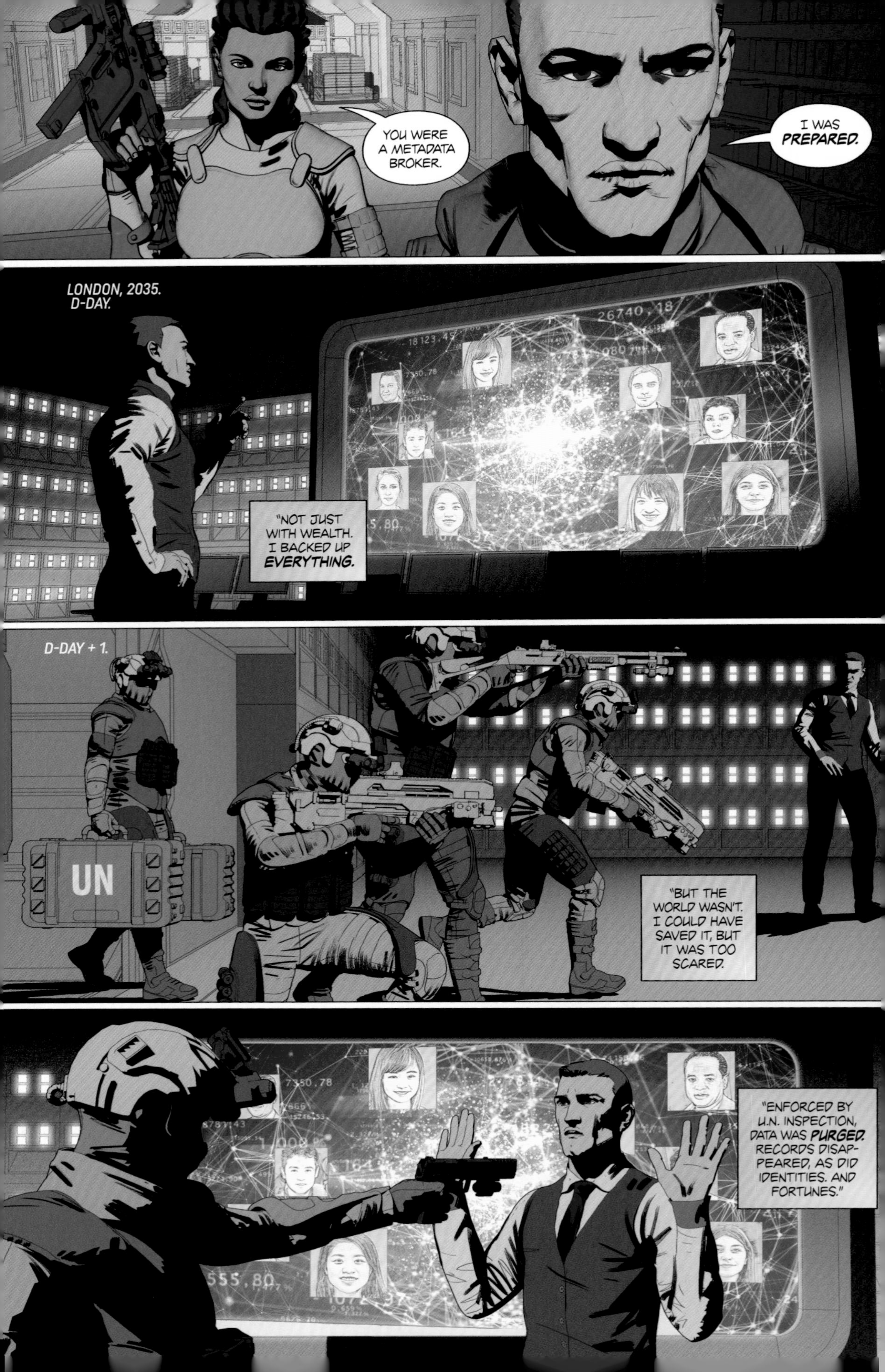
YOU WERE A METADATA BROKER.
I WAS **PREPARED.**
LONDON, 2035. D-DAY.
"NOT JUST WITH WEALTH. I BACKED UP **EVERYTHING.**
D-DAY + 1.
UN
"BUT THE WORLD WASN'T. I COULD HAVE SAVED IT, BUT IT WAS TOO SCARED.
"ENFORCED BY U.N. INSPECTION, DATA WAS **PURGED.** RECORDS DISAPPEARED, AS DID IDENTITIES. AND FORTUNES."

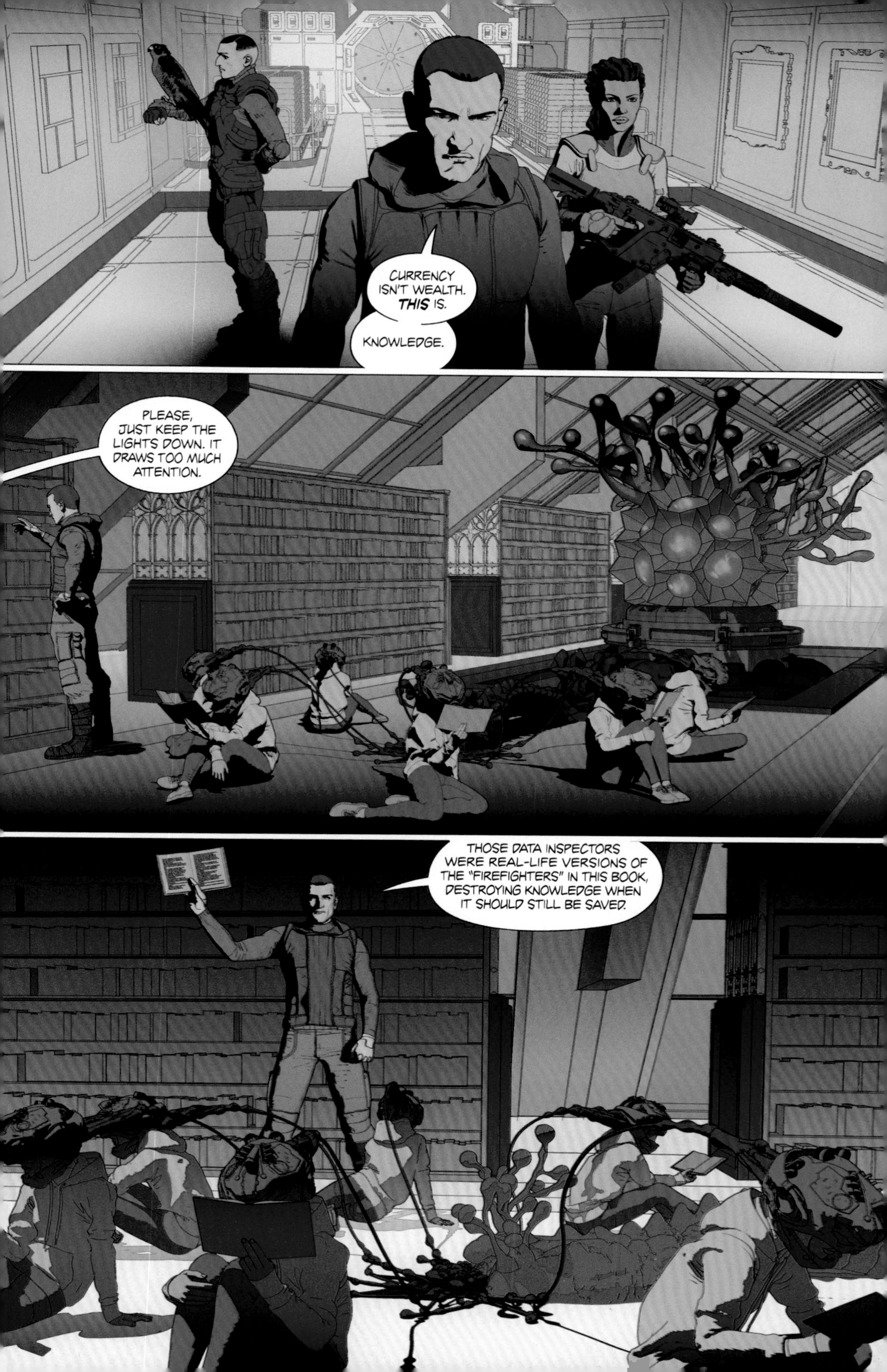
CURRENCY ISN'T WEALTH. THIS IS.
KNOWLEDGE.
PLEASE, JUST KEEP THE LIGHTS DOWN. IT DRAWS TOO MUCH ATTENTION.
THOSE DATA INSPECTORS WERE REAL-LIFE VERSIONS OF THE "FIREFIGHTERS" IN THIS BOOK, DESTROYING KNOWLEDGE WHEN IT SHOULD STILL BE SAVED.

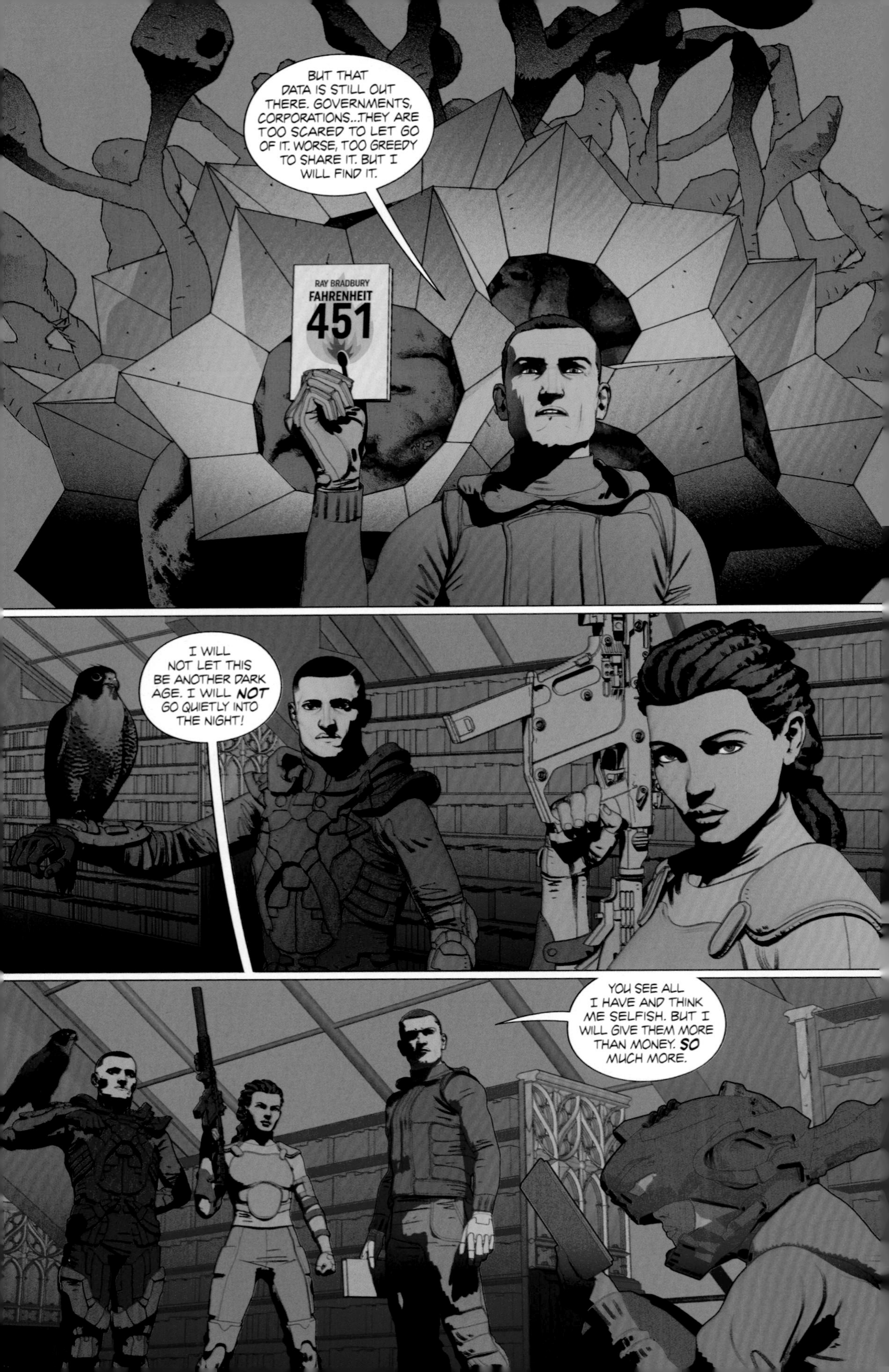
BUT THAT DATA IS STILL OUT THERE. GOVERNMENTS, CORPORATIONS...THEY ARE TOO SCARED TO LET GO OF IT. WORSE, TOO GREEDY TO SHARE IT. BUT I WILL FIND IT.
RAY BRADBURY
FAHRENHEIT
451
I WILL NOT LET THIS BE ANOTHER DARK AGE. I WILL **NOT** GO QUIETLY INTO THE NIGHT!
YOU SEE ALL I HAVE AND THINK ME SELFISH. BUT I WILL GIVE THEM MORE THAN MONEY. **SO** MUCH MORE.

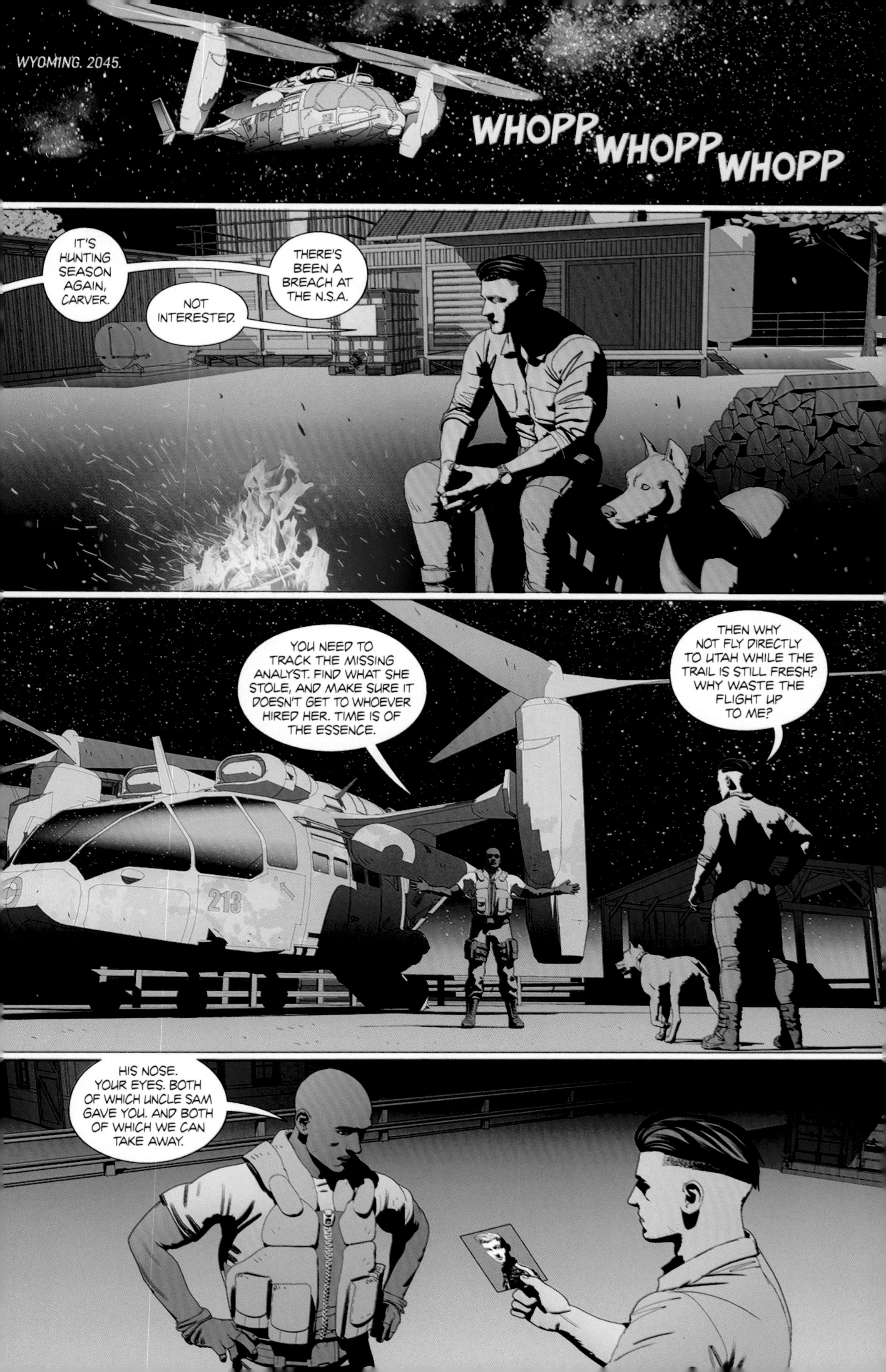
WYOMING. 2045.
WHOPP WHOPP WHOPP
IT'S HUNTING SEASON AGAIN, CARVER.
THERE'S BEEN A BREACH AT THE N.S.A.
NOT INTERESTED.
YOU NEED TO TRACK THE MISSING ANALYST. FIND WHAT SHE STOLE, AND MAKE SURE IT DOESN'T GET TO WHOEVER HIRED HER. TIME IS OF THE ESSENCE.
THEN WHY NOT FLY DIRECTLY TO UTAH WHILE THE TRAIL IS STILL FRESH? WHY WASTE THE FLIGHT UP TO ME?
213
HIS NOSE. YOUR EYES. BOTH OF WHICH UNCLE SAM GAVE YOU. AND BOTH OF WHICH WE CAN TAKE AWAY.

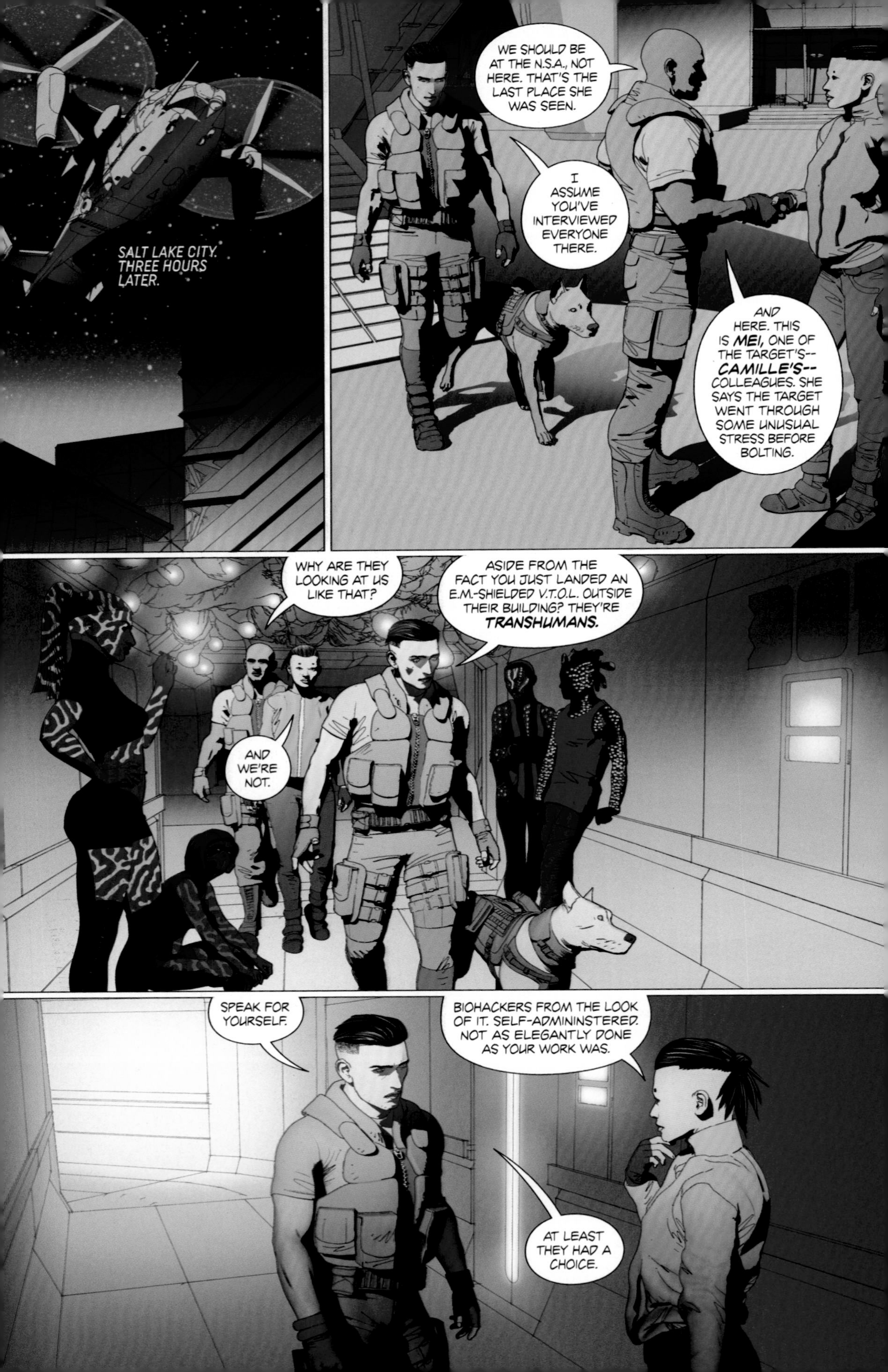
SALT LAKE CITY. THREE HOURS LATER.
WE SHOULD BE AT THE N.S.A., NOT HERE. THAT'S THE LAST PLACE SHE WAS SEEN.
I ASSUME YOU'VE INTERVIEWED EVERYONE THERE.
AND HERE. THIS IS MEI, ONE OF THE TARGET'S-- CAMILLE'S-- COLLEAGUES. SHE SAYS THE TARGET WENT THROUGH SOME UNUSUAL STRESS BEFORE BOLTING.
WHY ARE THEY LOOKING AT US LIKE THAT?
ASIDE FROM THE FACT YOU JUST LANDED AN E.M.-SHIELDED V.T.O.L. OUTSIDE THEIR BUILDING? THEY'RE TRANSHUMANS.
AND WE'RE NOT.
SPEAK FOR YOURSELF.
BIOHACKERS FROM THE LOOK OF IT. SELF-ADMININSTERED. NOT AS ELEGANTLY DONE AS YOUR WORK WAS.
AT LEAST THEY HAD A CHOICE.

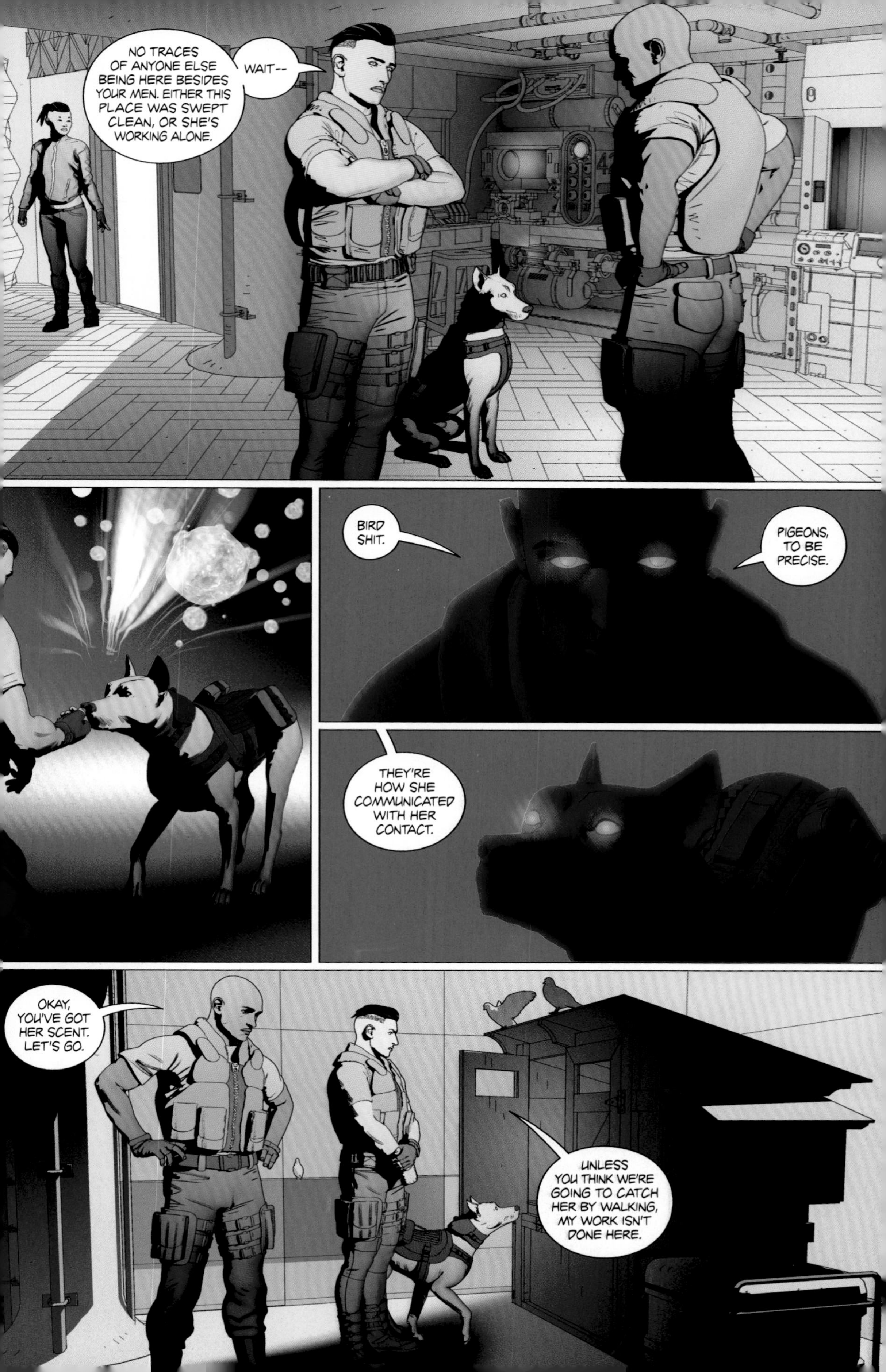
NO TRACES OF ANYONE ELSE BEING HERE BESIDES YOUR MEN. EITHER THIS PLACE WAS SWEPT CLEAN, OR SHE'S WORKING ALONE.
WAIT--
BIRD SHIT.
PIGEONS, TO BE PRECISE.
THEY'RE HOW SHE COMMUNICATED WITH HER CONTACT.
OKAY, YOU'VE GOT HER SCENT. LET'S GO.
UNLESS YOU THINK WE'RE GOING TO CATCH HER BY WALKING, MY WORK ISN'T DONE HERE.

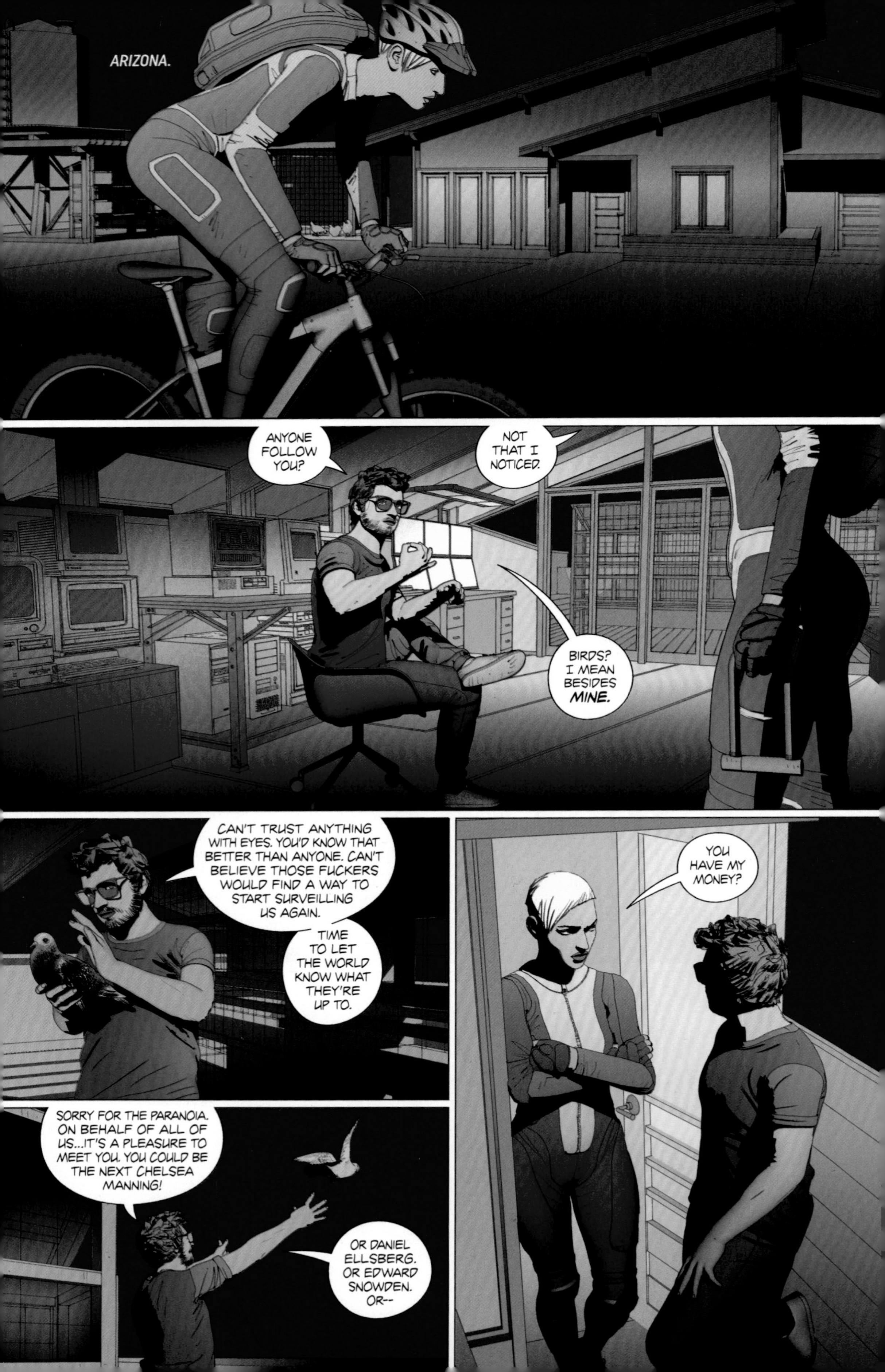
ARIZONA.
ANYONE FOLLOW YOU?
NOT THAT I NOTICED.
BIRDS? I MEAN BESIDES MINE.
CAN'T TRUST ANYTHING WITH EYES. YOU'D KNOW THAT BETTER THAN ANYONE. CAN'T BELIEVE THOSE FUCKERS WOULD FIND A WAY TO START SURVEILLING US AGAIN.
TIME TO LET THE WORLD KNOW WHAT THEY'RE UP TO.
SORRY FOR THE PARANOIA. ON BEHALF OF ALL OF US...IT'S A PLEASURE TO MEET YOU. YOU COULD BE THE NEXT CHELSEA MANNING!
OR DANIEL ELLSBERG. OR EDWARD SNOWDEN. OR--
YOU HAVE MY MONEY?

WAIT. I THOUGHT YOU WERE A TRUE BELIEVER.

YOU GUYS WANTED SOMEONE INSIDE. YOU CAN'T GET PICKY.

FUCKING MERCENARY.

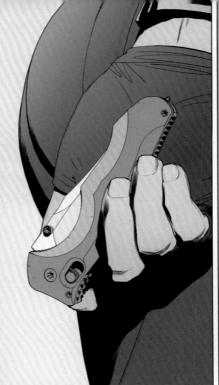

I'VE SEEN THE SHIT THEY'RE SURVEILLING. I DON'T THINK YOU'D BE SO QUICK TO BLOW THIS THING UP IF YOU SAW WHAT I DID. BUT I DON'T CARE.

I'M GOING TO ASK YOU ONE MORE TIME. WHERE'S MY MONEY?

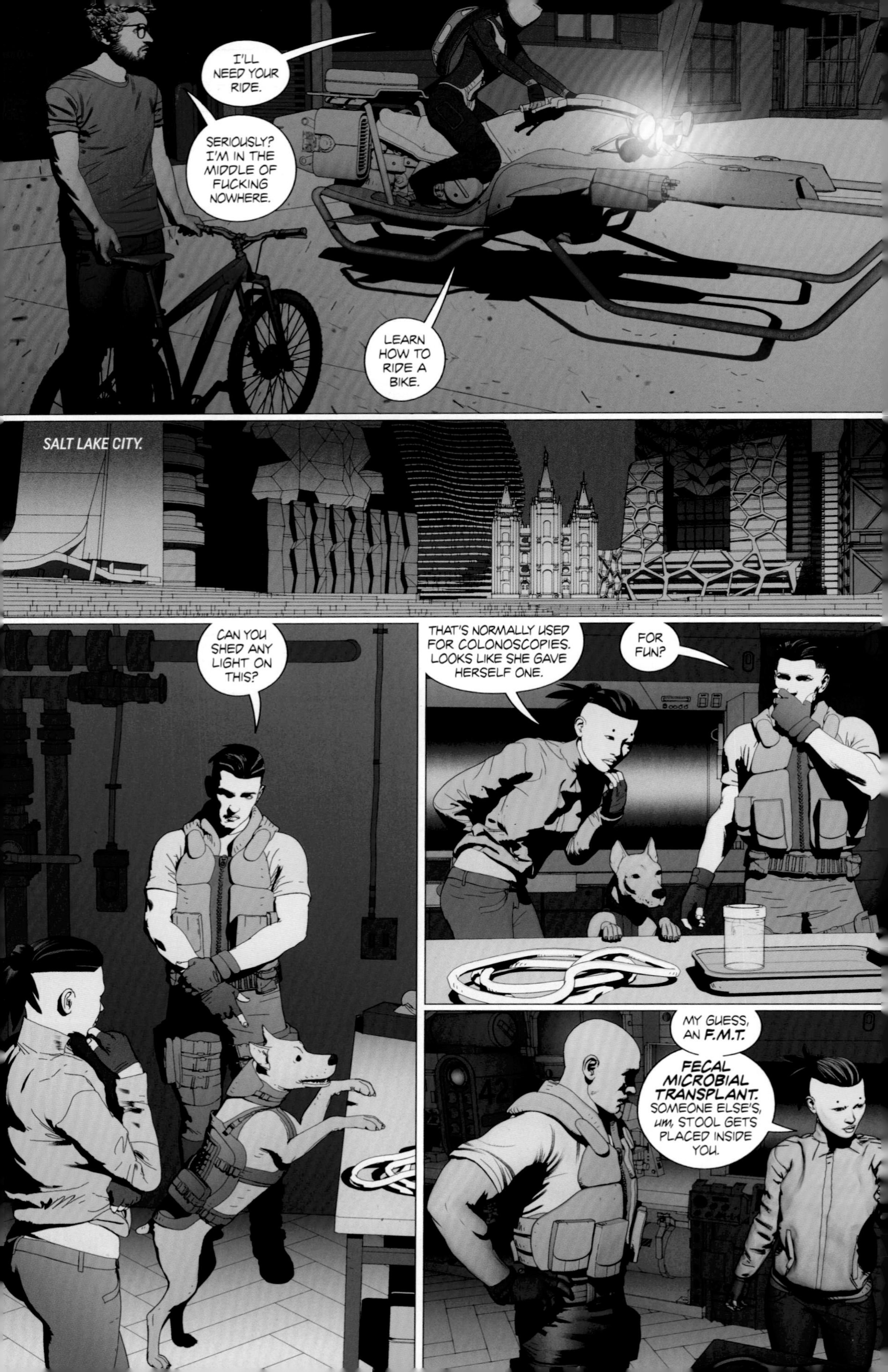
I'LL NEED YOUR RIDE.
SERIOUSLY? I'M IN THE MIDDLE OF FUCKING NOWHERE.
LEARN HOW TO RIDE A BIKE.
SALT LAKE CITY.
CAN YOU SHED ANY LIGHT ON THIS?
THAT'S NORMALLY USED FOR COLONOSCOPIES. LOOKS LIKE SHE GAVE HERSELF ONE.
FOR FUN?
MY GUESS, AN F.M.T.
FECAL MICROBIAL TRANSPLANT. SOMEONE ELSE'S, um, STOOL GETS PLACED INSIDE YOU.

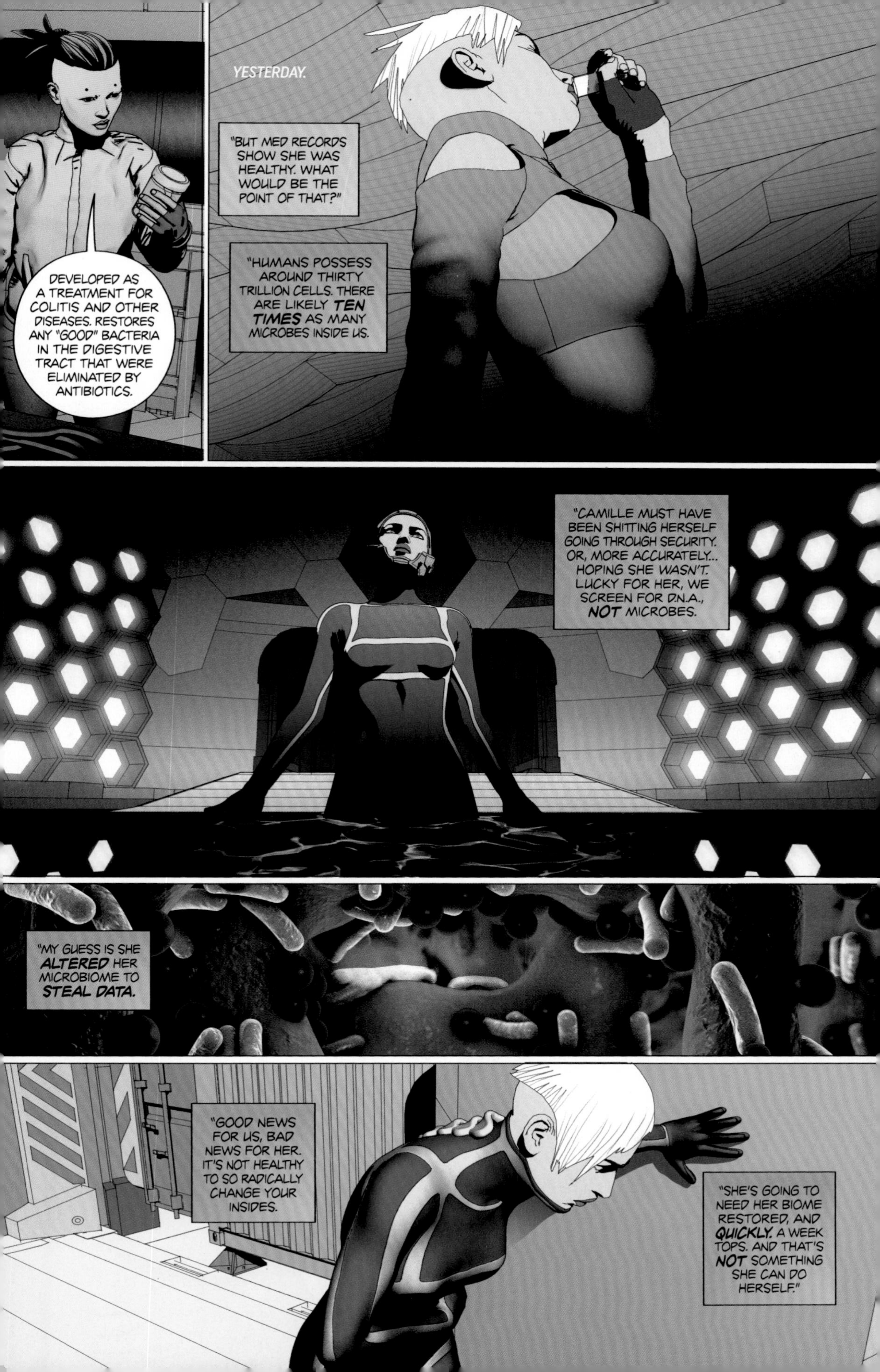
DEVELOPED AS A TREATMENT FOR COLITIS AND OTHER DISEASES. RESTORES ANY "GOOD" BACTERIA IN THE DIGESTIVE TRACT THAT WERE ELIMINATED BY ANTIBIOTICS.
YESTERDAY.
"BUT MED RECORDS SHOW SHE WAS HEALTHY. WHAT WOULD BE THE POINT OF THAT?"
"HUMANS POSSESS AROUND THIRTY TRILLION CELLS. THERE ARE LIKELY **TEN TIMES** AS MANY MICROBES INSIDE US.
"CAMILLE MUST HAVE BEEN SHITTING HERSELF GOING THROUGH SECURITY. OR, MORE ACCURATELY... HOPING SHE *WASN'T.* LUCKY FOR HER, WE SCREEN FOR D.N.A., **NOT** MICROBES.
"MY GUESS IS SHE **ALTERED** HER MICROBIOME TO **STEAL DATA.**
"GOOD NEWS FOR US, BAD NEWS FOR HER. IT'S NOT HEALTHY TO SO RADICALLY CHANGE YOUR INSIDES.
"SHE'S GOING TO NEED HER BIOME RESTORED, AND **QUICKLY.** A WEEK TOPS. AND THAT'S **NOT** SOMETHING SHE CAN DO HERSELF."

NOW.

WHO COULD HAVE DONE THIS?

SOMEONE WITH TREMENDOUS RESOURCES. I'M GUESSING A NATION-STATE. BUT SHE'S NEVER EVEN USED HER PASSPORT.

YOU'RE ASKING THE WRONG QUESTION. WHY GO THROUGH ALL THIS?

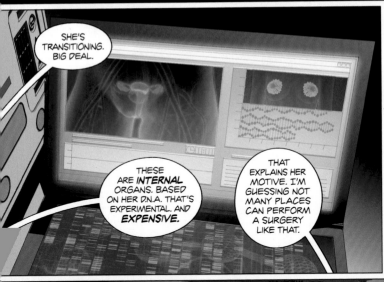

SHE'S TRANSITIONING. BIG DEAL.

THESE ARE **INTERNAL** ORGANS. BASED ON HER D.N.A. THAT'S EXPERIMENTAL. AND **EXPENSIVE.**

THAT EXPLAINS HER MOTIVE. I'M GUESSING NOT MANY PLACES CAN PERFORM A SURGERY LIKE THAT.

CHINA HAS BEEN GIVING INCENTIVES FOR REASSIGNMENT TO HELP WITH THEIR GENDER IMBALANCE.

SHE'S NOT GETTING TO CHINA IN A WEEK. MAYBE CUBA? THEY'VE GOT BETTER HEALTH CARE THAN WE DO.

THINK CLOSER.

THERE IS ONE PLACE I KNOW. A... FARM. IN--

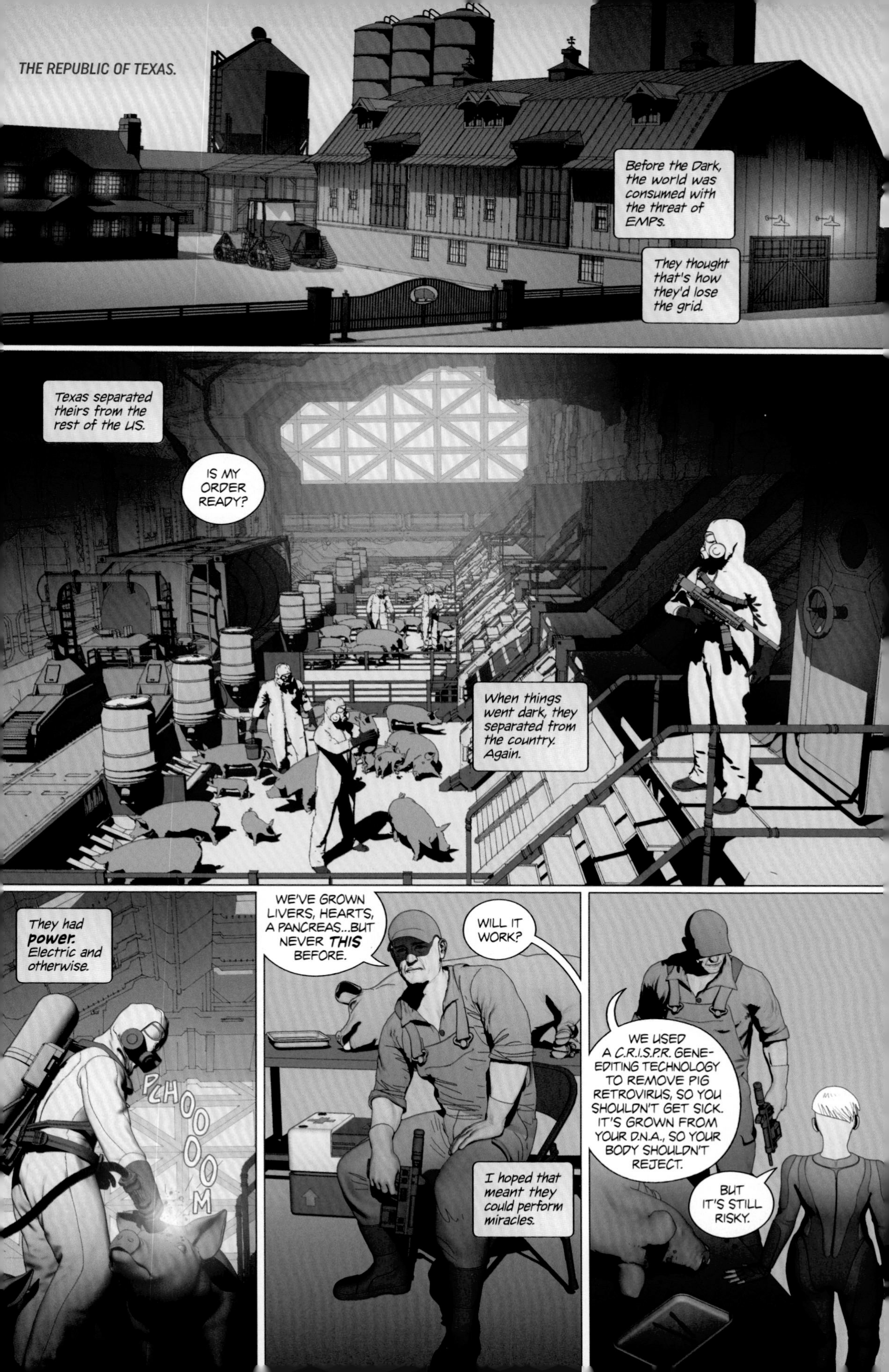

THE REPUBLIC OF TEXAS.
Before the Dark, the world was consumed with the threat of EMPs.
They thought that's how they'd lose the grid.
Texas separated theirs from the rest of the US.
IS MY ORDER READY?
When things went dark, they separated from the country. Again.
They had **power.** Electric and otherwise.
PLCHOOOOOM
WE'VE GROWN LIVERS, HEARTS, A PANCREAS...BUT NEVER **THIS** BEFORE.
WILL IT WORK?
I hoped that meant they could perform miracles.
WE USED A C.R.I.S.P.R. GENE-EDITING TECHNOLOGY TO REMOVE PIG RETROVIRUS, SO YOU SHOULDN'T GET SICK. IT'S GROWN FROM YOUR D.N.A., SO YOUR BODY SHOULDN'T REJECT.
BUT IT'S STILL RISKY.

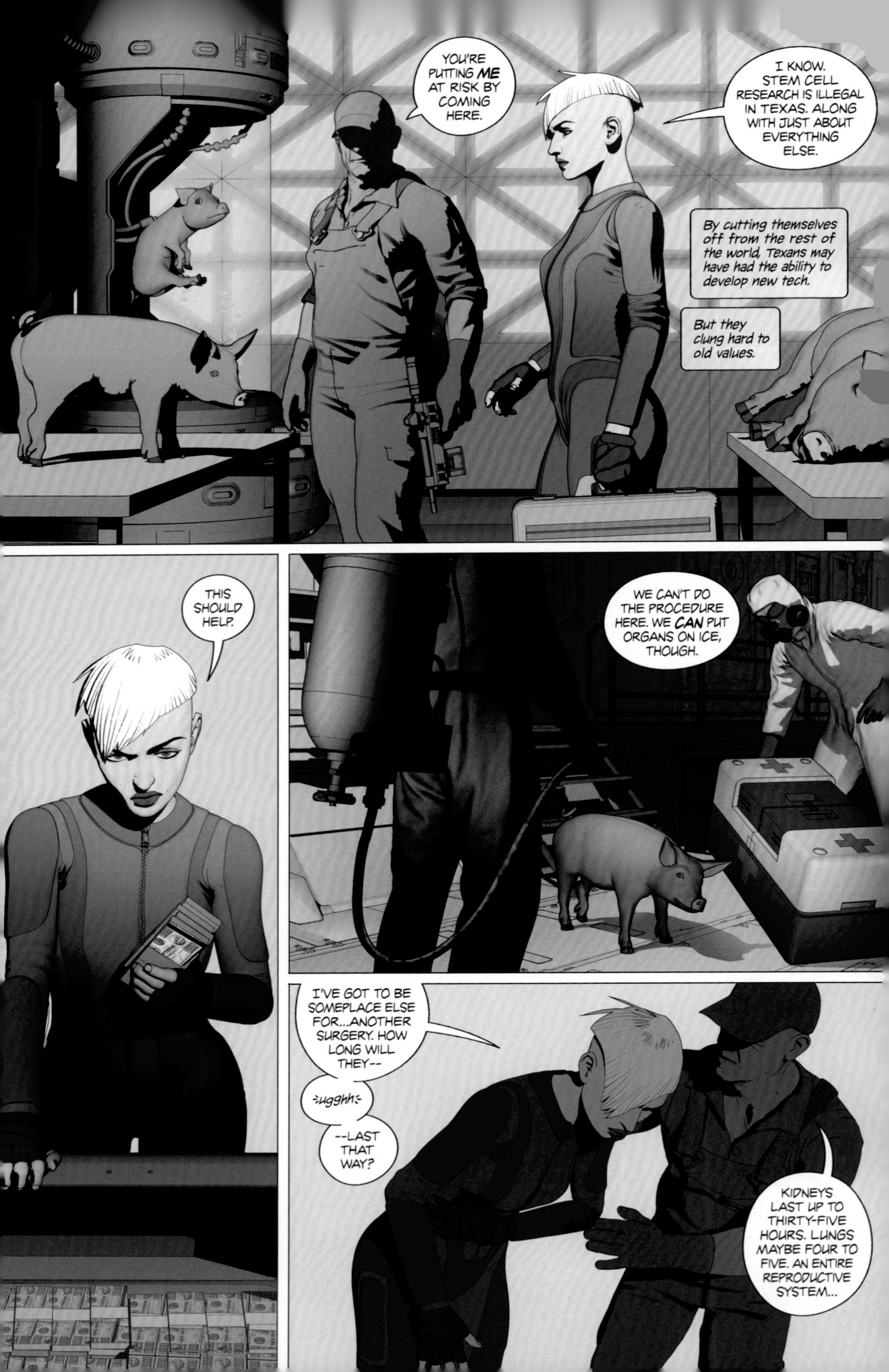
YOU'RE PUTTING ME AT RISK BY COMING HERE.
I KNOW. STEM CELL RESEARCH IS ILLEGAL IN TEXAS. ALONG WITH JUST ABOUT EVERYTHING ELSE.
By cutting themselves off from the rest of the world, Texans may have had the ability to develop new tech.
But they clung hard to old values.
THIS SHOULD HELP.
WE CAN'T DO THE PROCEDURE HERE. WE CAN PUT ORGANS ON ICE, THOUGH.
I'VE GOT TO BE SOMEPLACE ELSE FOR...ANOTHER SURGERY. HOW LONG WILL THEY--
ugghh
--LAST THAT WAY?
KIDNEYS LAST UP TO THIRTY-FIVE HOURS. LUNGS MAYBE FOUR TO FIVE. AN ENTIRE REPRODUCTIVE SYSTEM...

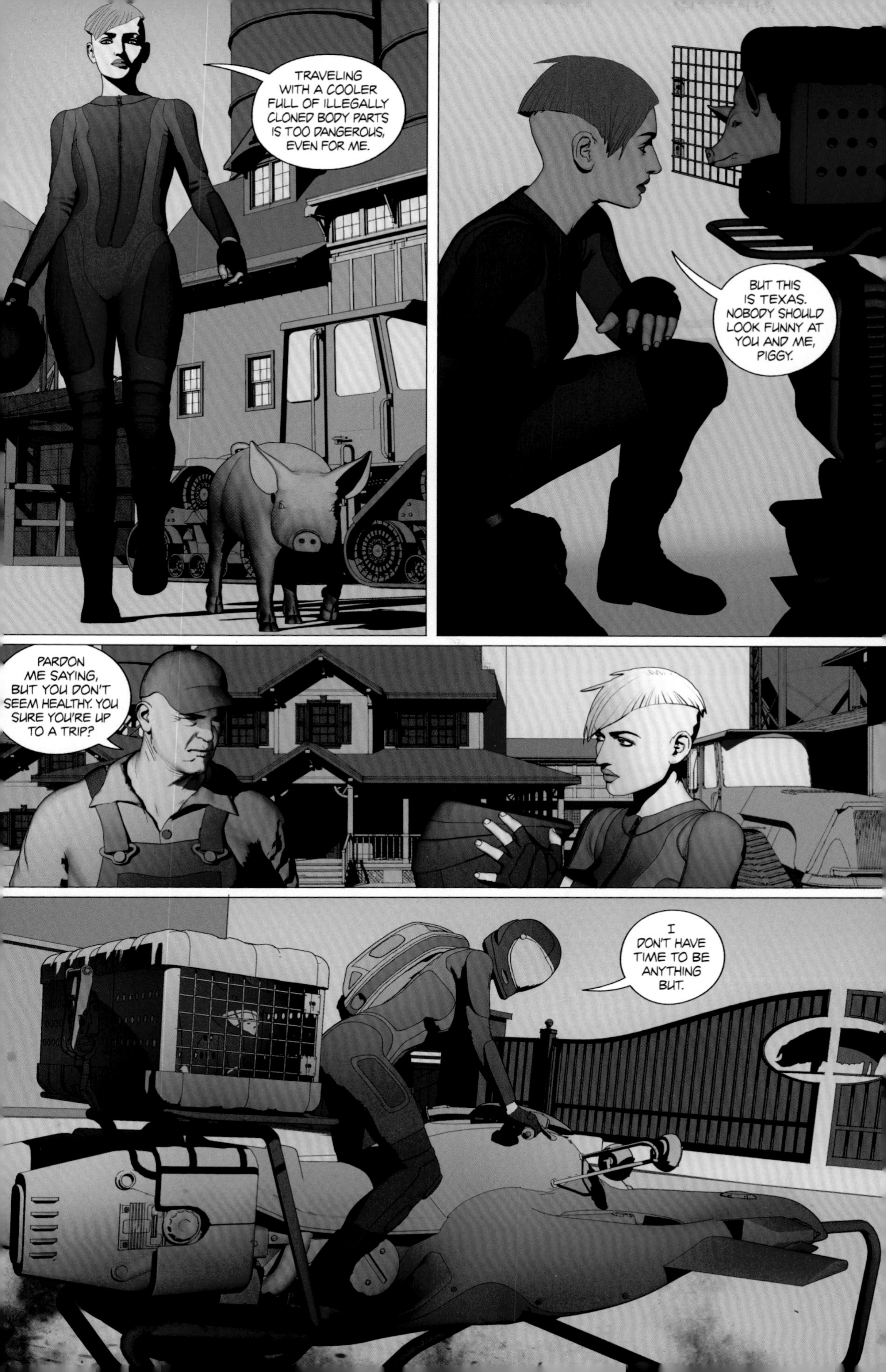

TRAVELING WITH A COOLER FULL OF ILLEGALLY CLONED BODY PARTS IS TOO DANGEROUS, EVEN FOR ME.
BUT THIS IS TEXAS. NOBODY SHOULD LOOK FUNNY AT YOU AND ME, PIGGY.
PARDON ME SAYING, BUT YOU DON'T SEEM HEALTHY. YOU SURE YOU'RE UP TO A TRIP?
I DON'T HAVE TIME TO BE ANYTHING BUT.

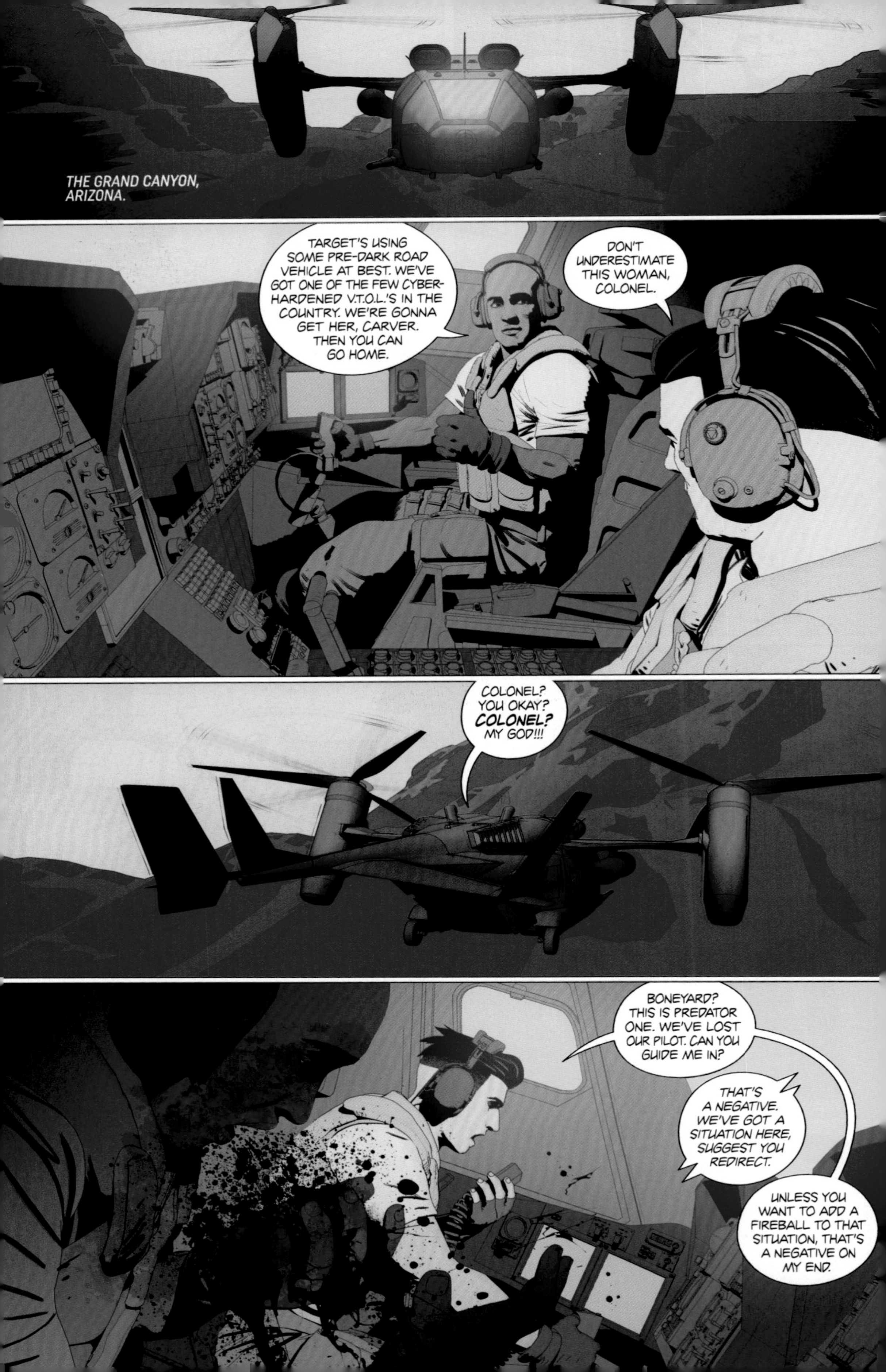
THE GRAND CANYON, ARIZONA.
TARGET'S USING SOME PRE-DARK ROAD VEHICLE AT BEST. WE'VE GOT ONE OF THE FEW CYBER-HARDENED V.T.O.L.'S IN THE COUNTRY. WE'RE GONNA GET HER, CARVER. THEN YOU CAN GO HOME.
DON'T UNDERESTIMATE THIS WOMAN, COLONEL.
COLONEL? YOU OKAY? ***COLONEL?*** MY GOD!!!
BONEYARD? THIS IS PREDATOR ONE. WE'VE LOST OUR PILOT. CAN YOU GUIDE ME IN?
THAT'S A NEGATIVE. WE'VE GOT A SITUATION HERE, SUGGEST YOU REDIRECT.
UNLESS YOU WANT TO ADD A FIREBALL TO THAT SITUATION, THAT'S A NEGATIVE ON MY END.

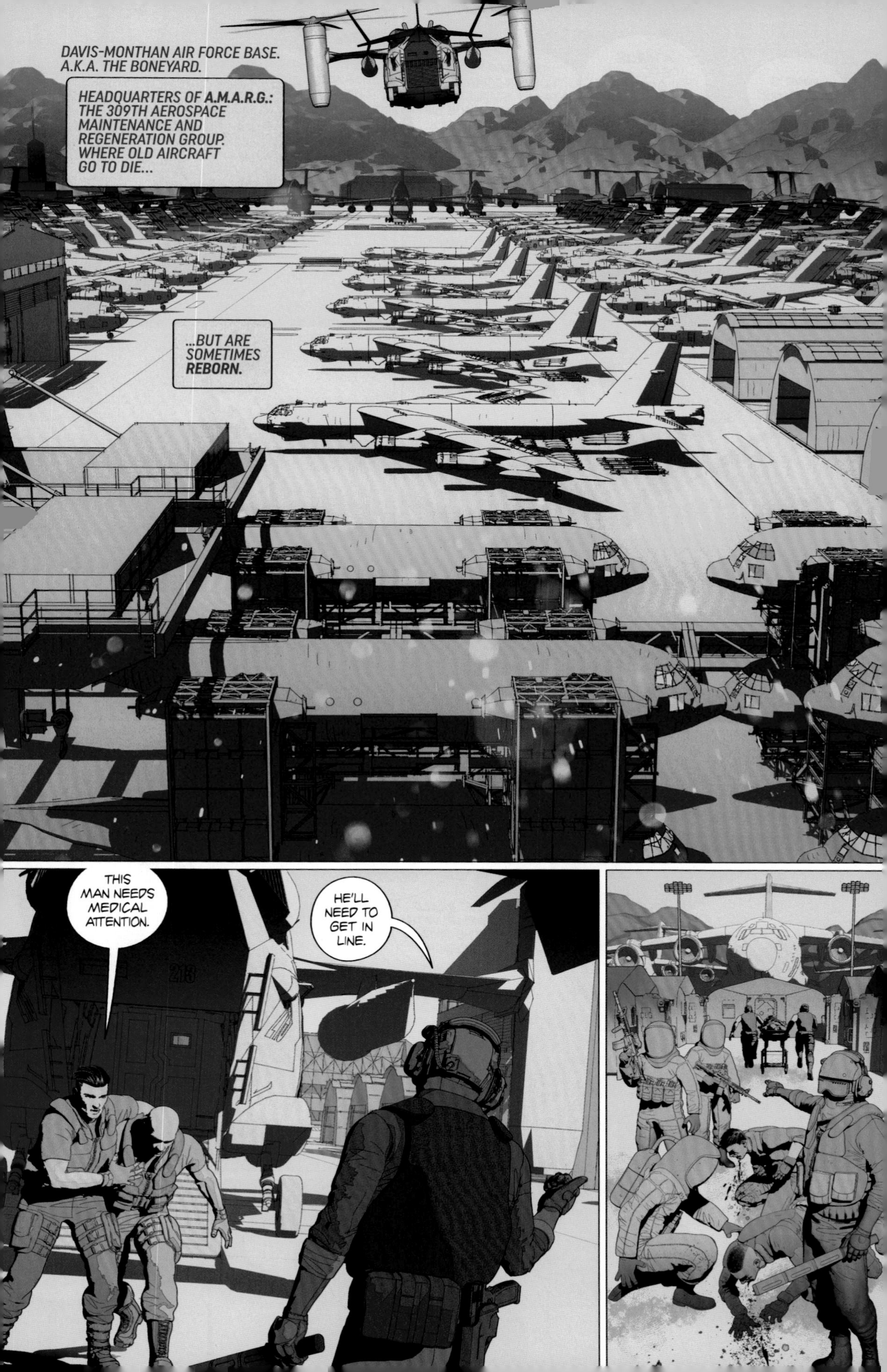
DAVIS-MONTHAN AIR FORCE BASE.
A.K.A. THE BONEYARD.
HEADQUARTERS OF **A.M.A.R.G.:** THE 309TH AEROSPACE MAINTENANCE AND REGENERATION GROUP. WHERE OLD AIRCRAFT GO TO DIE...
...BUT ARE SOMETIMES **REBORN.**
THIS MAN NEEDS MEDICAL ATTENTION.
HE'LL NEED TO GET IN LINE.
213

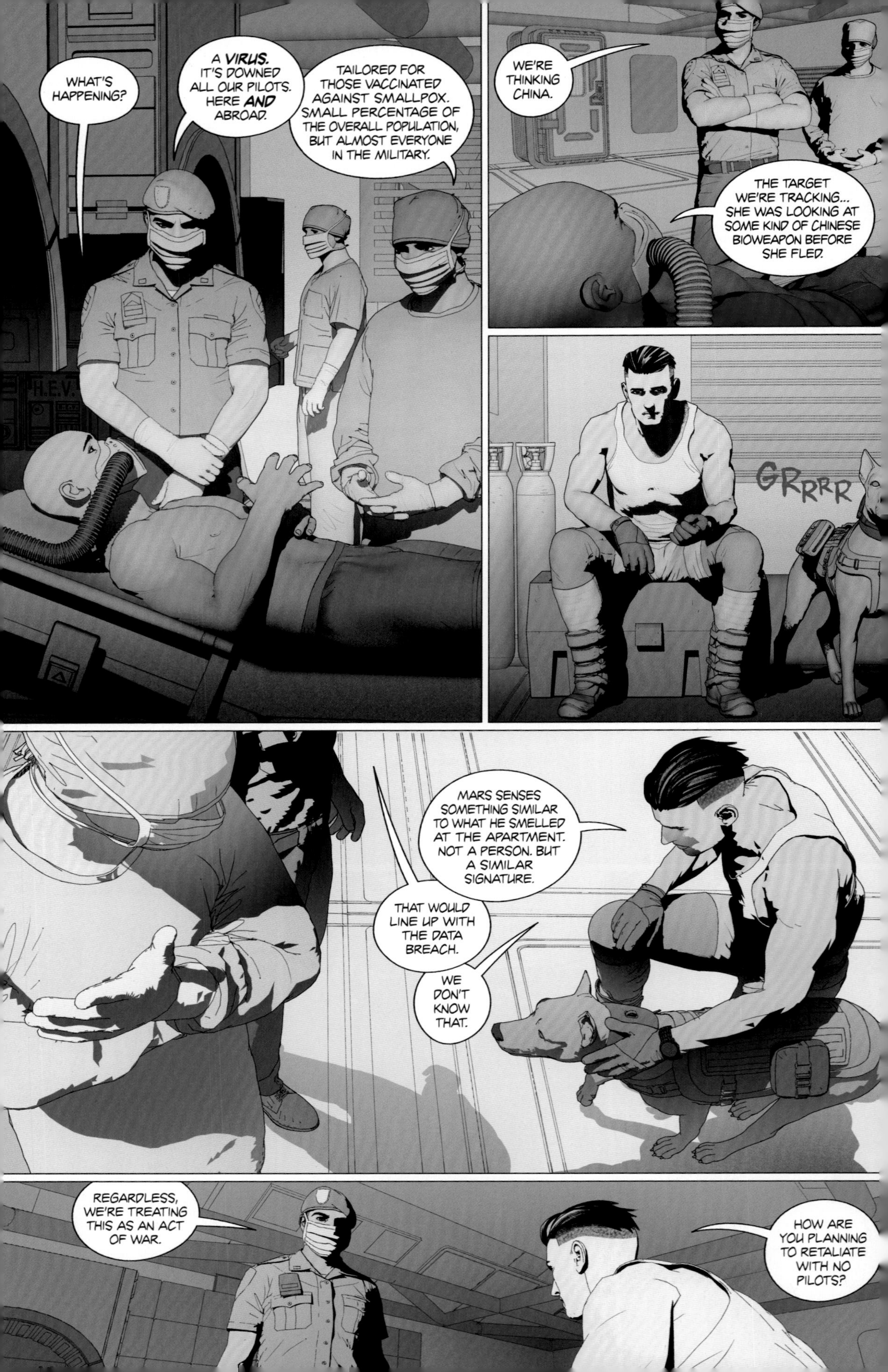
WHAT'S HAPPENING?
A **VIRUS.** IT'S DOWNED ALL OUR PILOTS. HERE **AND** ABROAD.
TAILORED FOR THOSE VACCINATED AGAINST SMALLPOX. SMALL PERCENTAGE OF THE OVERALL POPULATION, BUT ALMOST EVERYONE IN THE MILITARY.
H.E.V.
WE'RE THINKING CHINA.
THE TARGET WE'RE TRACKING... SHE WAS LOOKING AT SOME KIND OF CHINESE BIOWEAPON BEFORE SHE FLED.
GRRRR
MARS SENSES SOMETHING SIMILAR TO WHAT HE SMELLED AT THE APARTMENT. NOT A PERSON. BUT A SIMILAR SIGNATURE.
THAT WOULD LINE UP WITH THE DATA BREACH.
WE DON'T KNOW THAT.
REGARDLESS, WE'RE TREATING THIS AS AN ACT OF WAR.
HOW ARE YOU PLANNING TO RETALIATE WITH NO PILOTS?

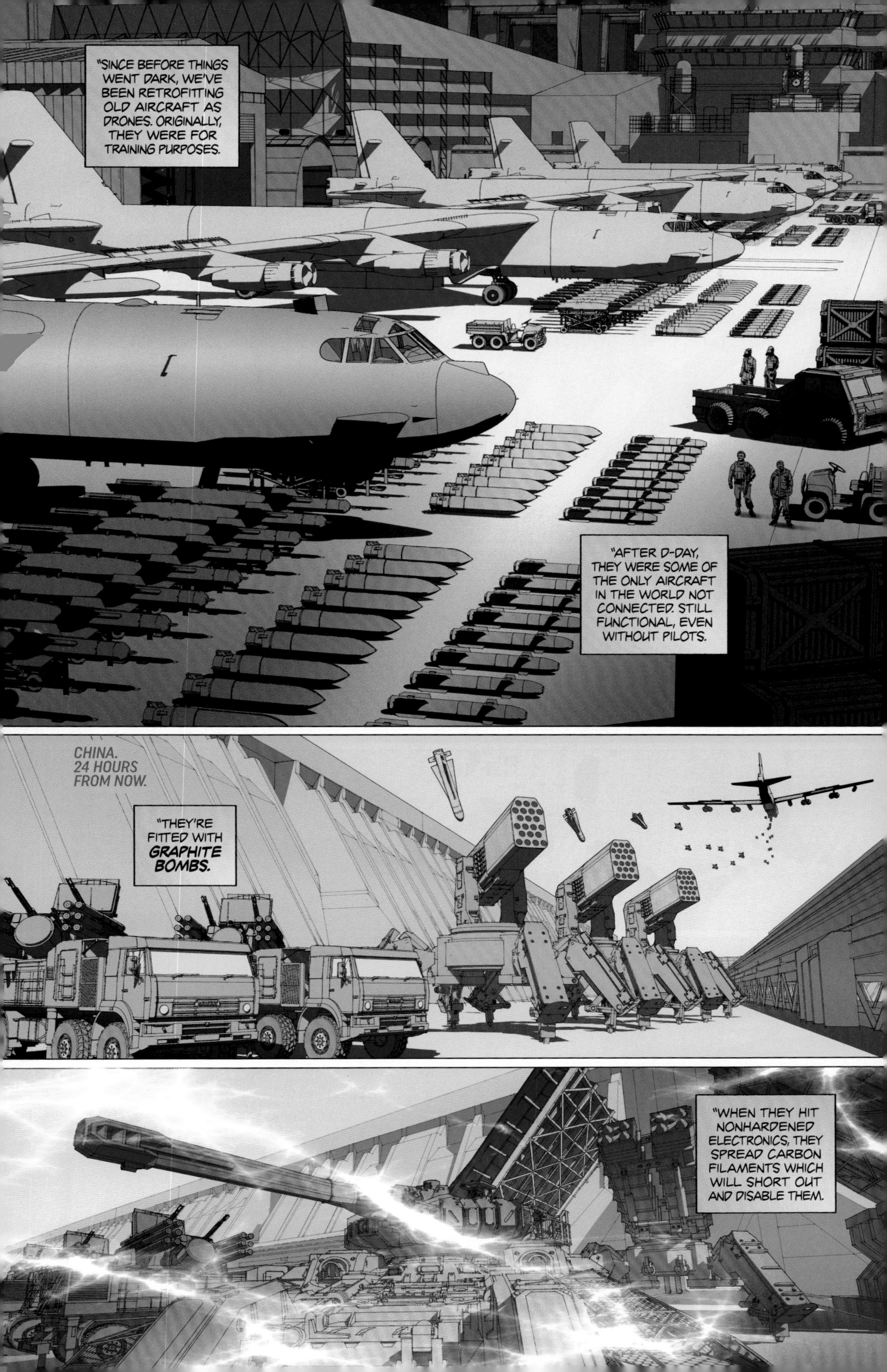
"SINCE BEFORE THINGS WENT DARK, WE'VE BEEN RETROFITTING OLD AIRCRAFT AS DRONES. ORIGINALLY, THEY WERE FOR TRAINING PURPOSES.
"AFTER D-DAY, THEY WERE SOME OF THE ONLY AIRCRAFT IN THE WORLD NOT CONNECTED. STILL FUNCTIONAL, EVEN WITHOUT PILOTS.
CHINA. 24 HOURS FROM NOW.
"THEY'RE FITTED WITH ***GRAPHITE BOMBS.***
"WHEN THEY HIT NONHARDENED ELECTRONICS, THEY SPREAD CARBON FILAMENTS WHICH WILL SHORT OUT AND DISABLE THEM.

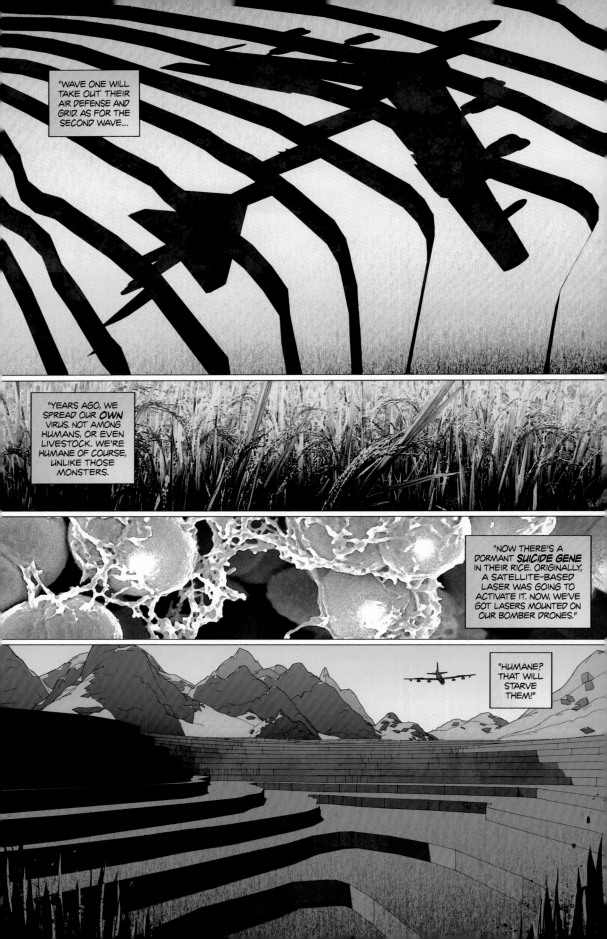

"WAVE ONE WILL TAKE OUT THEIR AIR DEFENSE AND GRID. AS FOR THE SECOND WAVE...

"YEARS AGO, WE SPREAD OUR *OWN* VIRUS. NOT AMONG HUMANS, OR EVEN LIVESTOCK. WE'RE HUMANE OF COURSE, UNLIKE THOSE MONSTERS.

"NOW THERE'S A DORMANT *SUICIDE GENE* IN THEIR RICE. ORIGINALLY, A SATELLITE-BASED LASER WAS GOING TO ACTIVATE IT. NOW, WE'VE GOT LASERS MOUNTED ON OUR BOMBER DRONES."

"HUMANE? THAT WILL STARVE THEM!"

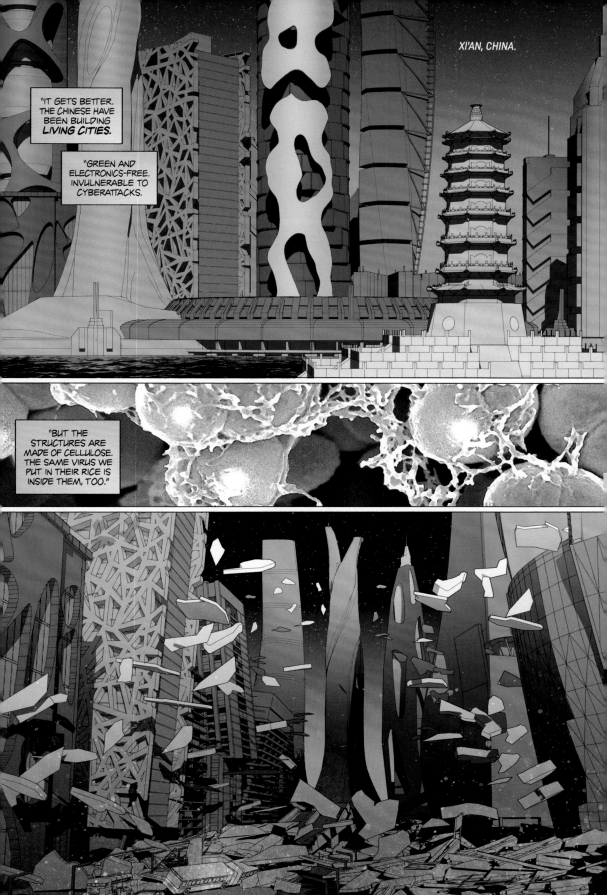

XI'AN, CHINA.

"IT GETS BETTER. THE CHINESE HAVE BEEN BUILDING *LIVING CITIES*.

"GREEN AND ELECTRONICS-FREE. INVULNERABLE TO CYBERATTACKS.

"BUT THE STRUCTURES ARE MADE OF CELLULOSE. THE SAME VIRUS WE PUT IN THEIR RICE IS INSIDE THEM, TOO."

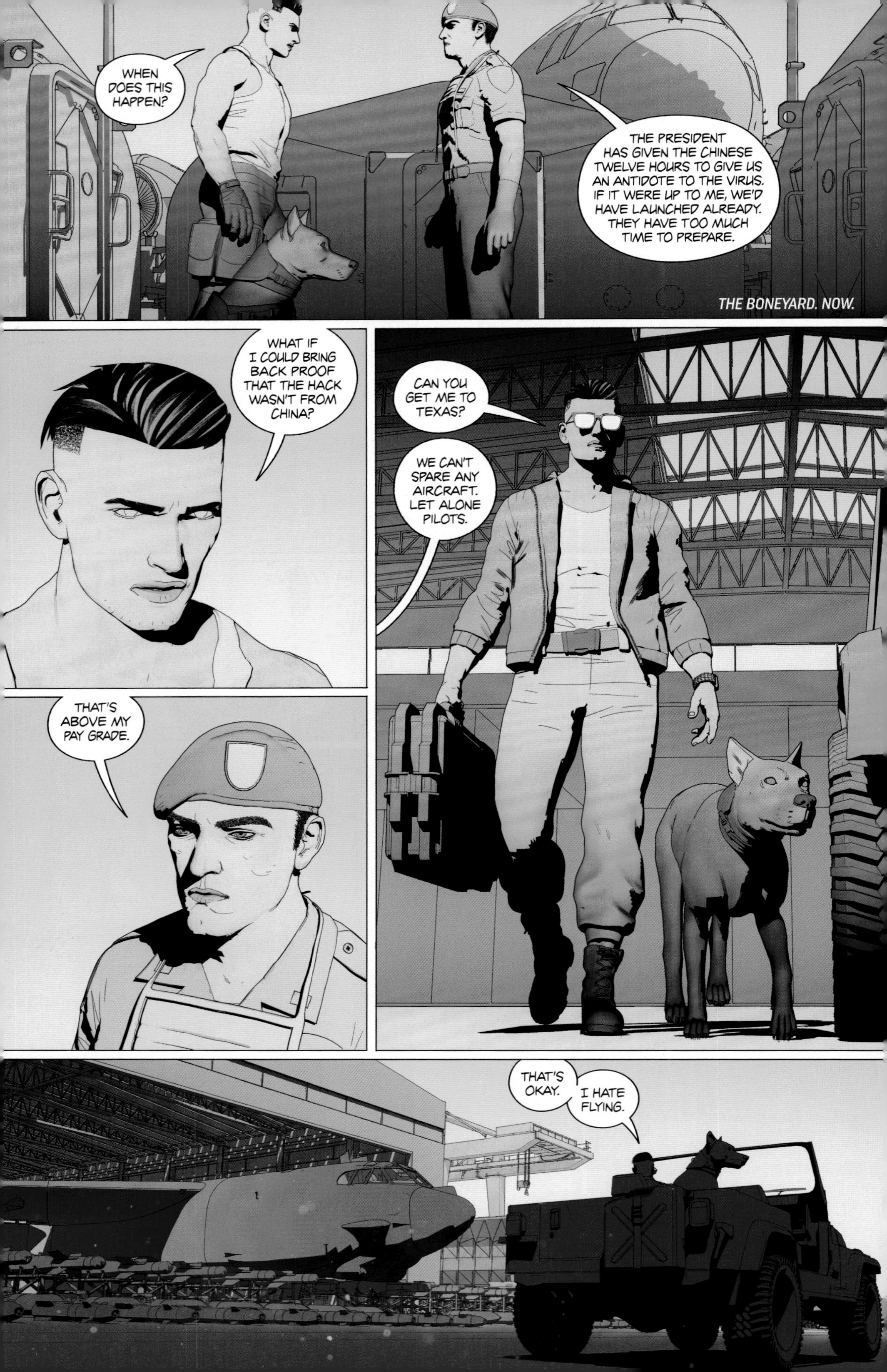
WHEN DOES THIS HAPPEN?
THE PRESIDENT HAS GIVEN THE CHINESE TWELVE HOURS TO GIVE US AN ANTIDOTE TO THE VIRUS. IF IT WERE UP TO ME, WE'D HAVE LAUNCHED ALREADY. THEY HAVE TOO MUCH TIME TO PREPARE.
THE BONEYARD. NOW.
WHAT IF I COULD BRING BACK PROOF THAT THE HACK WASN'T FROM CHINA?
THAT'S ABOVE MY PAY GRADE.
CAN YOU GET ME TO TEXAS?
WE CAN'T SPARE ANY AIRCRAFT. LET ALONE PILOTS.
THAT'S OKAY.
I HATE FLYING.

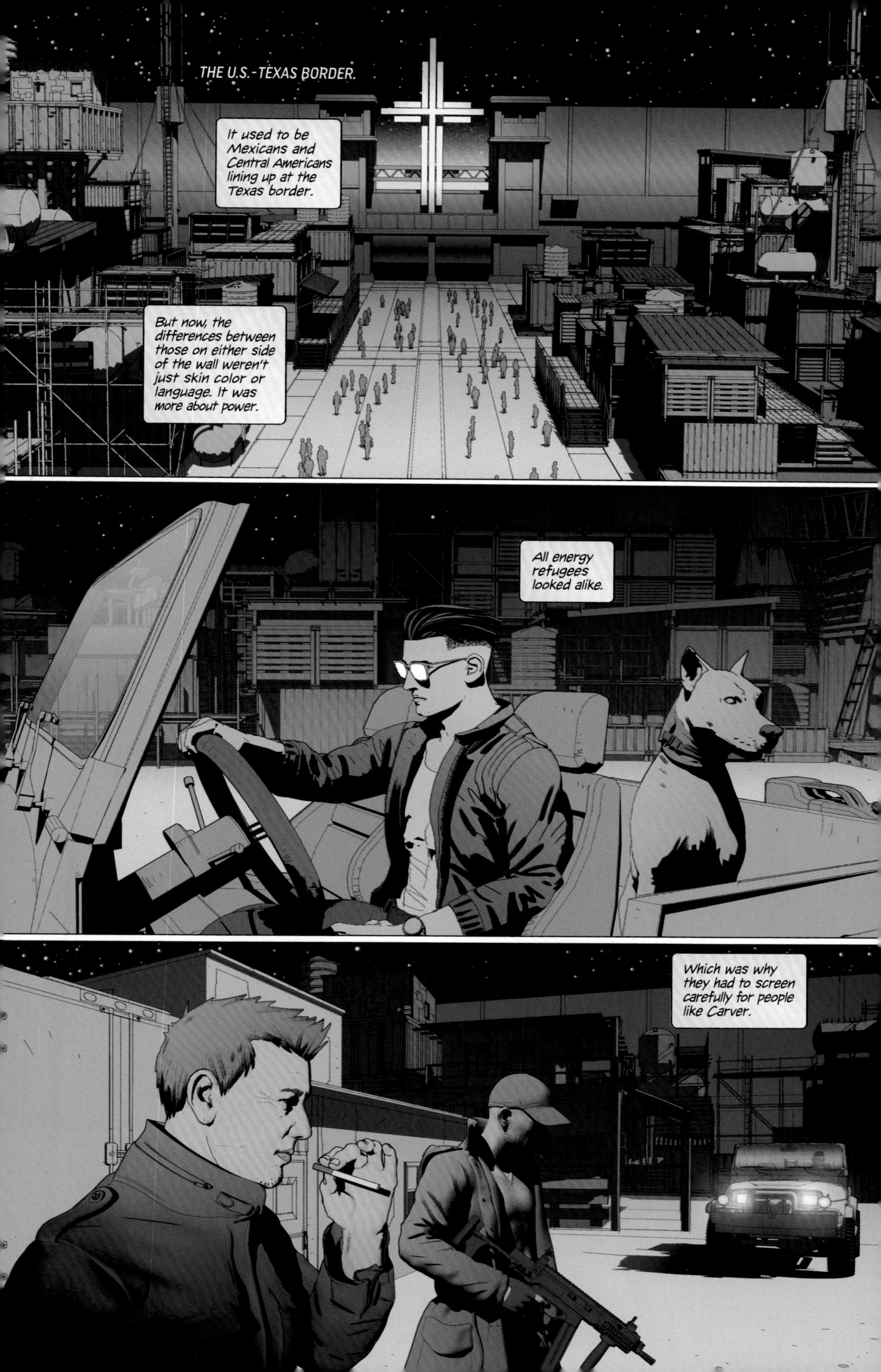
THE U.S.-TEXAS BORDER.
It used to be Mexicans and Central Americans lining up at the Texas border.
But now, the differences between those on either side of the wall weren't just skin color or language. It was more about power.
All energy refugees looked alike.
Which was why they had to screen carefully for people like Carver.

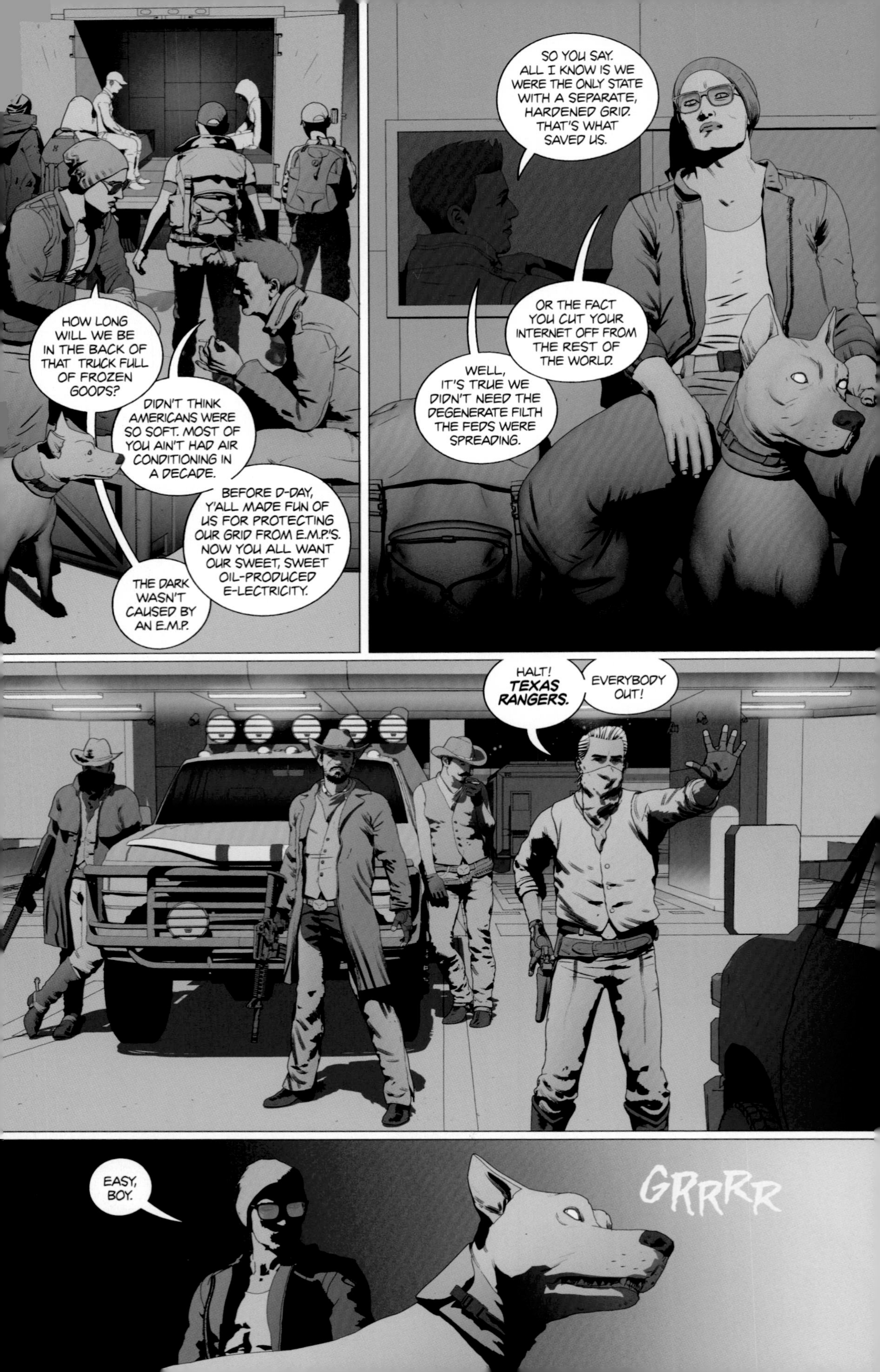
HOW LONG WILL WE BE IN THE BACK OF THAT TRUCK FULL OF FROZEN GOODS?
DIDN'T THINK AMERICANS WERE SO SOFT. MOST OF YOU AIN'T HAD AIR CONDITIONING IN A DECADE.
BEFORE D-DAY, Y'ALL MADE FUN OF US FOR PROTECTING OUR GRID FROM E.M.P.'S. NOW YOU ALL WANT OUR SWEET, SWEET OIL-PRODUCED E-LECTRICITY.
THE DARK WASN'T CAUSED BY AN E.M.P.
SO YOU SAY. ALL I KNOW IS WE WERE THE ONLY STATE WITH A SEPARATE, HARDENED GRID. THAT'S WHAT SAVED US.
OR THE FACT YOU CUT YOUR INTERNET OFF FROM THE REST OF THE WORLD.
WELL, IT'S TRUE WE DIDN'T NEED THE DEGENERATE FILTH THE FEDS WERE SPREADING.
HALT! **TEXAS RANGERS.**
EVERYBODY OUT!
EASY, BOY.
GRRRR

RELAX. YOUR COYOTE PAID HIS TOLL.

JUST GONNA COLLECT SOME BLOOD SAMPLES. YOU'LL BE FINE--

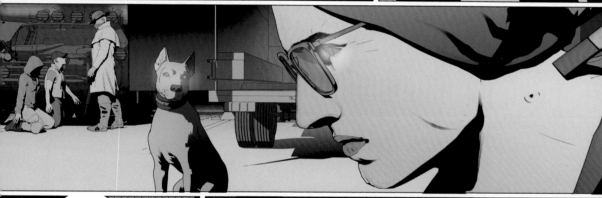

AS LONG AS YOU'RE HUMAN.

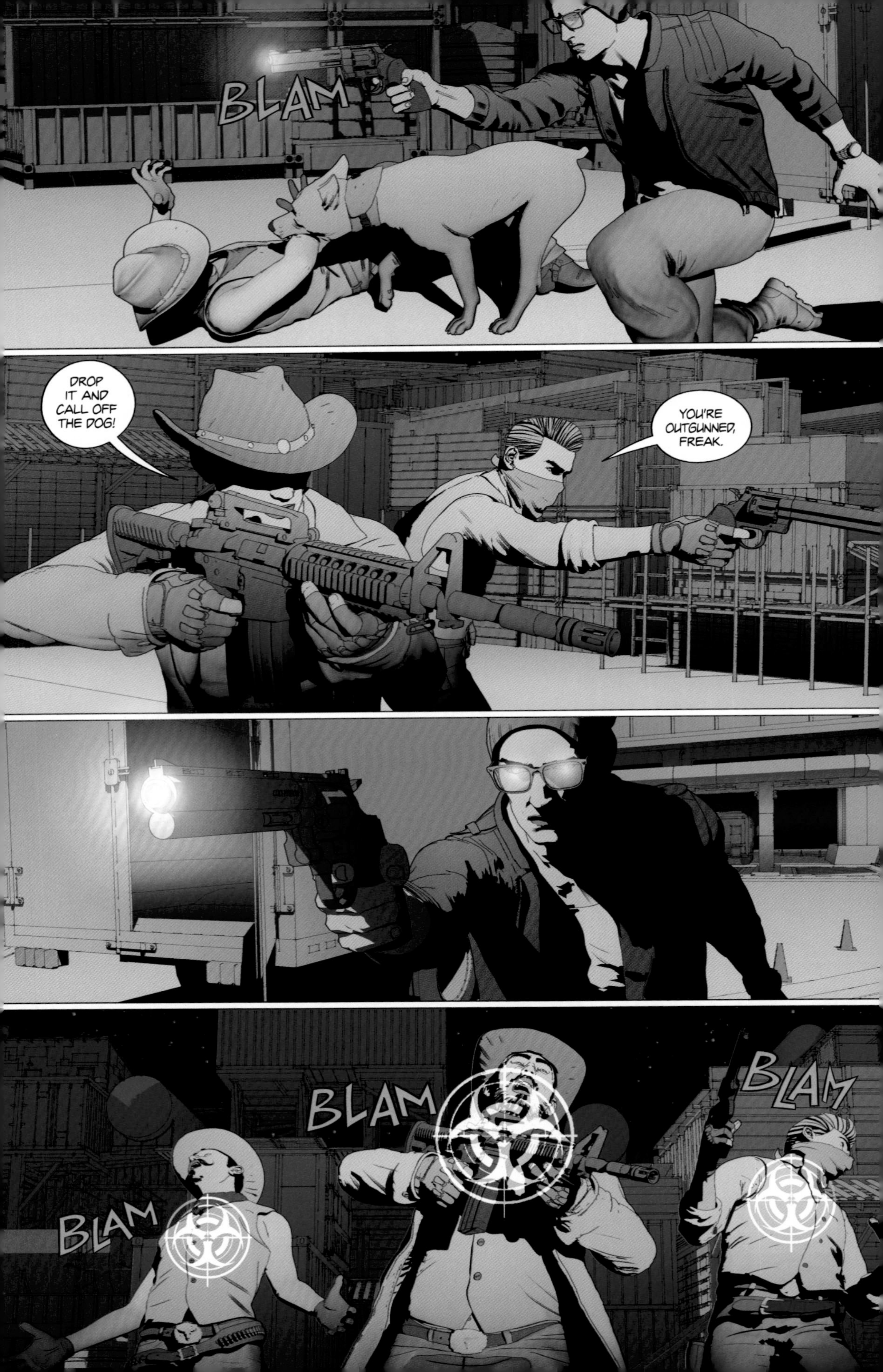
BLAM
DROP IT AND CALL OFF THE DOG!
YOU'RE OUTGUNNED, FREAK.
BLAM
BLAM
BLAM

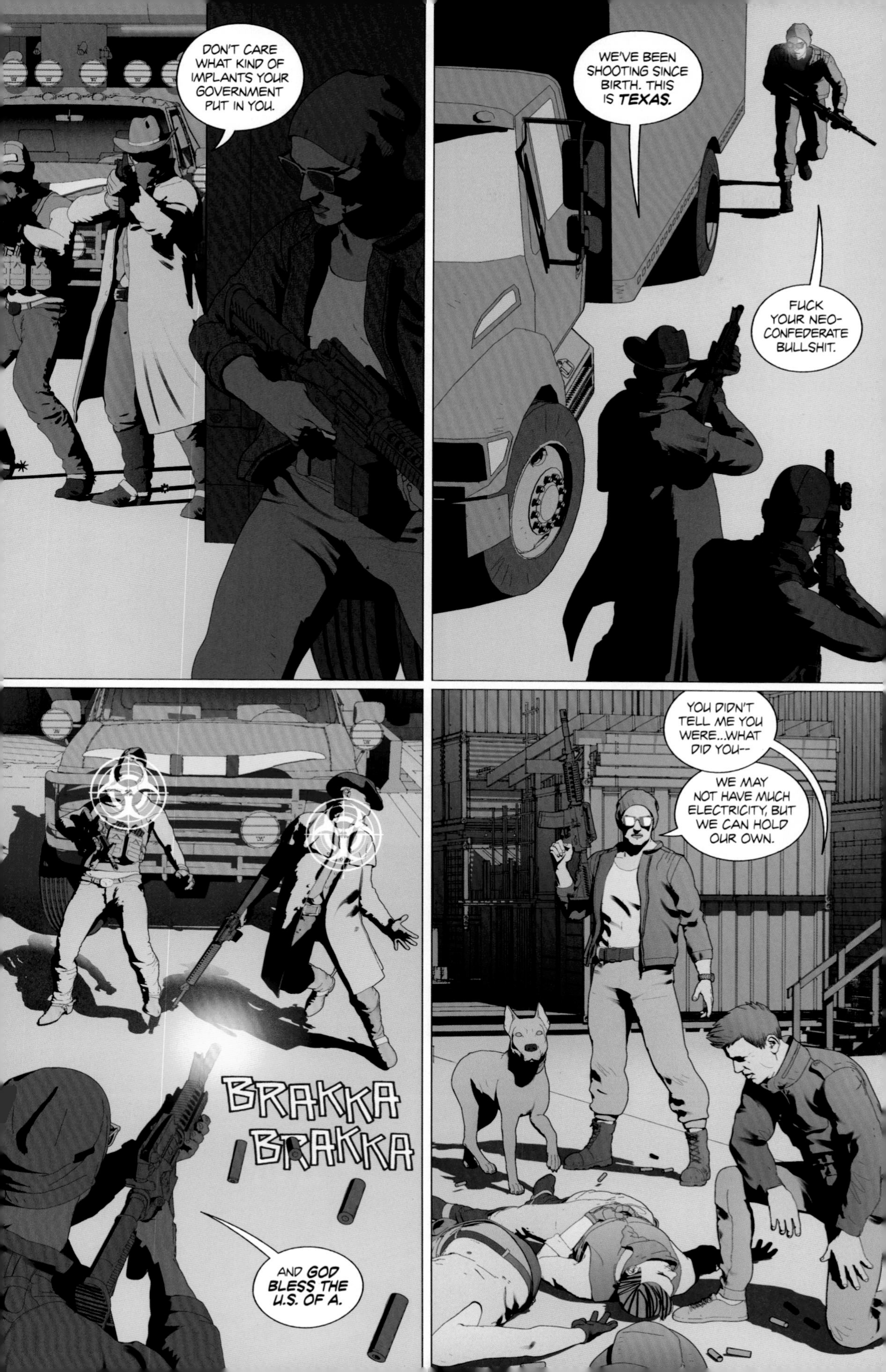
DON'T CARE WHAT KIND OF IMPLANTS YOUR GOVERNMENT PUT IN YOU.
WE'VE BEEN SHOOTING SINCE BIRTH. THIS IS ***TEXAS.***
FUCK YOUR NEO-CONFEDERATE BULLSHIT.
BRAKKA BRAKKA
AND ***GOD*** BLESS THE ***U.S. OF A.***
YOU DIDN'T TELL ME YOU WERE...WHAT DID YOU--
WE MAY NOT HAVE MUCH ELECTRICITY, BUT WE CAN HOLD OUR OWN.

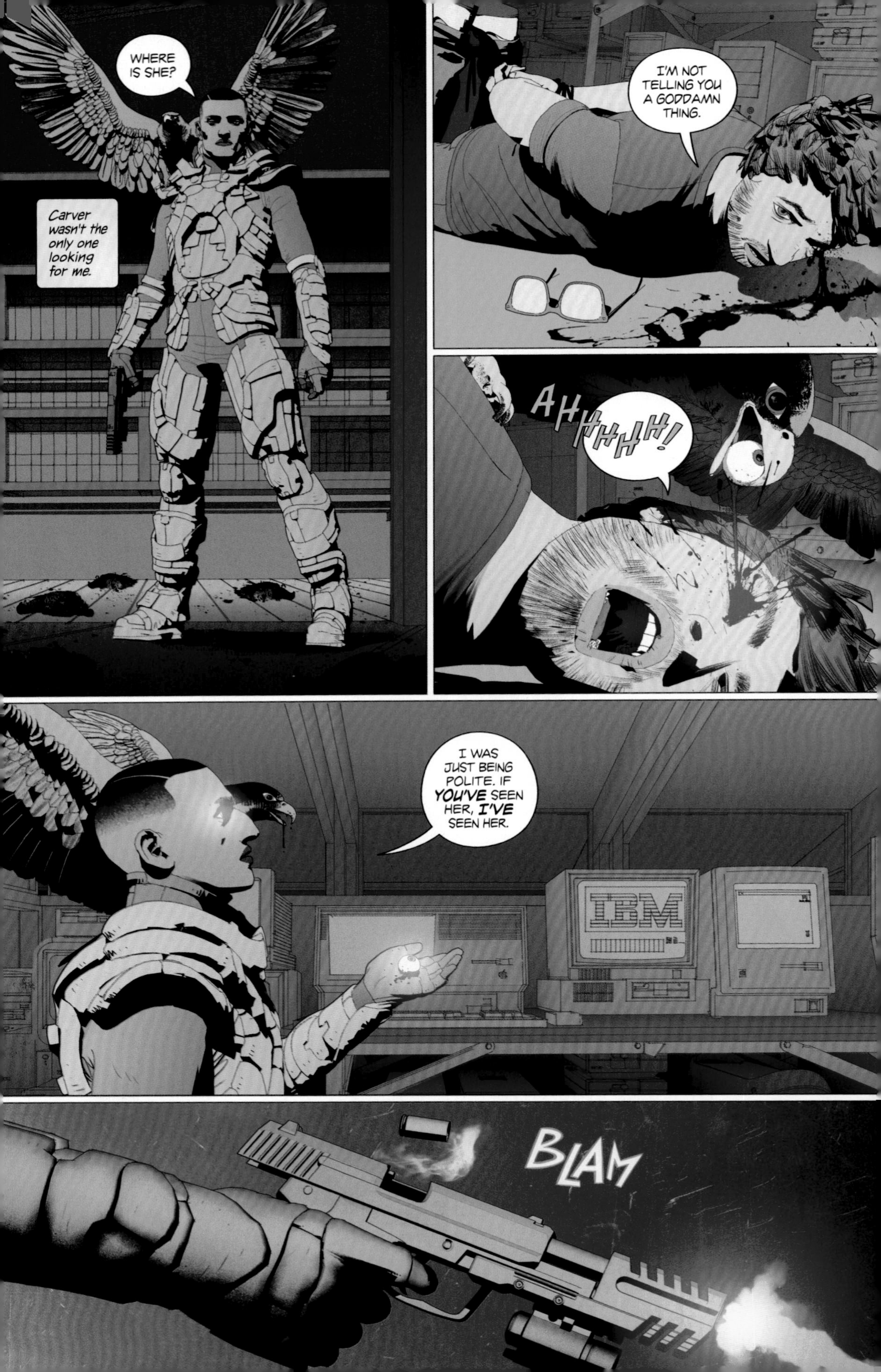
WHERE IS SHE?
Carver wasn't the only one looking for me.
I'M NOT TELLING YOU A GODDAMN THING.
AHHHHHH!
I WAS JUST BEING POLITE. IF YOU'VE SEEN HER, I'VE SEEN HER.
IBM
BLAM

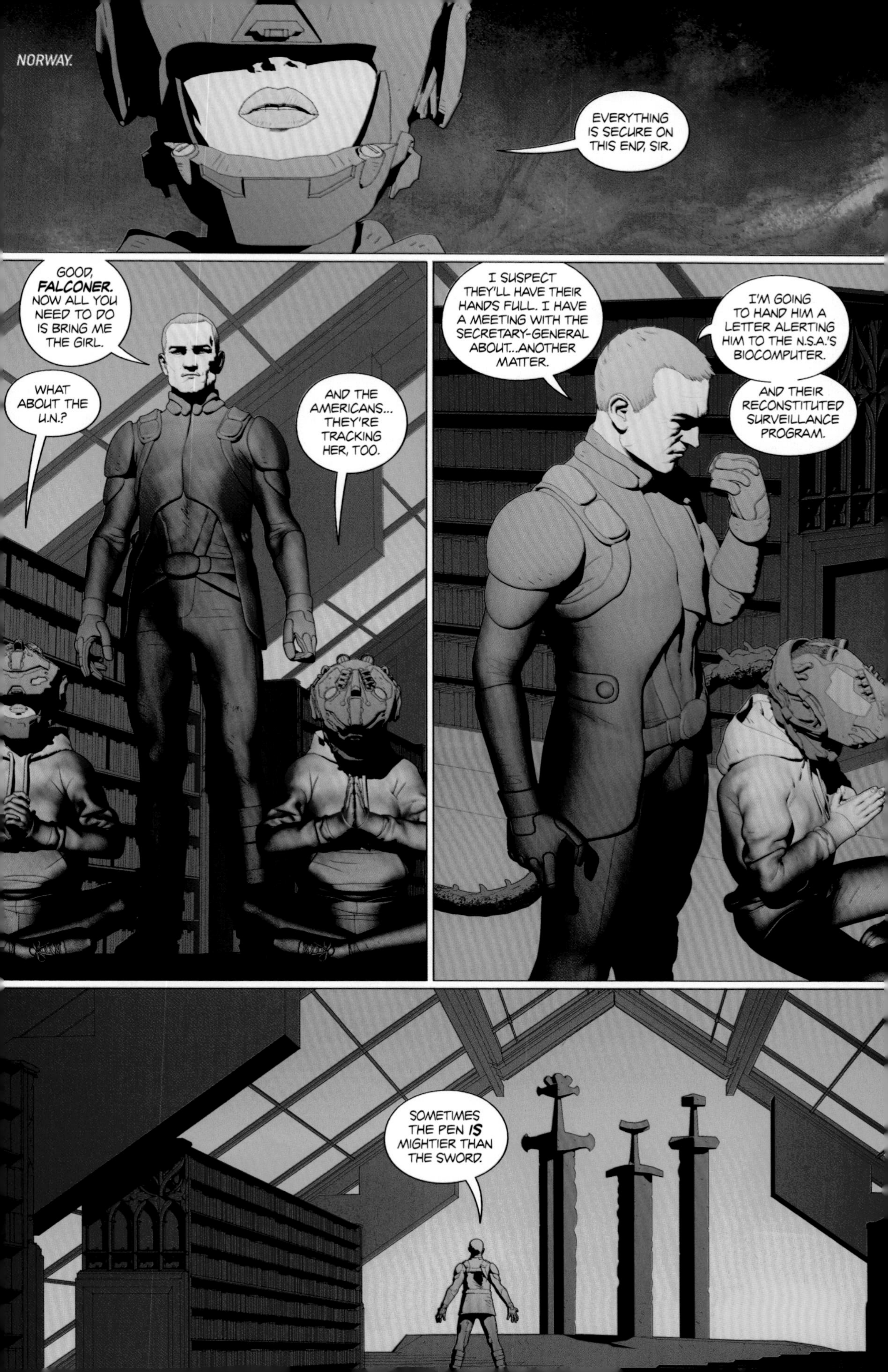
NORWAY.
EVERYTHING IS SECURE ON THIS END, SIR.
GOOD, FALCONER. NOW ALL YOU NEED TO DO IS BRING ME THE GIRL.
WHAT ABOUT THE U.N.?
AND THE AMERICANS... THEY'RE TRACKING HER, TOO.
I SUSPECT THEY'LL HAVE THEIR HANDS FULL. I HAVE A MEETING WITH THE SECRETARY-GENERAL ABOUT...ANOTHER MATTER.
I'M GOING TO HAND HIM A LETTER ALERTING HIM TO THE N.S.A.'S BIOCOMPUTER.
AND THEIR RECONSTITUTED SURVEILLANCE PROGRAM.
SOMETIMES THE PEN IS MIGHTIER THAN THE SWORD.

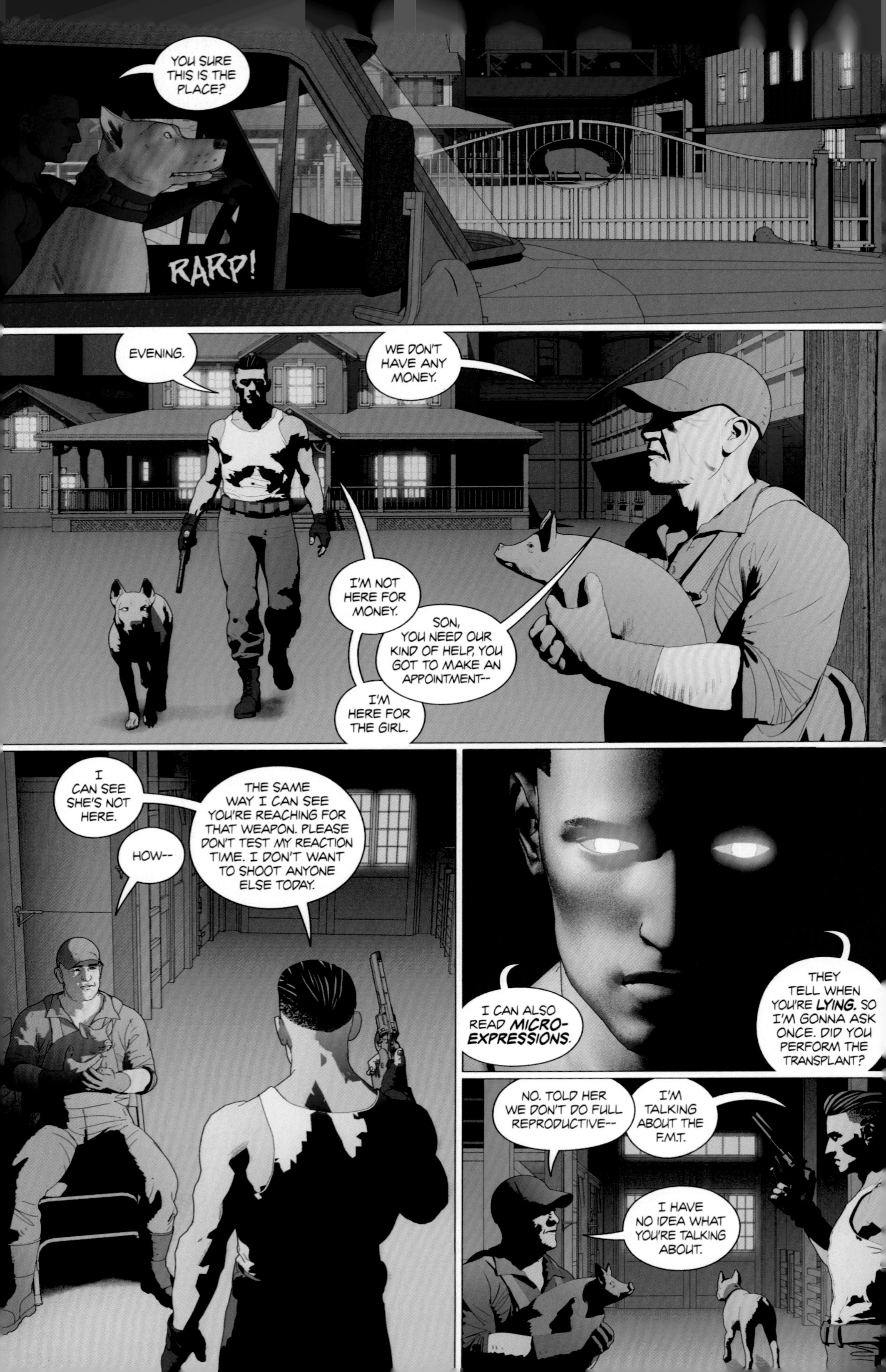
YOU SURE THIS IS THE PLACE?
RARP!
EVENING.
WE DON'T HAVE ANY MONEY.
I'M NOT HERE FOR MONEY.
SON, YOU NEED OUR KIND OF HELP, YOU GOT TO MAKE AN APPOINTMENT--
I'M HERE FOR THE GIRL.
I CAN SEE SHE'S NOT HERE.
HOW--
THE SAME WAY I CAN SEE YOU'RE REACHING FOR THAT WEAPON. PLEASE DON'T TEST MY REACTION TIME. I DON'T WANT TO SHOOT ANYONE ELSE TODAY.
I CAN ALSO READ MICRO-EXPRESSIONS.
THEY TELL WHEN YOU'RE LYING. SO I'M GONNA ASK ONCE. DID YOU PERFORM THE TRANSPLANT?
NO. TOLD HER WE DON'T DO FULL REPRODUCTIVE--
I'M TALKING ABOUT THE F.M.T.
I HAVE NO IDEA WHAT YOU'RE TALKING ABOUT.

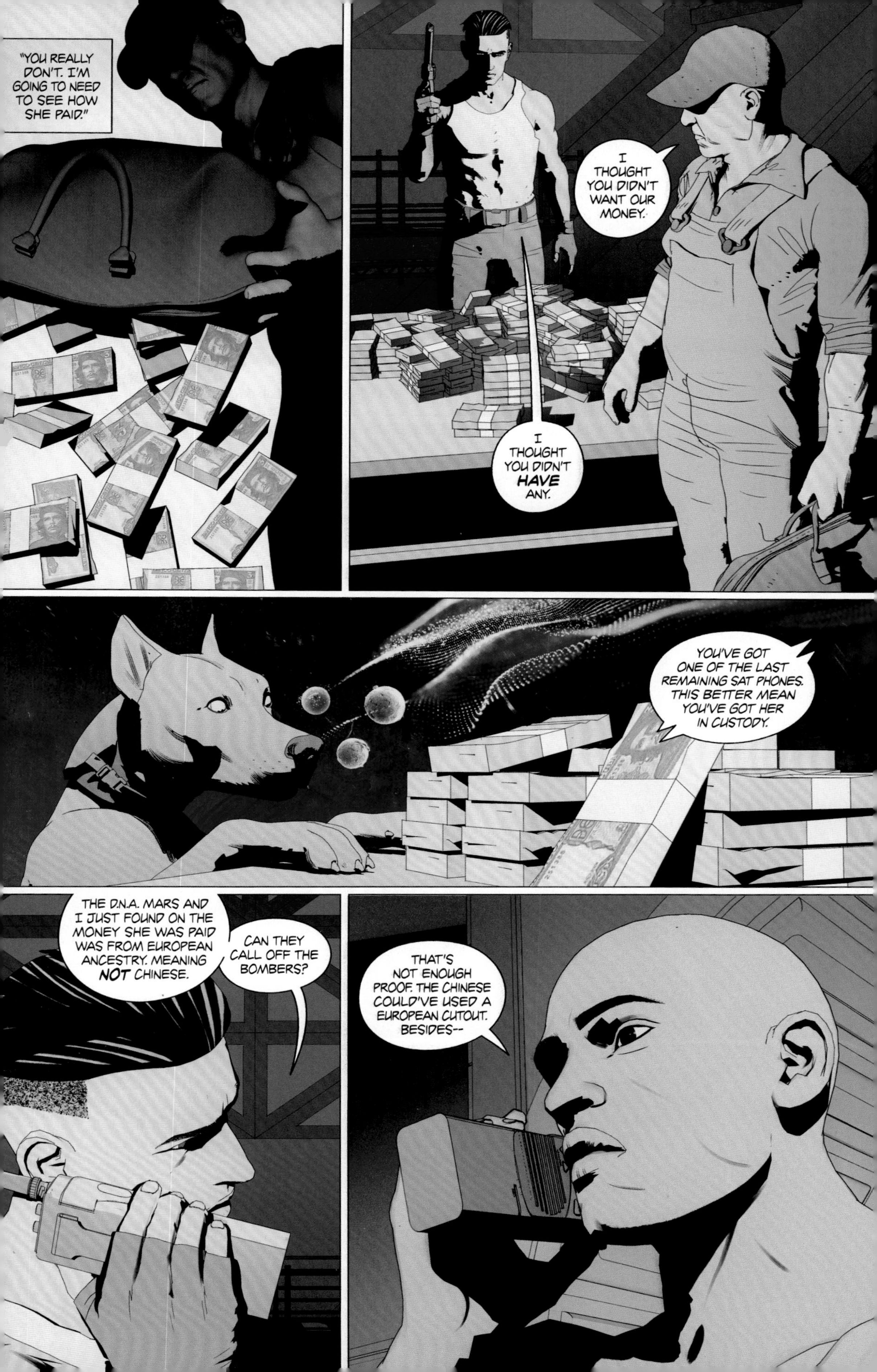
"YOU REALLY DON'T. I'M GOING TO NEED TO SEE HOW SHE PAID."
I THOUGHT YOU DIDN'T WANT OUR MONEY.
I THOUGHT YOU DIDN'T **HAVE** ANY.
YOU'VE GOT ONE OF THE LAST REMAINING SAT PHONES. THIS BETTER MEAN YOU'VE GOT HER IN CUSTODY.
THE D.N.A. MARS AND I JUST FOUND ON THE MONEY SHE WAS PAID WAS FROM EUROPEAN ANCESTRY. MEANING **NOT** CHINESE.
CAN THEY CALL OFF THE BOMBERS?
THAT'S NOT ENOUGH PROOF. THE CHINESE COULD'VE USED A EUROPEAN CUTOUT. BESIDES--

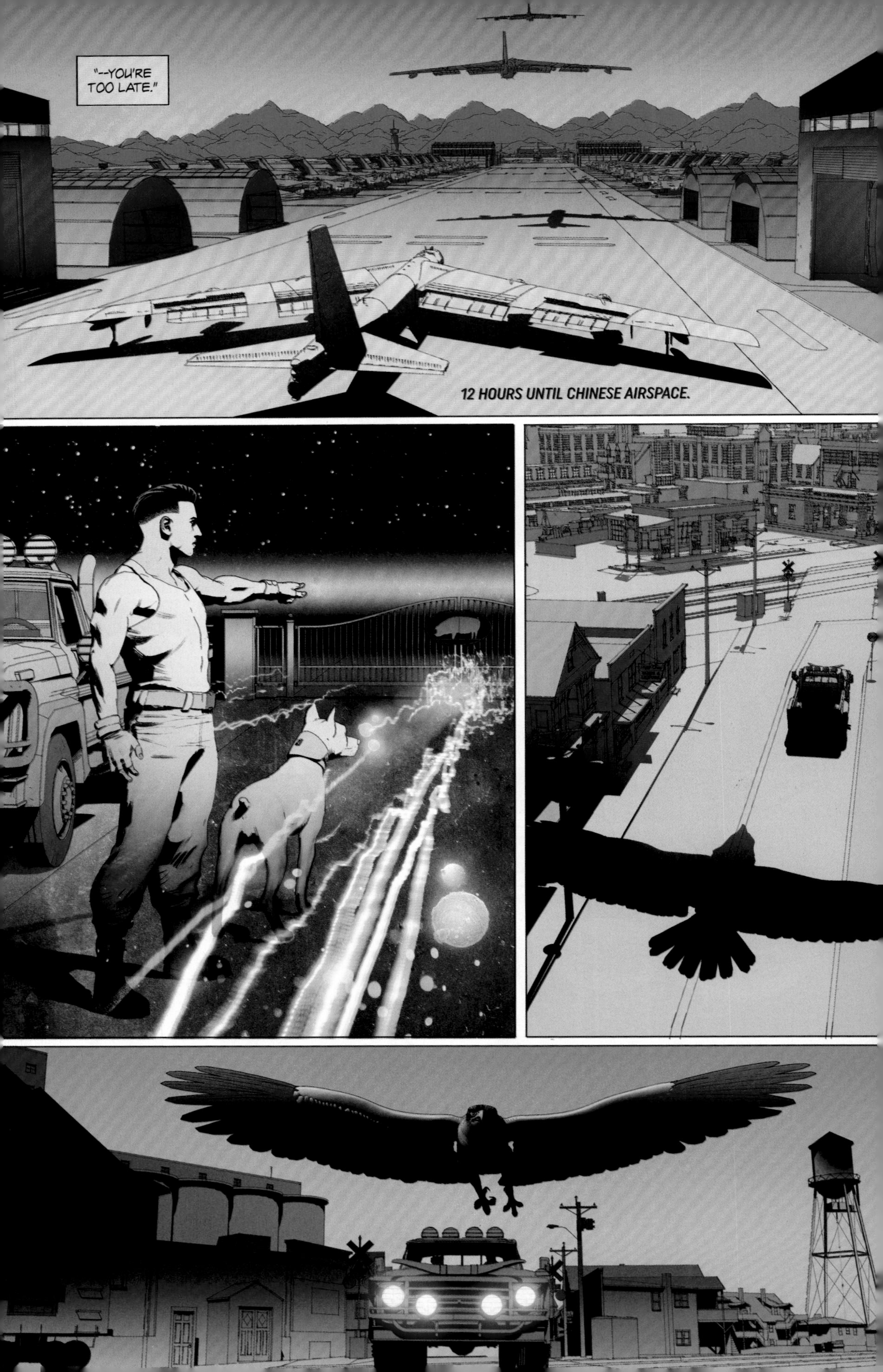
"--YOU'RE TOO LATE."
12 HOURS UNTIL CHINESE AIRSPACE.

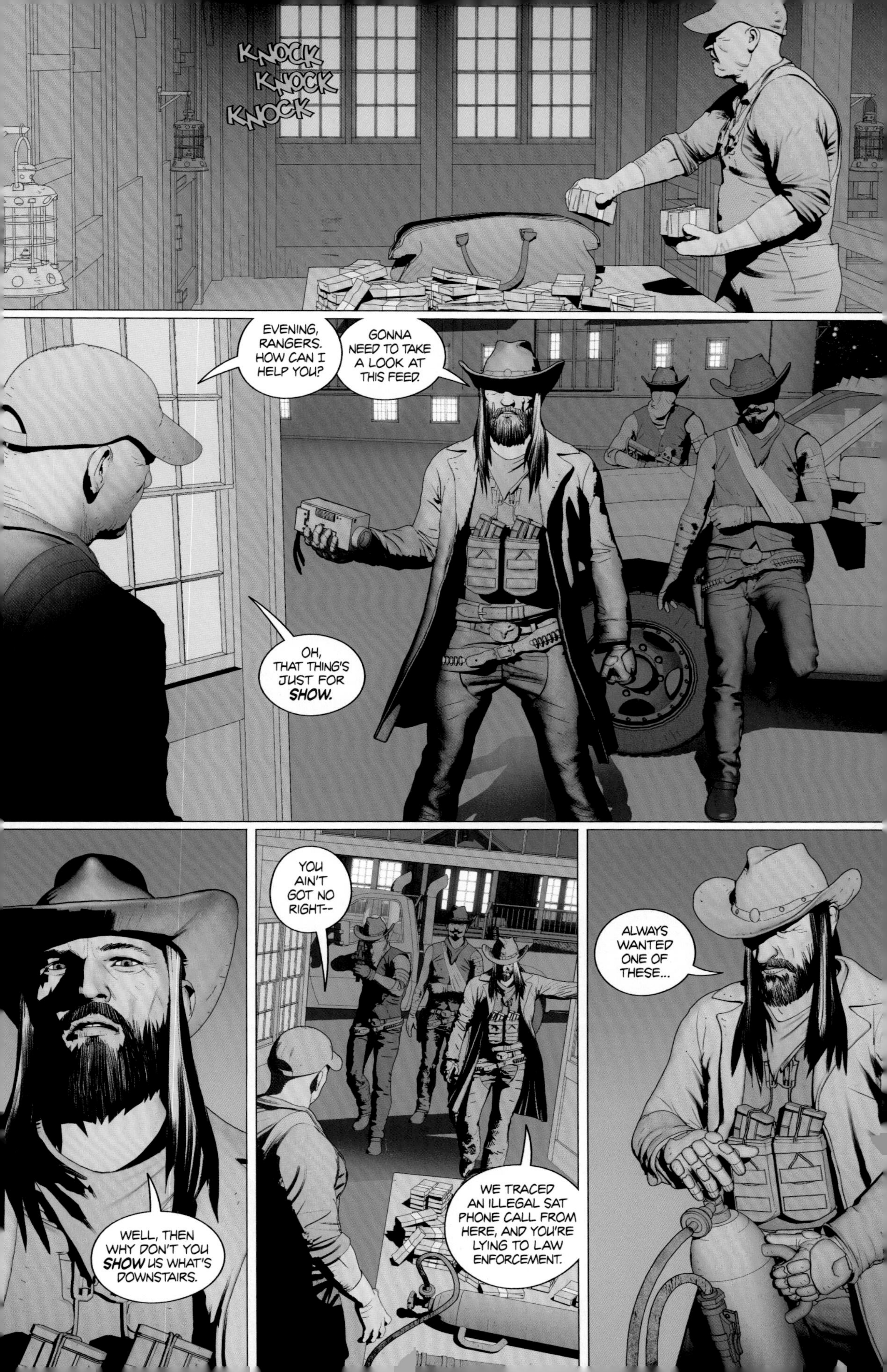
KNOCK
KNOCK
KNOCK
EVENING, RANGERS. HOW CAN I HELP YOU?
GONNA NEED TO TAKE A LOOK AT THIS FEED.
OH, THAT THING'S JUST FOR SHOW.
WELL, THEN WHY DON'T YOU SHOW US WHAT'S DOWNSTAIRS.
YOU AIN'T GOT NO RIGHT--
WE TRACED AN ILLEGAL SAT PHONE CALL FROM HERE, AND YOU'RE LYING TO LAW ENFORCEMENT.
ALWAYS WANTED ONE OF THESE...

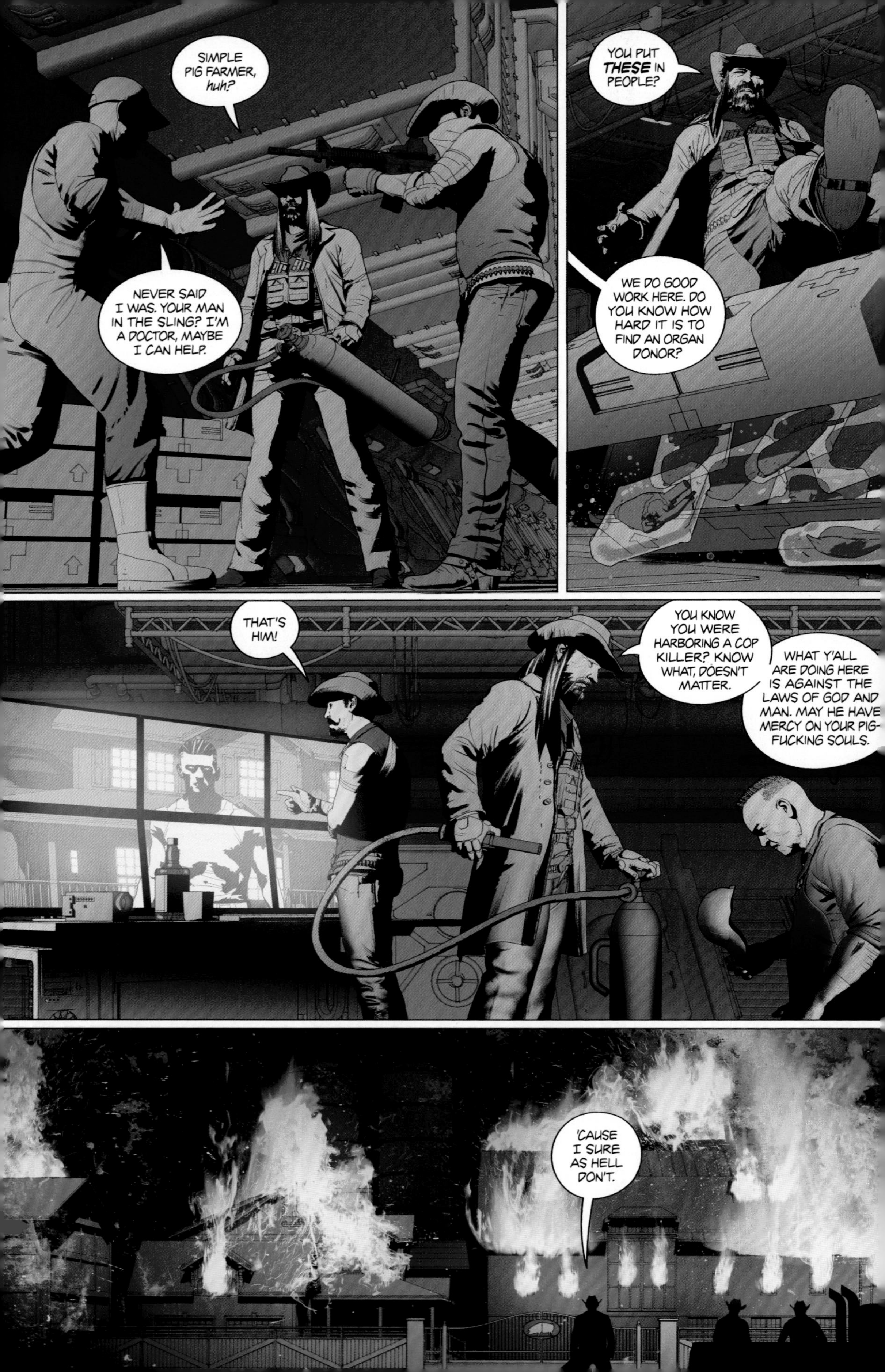
SIMPLE PIG FARMER, *huh?*
NEVER SAID I WAS. YOUR MAN IN THE SLING? I'M A DOCTOR, MAYBE I CAN HELP.
YOU PUT **THESE** IN PEOPLE?
WE DO GOOD WORK HERE. DO YOU KNOW HOW HARD IT IS TO FIND AN ORGAN DONOR?
THAT'S HIM!
YOU KNOW YOU WERE HARBORING A COP KILLER? KNOW WHAT, DOESN'T MATTER.
WHAT Y'ALL ARE DOING HERE IS AGAINST THE LAWS OF GOD AND MAN. MAY HE HAVE MERCY ON YOUR PIG-FUCKING SOULS.
'CAUSE I SURE AS HELL DON'T.

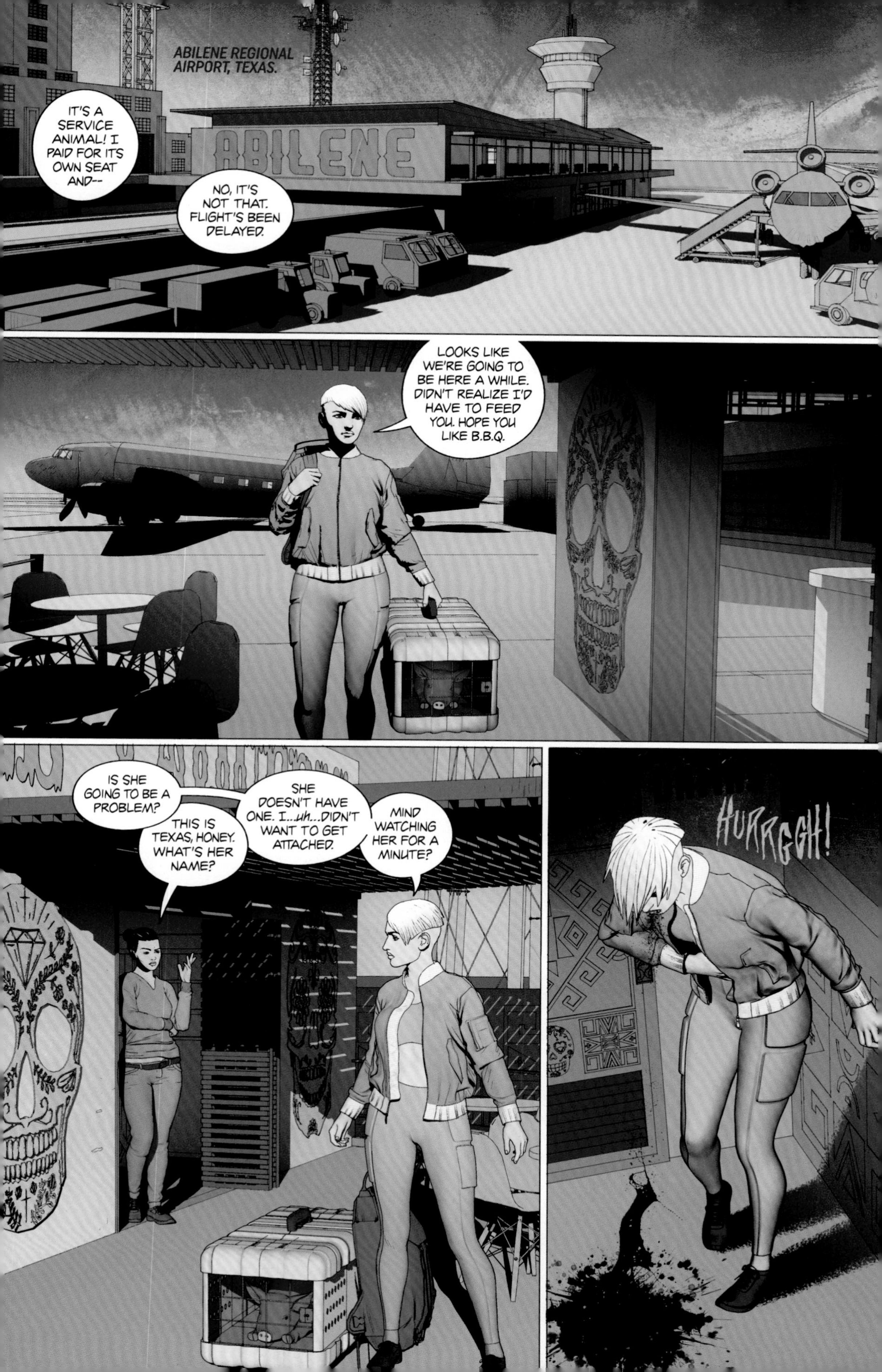
ABILENE REGIONAL AIRPORT, TEXAS.
ABILENE
IT'S A SERVICE ANIMAL! I PAID FOR ITS OWN SEAT AND--
NO, IT'S NOT THAT. FLIGHT'S BEEN DELAYED.
LOOKS LIKE WE'RE GOING TO BE HERE A WHILE. DIDN'T REALIZE I'D HAVE TO FEED YOU. HOPE YOU LIKE B.B.Q.
IS SHE GOING TO BE A PROBLEM?
THIS IS TEXAS, HONEY. WHAT'S HER NAME?
SHE DOESN'T HAVE ONE. I...uh...DIDN'T WANT TO GET ATTACHED.
MIND WATCHING HER FOR A MINUTE?
HURRGGH!

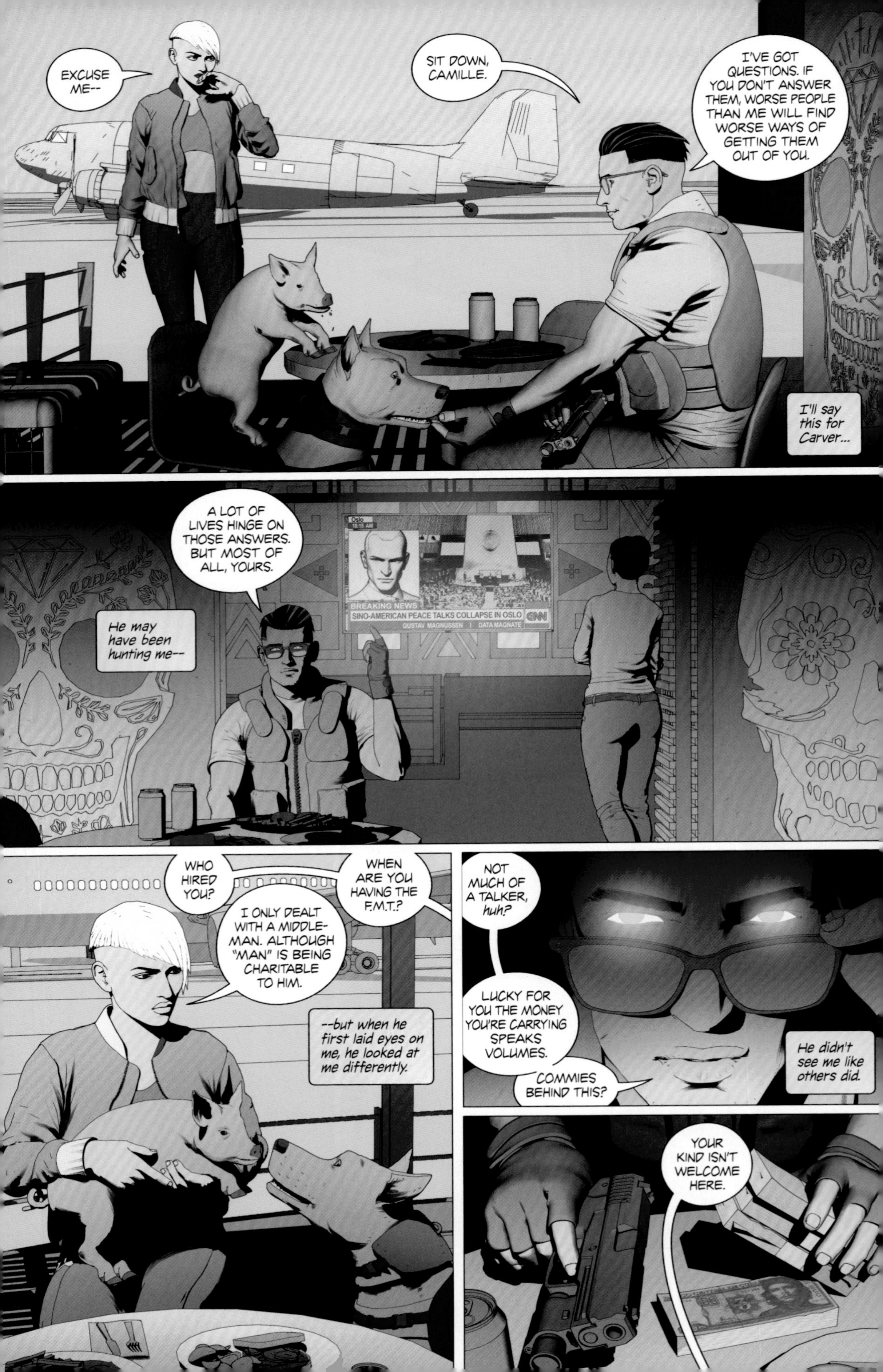
EXCUSE ME--
SIT DOWN, CAMILLE.
I'VE GOT QUESTIONS. IF YOU DON'T ANSWER THEM, WORSE PEOPLE THAN ME WILL FIND WORSE WAYS OF GETTING THEM OUT OF YOU.
I'll say this for Carver...
A LOT OF LIVES HINGE ON THOSE ANSWERS. BUT MOST OF ALL, YOURS.
Oslo
10:15 AM
BREAKING NEWS
SINO-AMERICAN PEACE TALKS COLLAPSE IN OSLO
GUSTAV MAGNUSSEN | DATA MAGNATE
CNN
He may have been hunting me--
WHO HIRED YOU?
WHEN ARE YOU HAVING THE F.M.T.?
I ONLY DEALT WITH A MIDDLE-MAN. ALTHOUGH "MAN" IS BEING CHARITABLE TO HIM.
--but when he first laid eyes on me, he looked at me differently.
NOT MUCH OF A TALKER, huh?
LUCKY FOR YOU THE MONEY YOU'RE CARRYING SPEAKS VOLUMES.
COMMIES BEHIND THIS?
He didn't see me like others did.
YOUR KIND ISN'T WELCOME HERE.

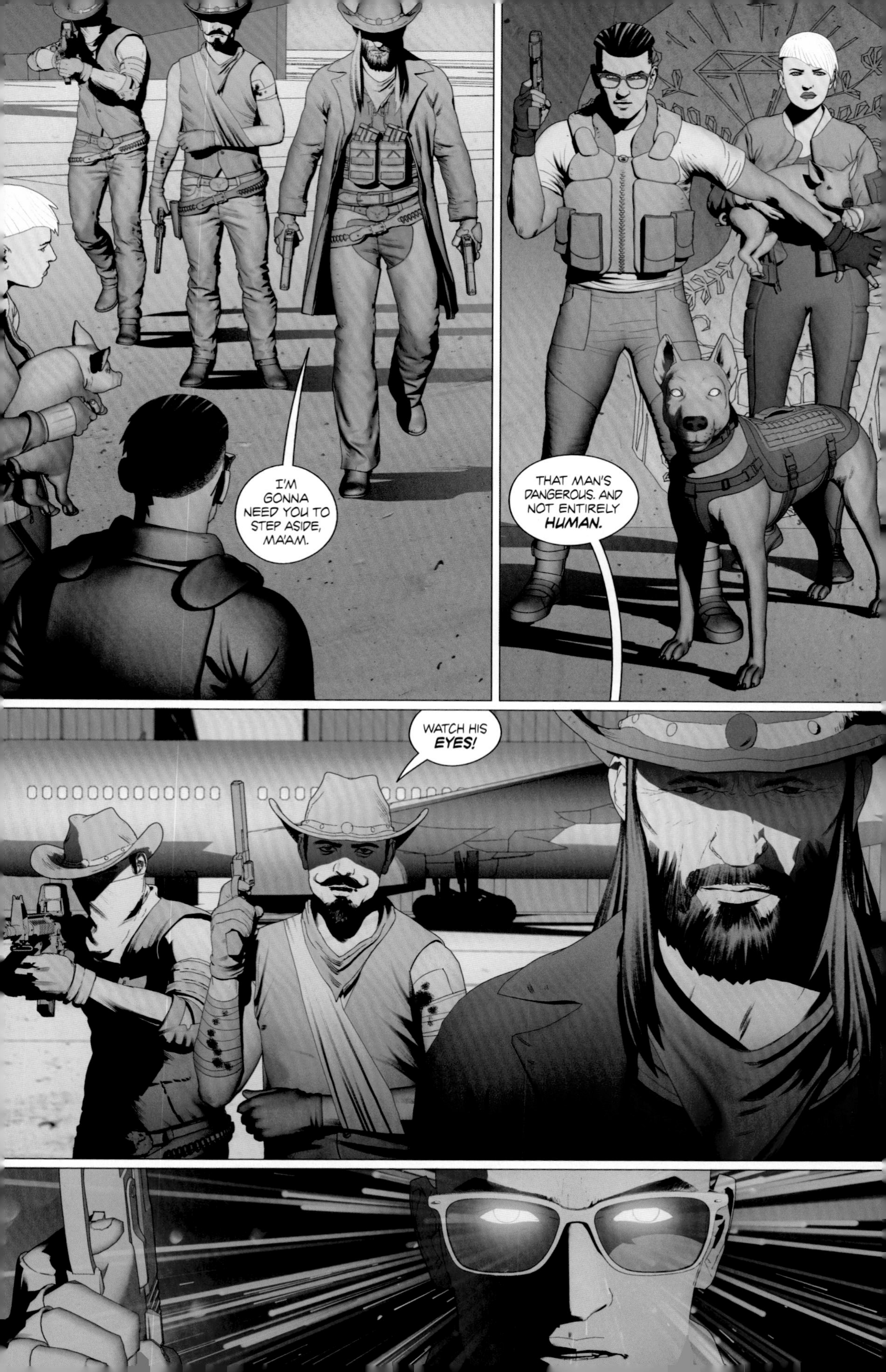
I'M GONNA NEED YOU TO STEP ASIDE, MA'AM.
THAT MAN'S DANGEROUS. AND NOT ENTIRELY **HUMAN.**
WATCH HIS ***EYES!***

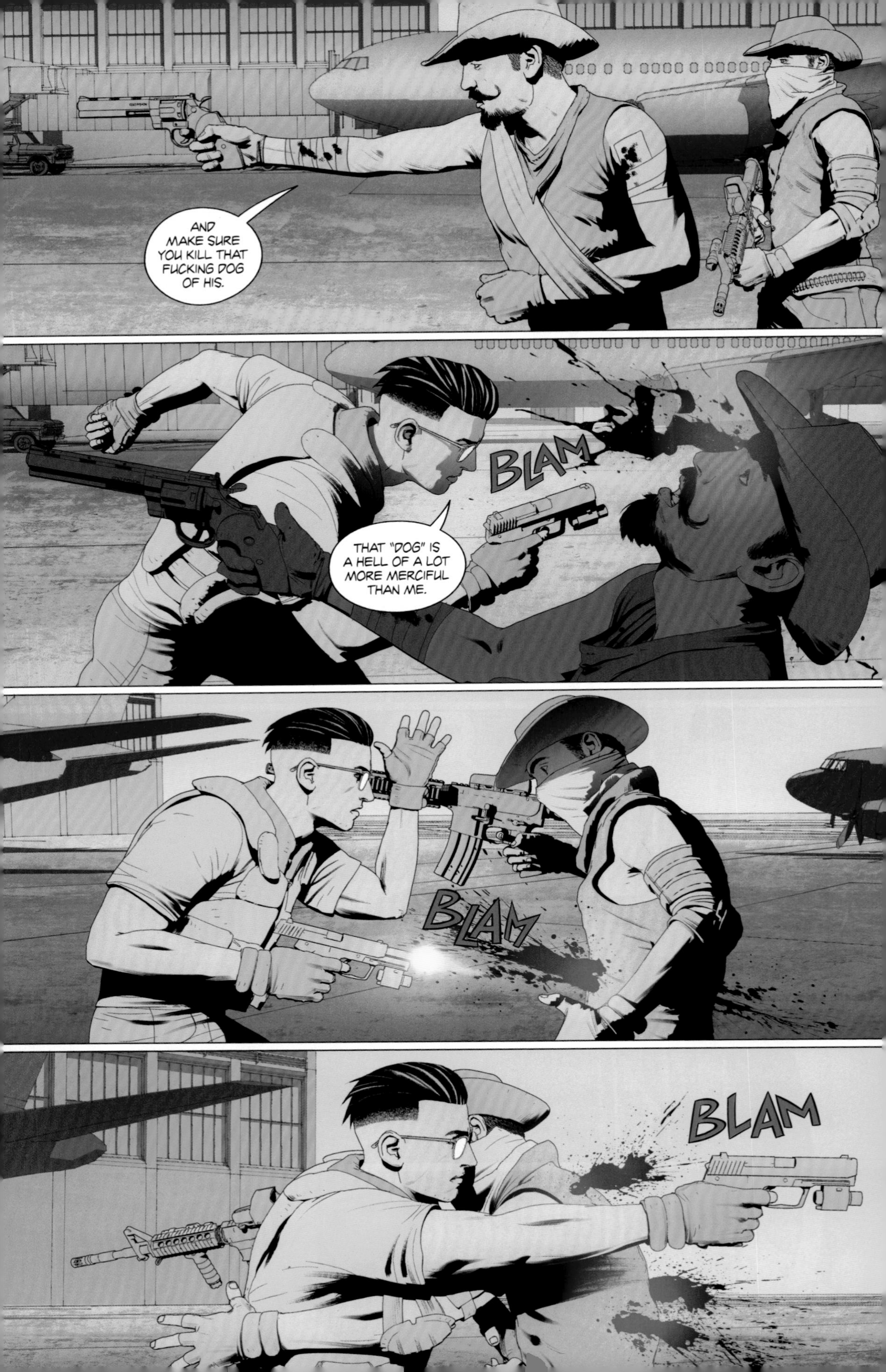
AND MAKE SURE YOU KILL THAT FUCKING DOG OF HIS.
BLAM
THAT "DOG" IS A HELL OF A LOT MORE MERCIFUL THAN ME.
BLAM
BLAM

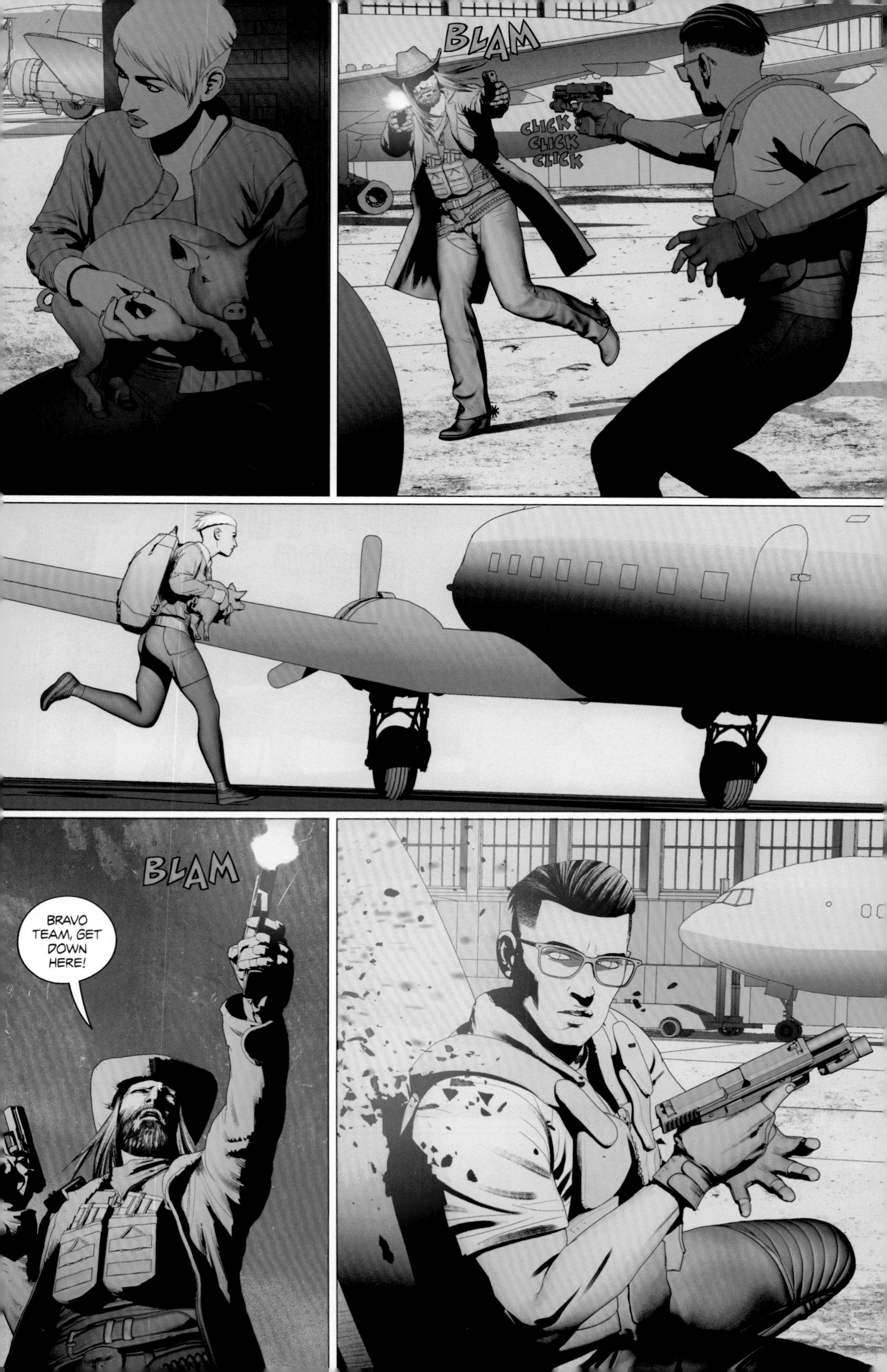
BLAM
CLICK CLICK CLICK
BLAM
BRAVO TEAM, GET DOWN HERE!

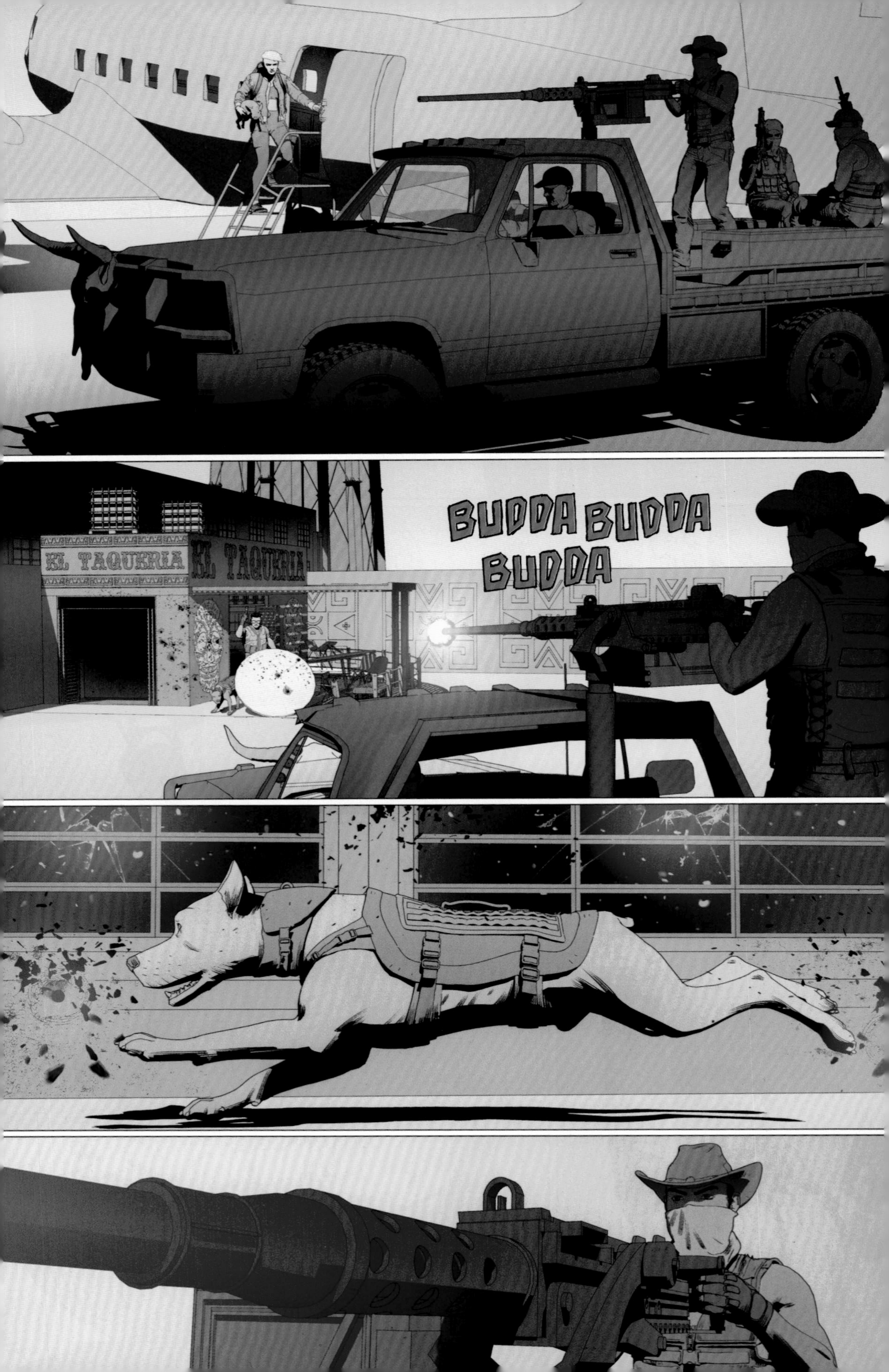
EL TAQUERIA
EL TAQUERIA
BUDDA BUDDA
BUDDA

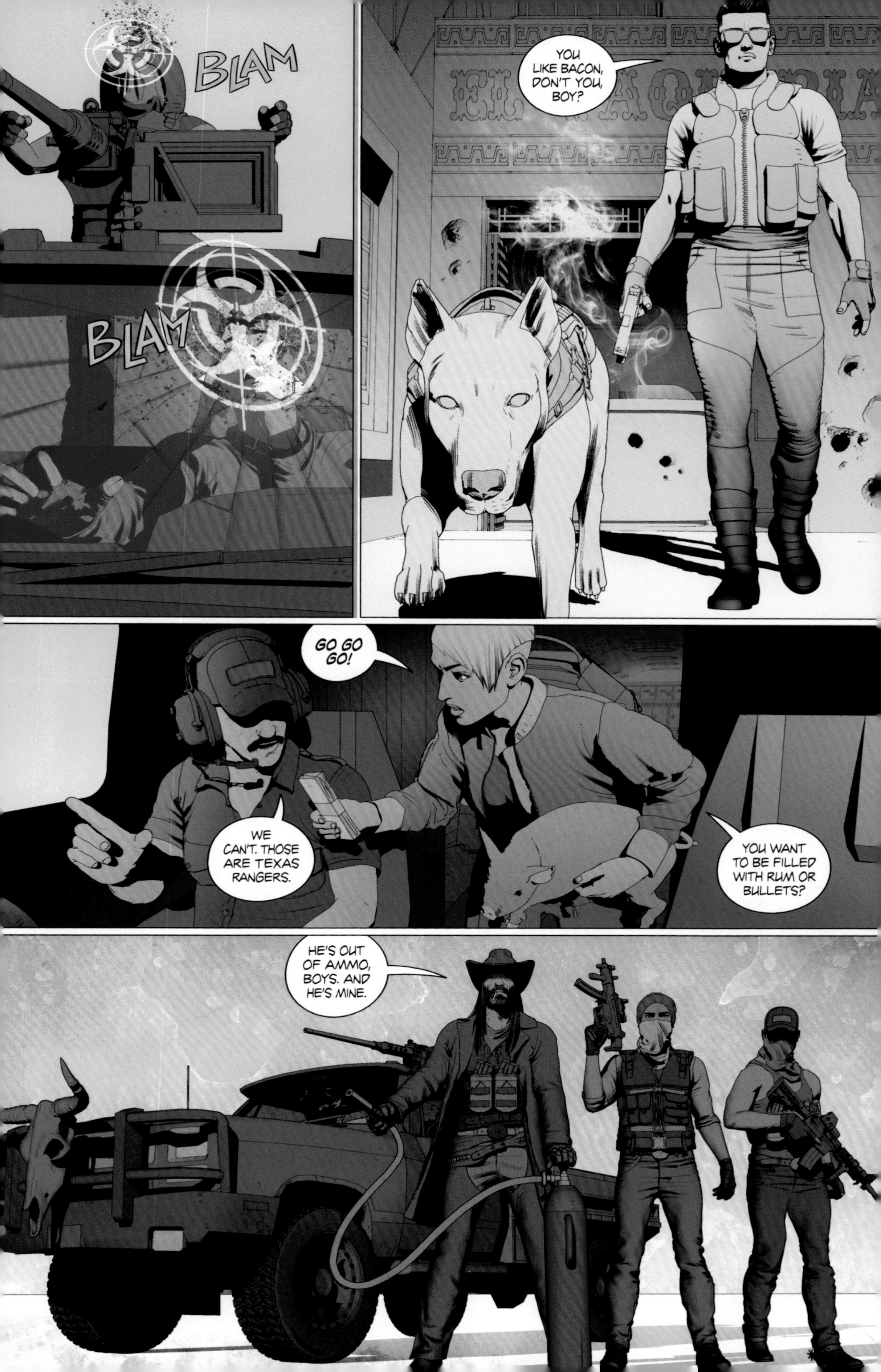

BLAM
BLAM
YOU LIKE BACON, DON'T YOU, BOY?
GO GO GO!
WE CAN'T. THOSE ARE TEXAS RANGERS.
YOU WANT TO BE FILLED WITH RUM OR BULLETS?
HE'S OUT OF AMMO, BOYS. AND HE'S MINE.

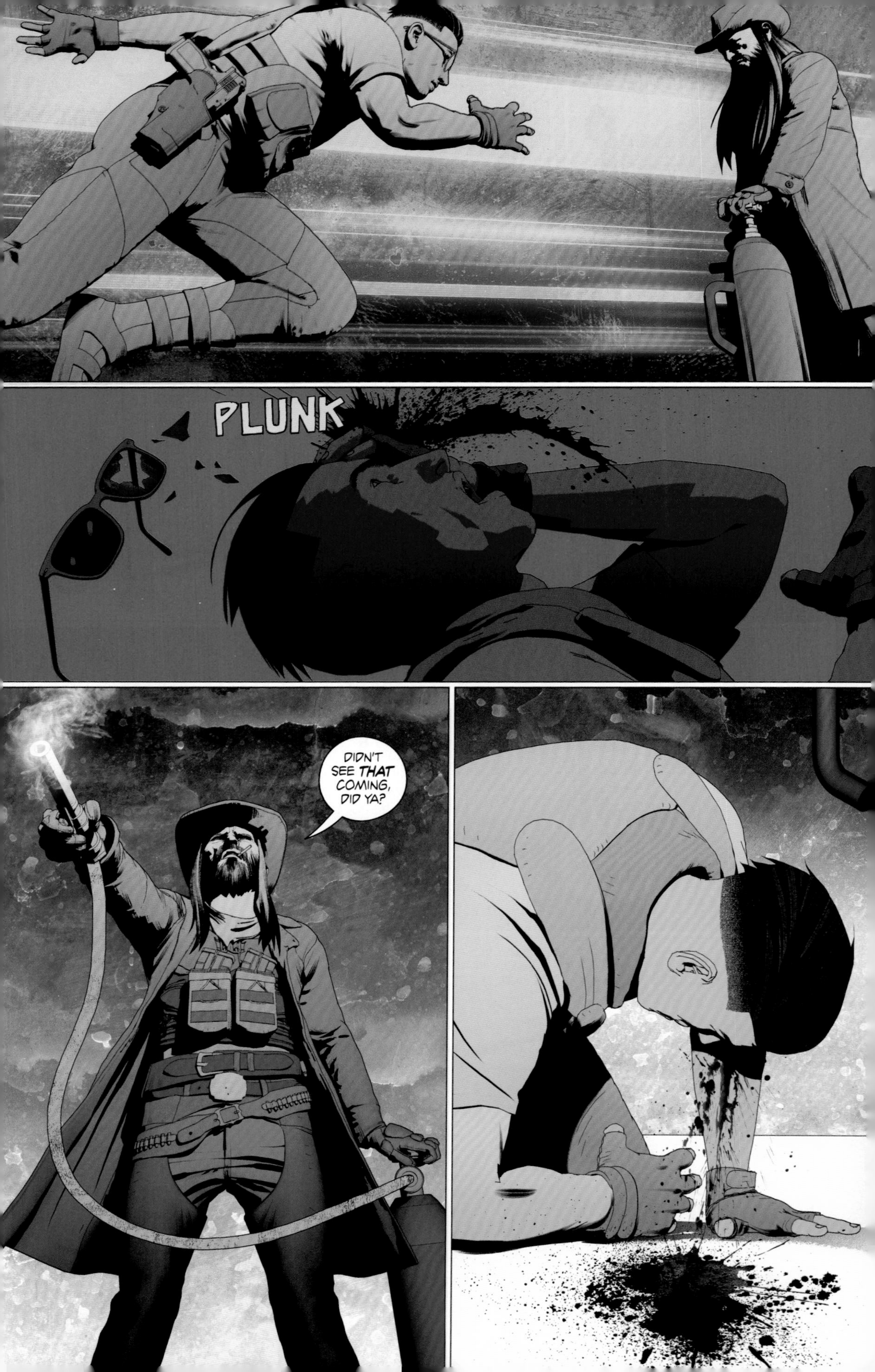
PLUNK
DIDN'T SEE THAT COMING, DID YA?

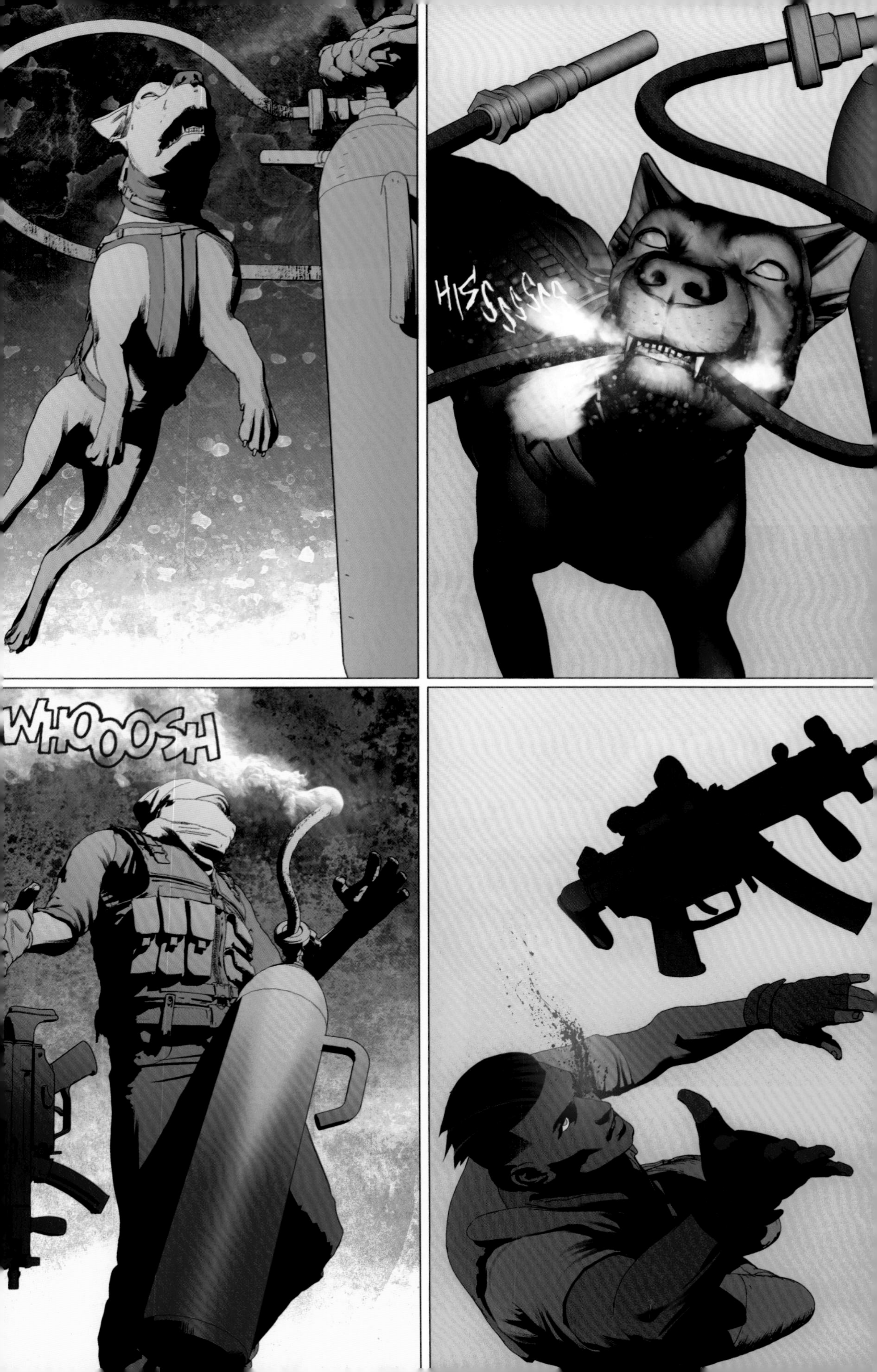
HISSSSSSS
WHOOOSH

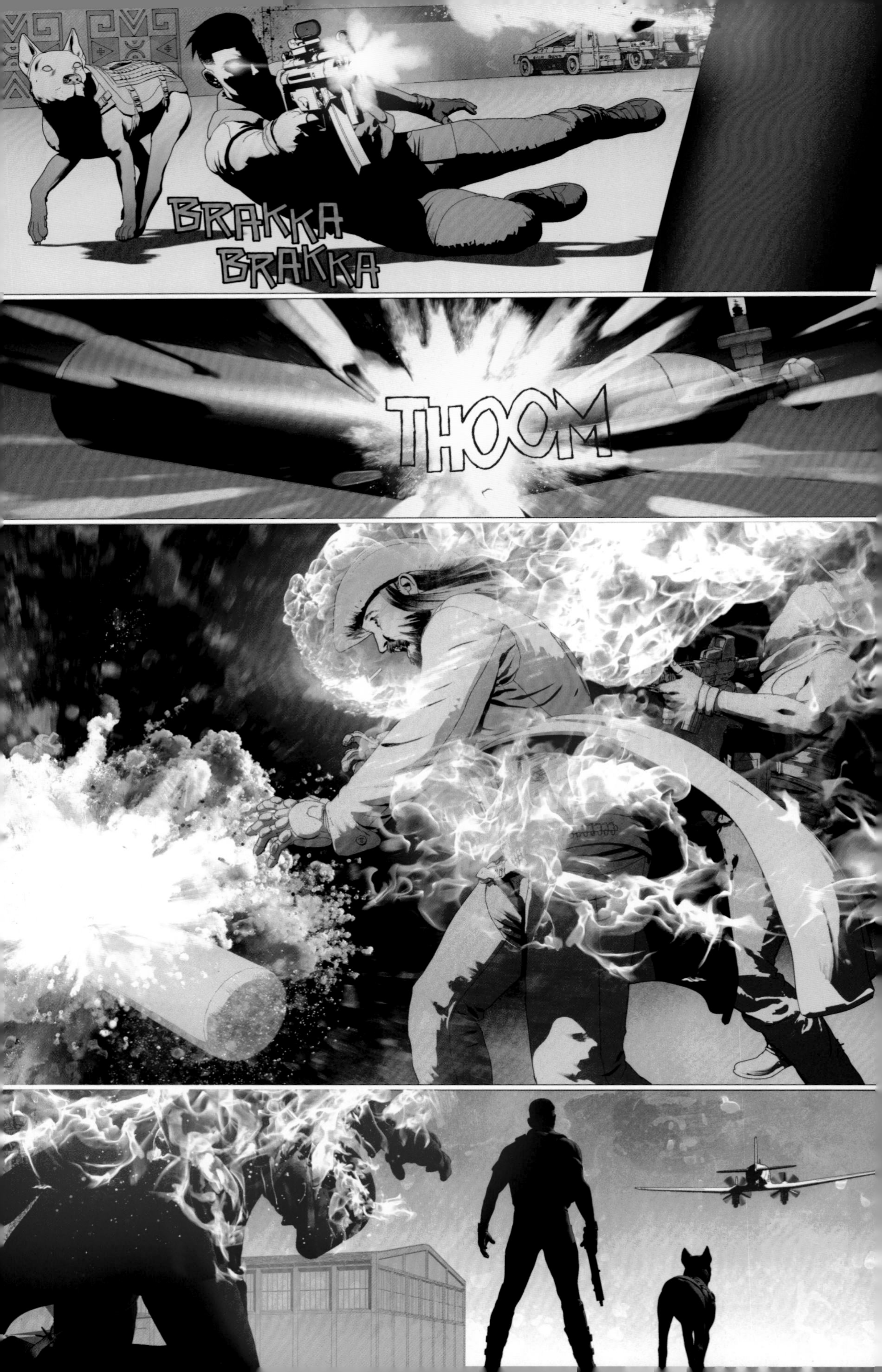
BRAKKA
BRAKKA
THOOM

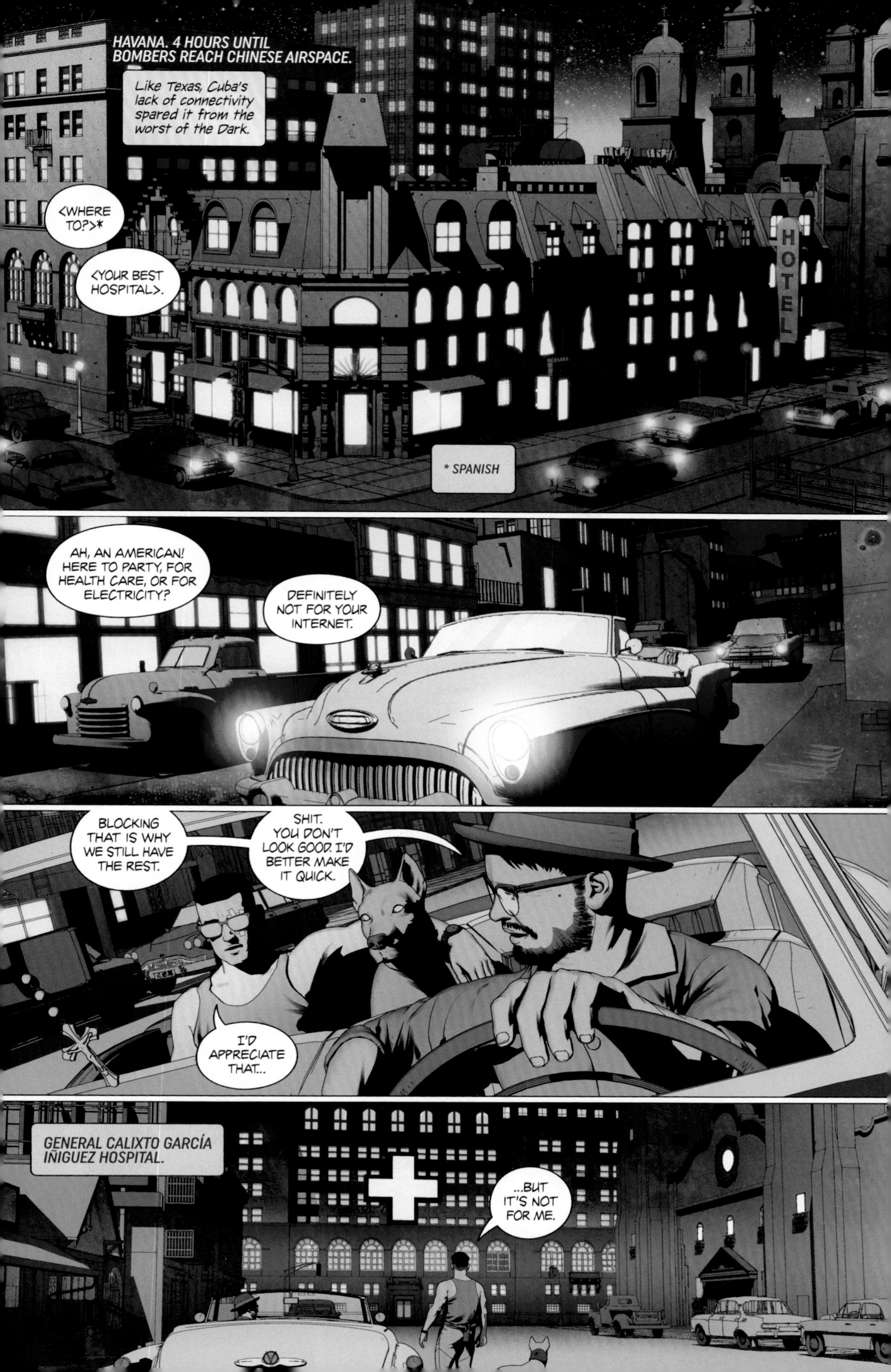

HAVANA. 4 HOURS UNTIL BOMBERS REACH CHINESE AIRSPACE.
Like Texas, Cuba's lack of connectivity spared it from the worst of the Dark.
<WHERE TO?>*
<YOUR BEST HOSPITAL>.
* SPANISH
AH, AN AMERICAN! HERE TO PARTY, FOR HEALTH CARE, OR FOR ELECTRICITY?
DEFINITELY NOT FOR YOUR INTERNET.
BLOCKING THAT IS WHY WE STILL HAVE THE REST.
SHIT. YOU DON'T LOOK GOOD. I'D BETTER MAKE IT QUICK.
I'D APPRECIATE THAT...
HOTEL
GENERAL CALIXTO GARCÍA IÑIGUEZ HOSPITAL.
...BUT IT'S NOT FOR ME.

THIS PLACE SMELLS AWFUL. I'M SORRY, BOY.

WAIT, WHAT'S THAT?

And like the Lone Star Republic, its citizens traded their freedom for power.

<I'M SORRY, THERE'S BEEN A CHANGE IN PLANS.>

<OKAY, OKAY! I WON'T OPERATE. JUST DON'T-->

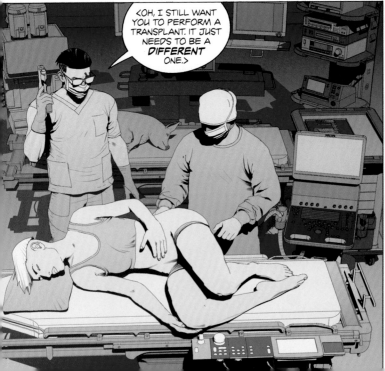

<OH, I STILL WANT YOU TO PERFORM A TRANSPLANT. IT JUST NEEDS TO BE A *DIFFERENT* ONE.>

ALL RIGHT, THIS IS WHAT WE PULLED OUT OF HER, MARS. TELL ME WHAT SHE STOLE.

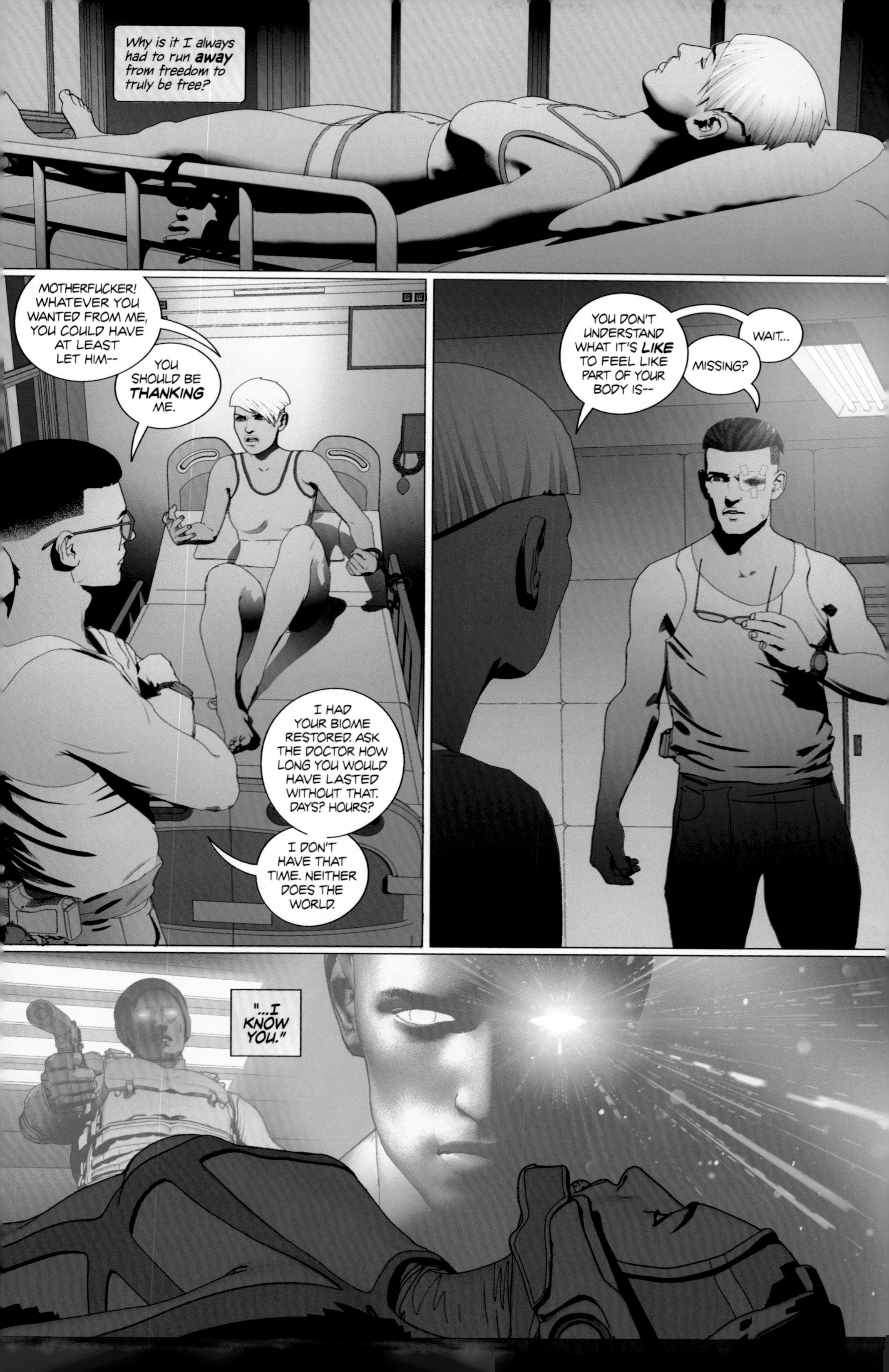

Why is it I always had to run **away** from freedom to truly be free?
MOTHERFUCKER! WHATEVER YOU WANTED FROM ME, YOU COULD HAVE AT LEAST LET HIM--
YOU SHOULD BE ***THANKING*** ME.
I HAD YOUR BIOME RESTORED. ASK THE DOCTOR HOW LONG YOU WOULD HAVE LASTED WITHOUT THAT. DAYS? HOURS?
I DON'T HAVE THAT TIME. NEITHER DOES THE WORLD.
YOU DON'T UNDERSTAND WHAT IT'S ***LIKE*** TO FEEL LIKE PART OF YOUR BODY IS--
WAIT...
MISSING?
"...I KNOW YOU."

THEN YOU KNOW WHAT I'M CAPABLE OF.

I ALSO KNOW YOU WOULDN'T BE DOING THIS IF YOU WEREN'T FORCED TO.

THIS IS ABOUT MORE THAN JUST ME. THE BOMBERS HEADING TO CHINA, AND WHATEVER THEY DO TO RETALIATE...THAT'S ALL BECAUSE OF WHAT YOU STOLE. ALL THAT'S ON YOU.

I DIDN'T STEAL ANYTHING.

THAT'S WHAT YOU SAID WHEN WE TALKED IN TEXAS.

YOUR EYES--

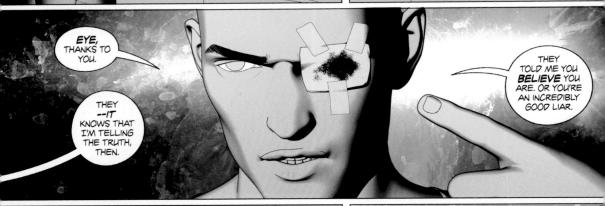

EYE, THANKS TO YOU.

THEY --IT KNOWS THAT I'M TELLING THE TRUTH, THEN.

THEY TOLD ME YOU BELIEVE YOU ARE. OR YOU'RE AN INCREDIBLY GOOD LIAR.

ROWF! ROWF! ROWF!

BUT THE DATA DOESN'T LIE.

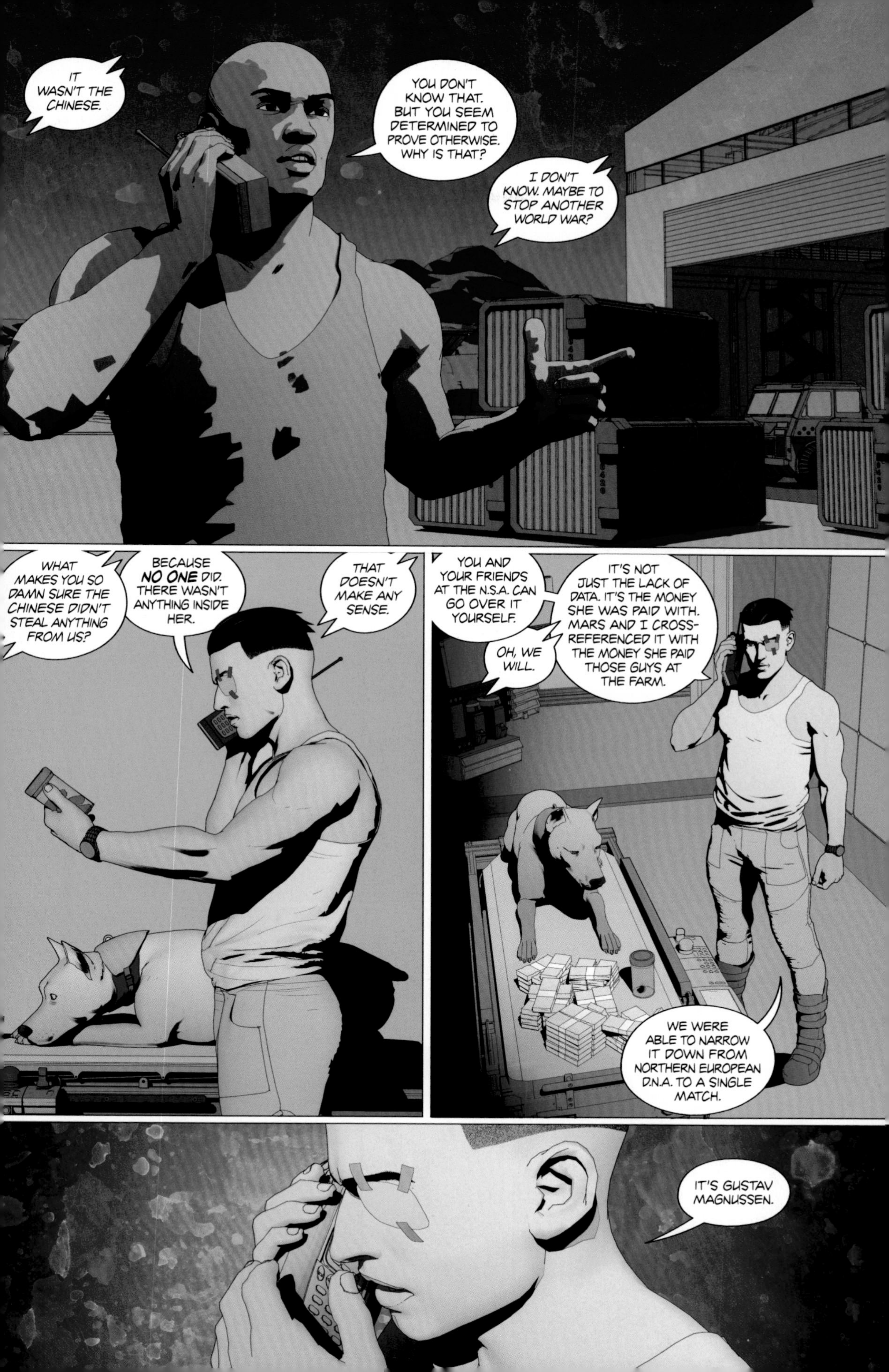
IT WASN'T THE CHINESE.
YOU DON'T KNOW THAT. BUT YOU SEEM DETERMINED TO PROVE OTHERWISE. WHY IS THAT?
I DON'T KNOW. MAYBE TO STOP ANOTHER WORLD WAR?
WHAT MAKES YOU SO DAMN SURE THE CHINESE DIDN'T STEAL ANYTHING FROM US?
BECAUSE **NO ONE** DID. THERE WASN'T ANYTHING INSIDE HER.
THAT DOESN'T MAKE ANY SENSE.
YOU AND YOUR FRIENDS AT THE N.S.A. CAN GO OVER IT YOURSELF.
OH, WE WILL.
IT'S NOT JUST THE LACK OF DATA. IT'S THE MONEY SHE WAS PAID WITH. MARS AND I CROSS-REFERENCED IT WITH THE MONEY SHE PAID THOSE GUYS AT THE FARM.
WE WERE ABLE TO NARROW IT DOWN FROM NORTHERN EUROPEAN D.N.A. TO A SINGLE MATCH.
IT'S GUSTAV MAGNUSSEN.

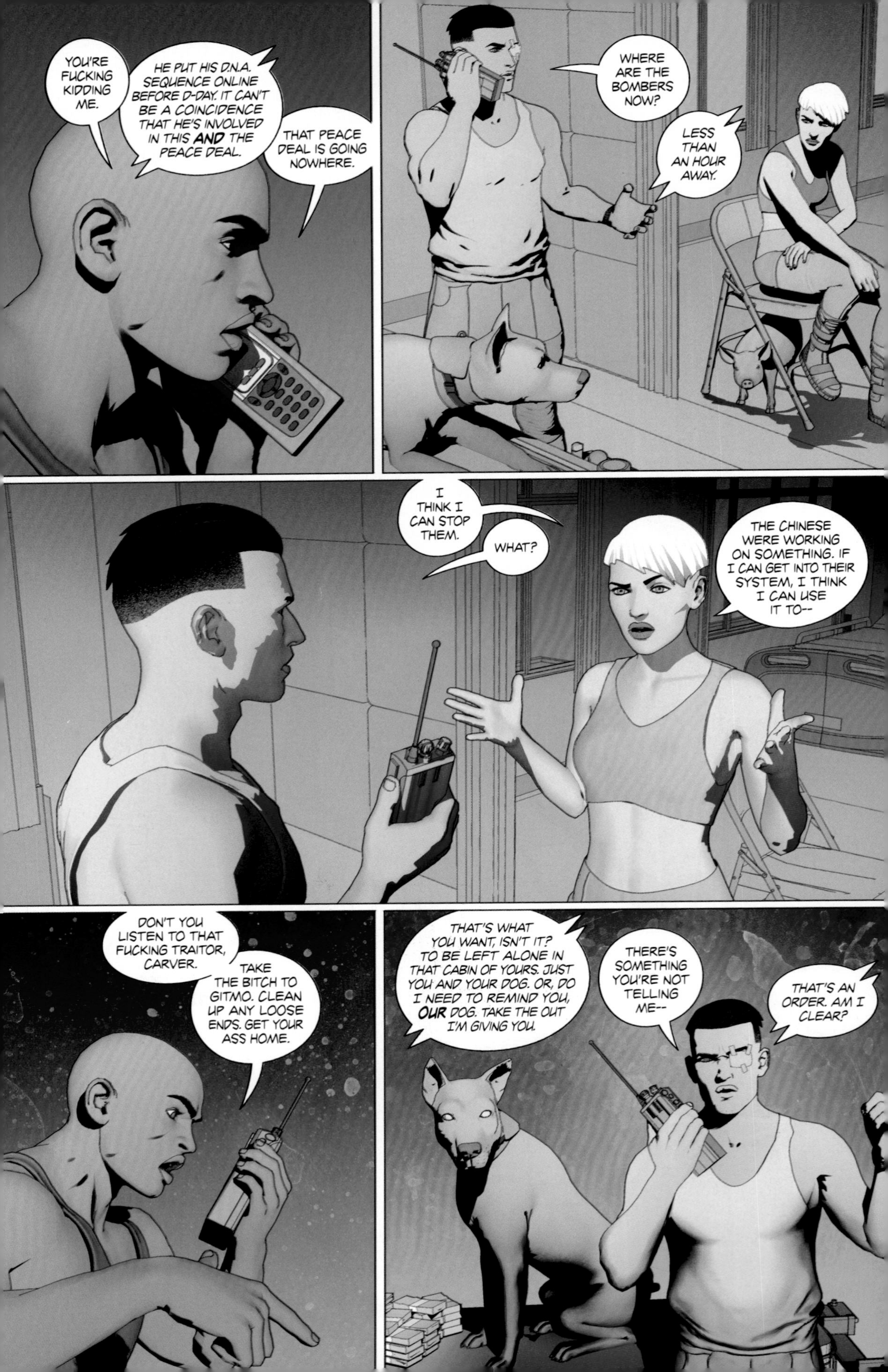
YOU'RE FUCKING KIDDING ME.
HE PUT HIS D.N.A. SEQUENCE ONLINE BEFORE D-DAY. IT CAN'T BE A COINCIDENCE THAT HE'S INVOLVED IN THIS AND THE PEACE DEAL.
THAT PEACE DEAL IS GOING NOWHERE.
WHERE ARE THE BOMBERS NOW?
LESS THAN AN HOUR AWAY.
I THINK I CAN STOP THEM.
WHAT?
THE CHINESE WERE WORKING ON SOMETHING. IF I CAN GET INTO THEIR SYSTEM, I THINK I CAN USE IT TO--
DON'T YOU LISTEN TO THAT FUCKING TRAITOR, CARVER.
TAKE THE BITCH TO GITMO. CLEAN UP ANY LOOSE ENDS. GET YOUR ASS HOME.
THAT'S WHAT YOU WANT, ISN'T IT? TO BE LEFT ALONE IN THAT CABIN OF YOURS. JUST YOU AND YOUR DOG. OR, DO I NEED TO REMIND YOU, OUR DOG. TAKE THE OUT I'M GIVING YOU.
THERE'S SOMETHING YOU'RE NOT TELLING ME--
THAT'S AN ORDER. AM I CLEAR?

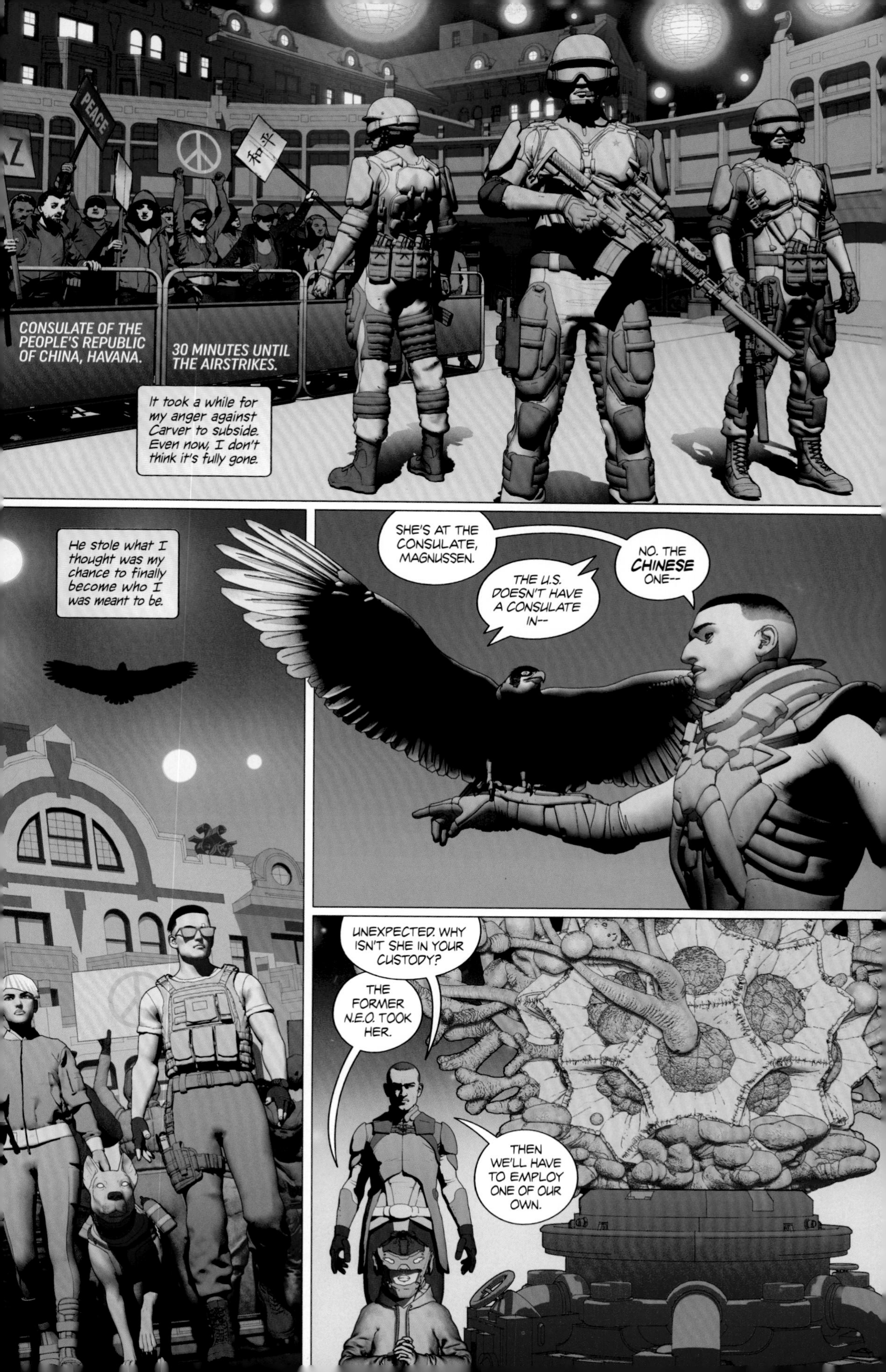

PEACE
和平
CONSULATE OF THE PEOPLE'S REPUBLIC OF CHINA, HAVANA.
30 MINUTES UNTIL THE AIRSTRIKES.
It took a while for my anger against Carver to subside. Even now, I don't think it's fully gone.
He stole what I thought was my chance to finally become who I was meant to be.
SHE'S AT THE CONSULATE, MAGNUSSEN.
THE U.S. DOESN'T HAVE A CONSULATE IN--
NO. THE **CHINESE** ONE--
UNEXPECTED. WHY ISN'T SHE IN YOUR CUSTODY?
THE FORMER N.E.O. TOOK HER.
THEN WE'LL HAVE TO EMPLOY ONE OF OUR OWN.

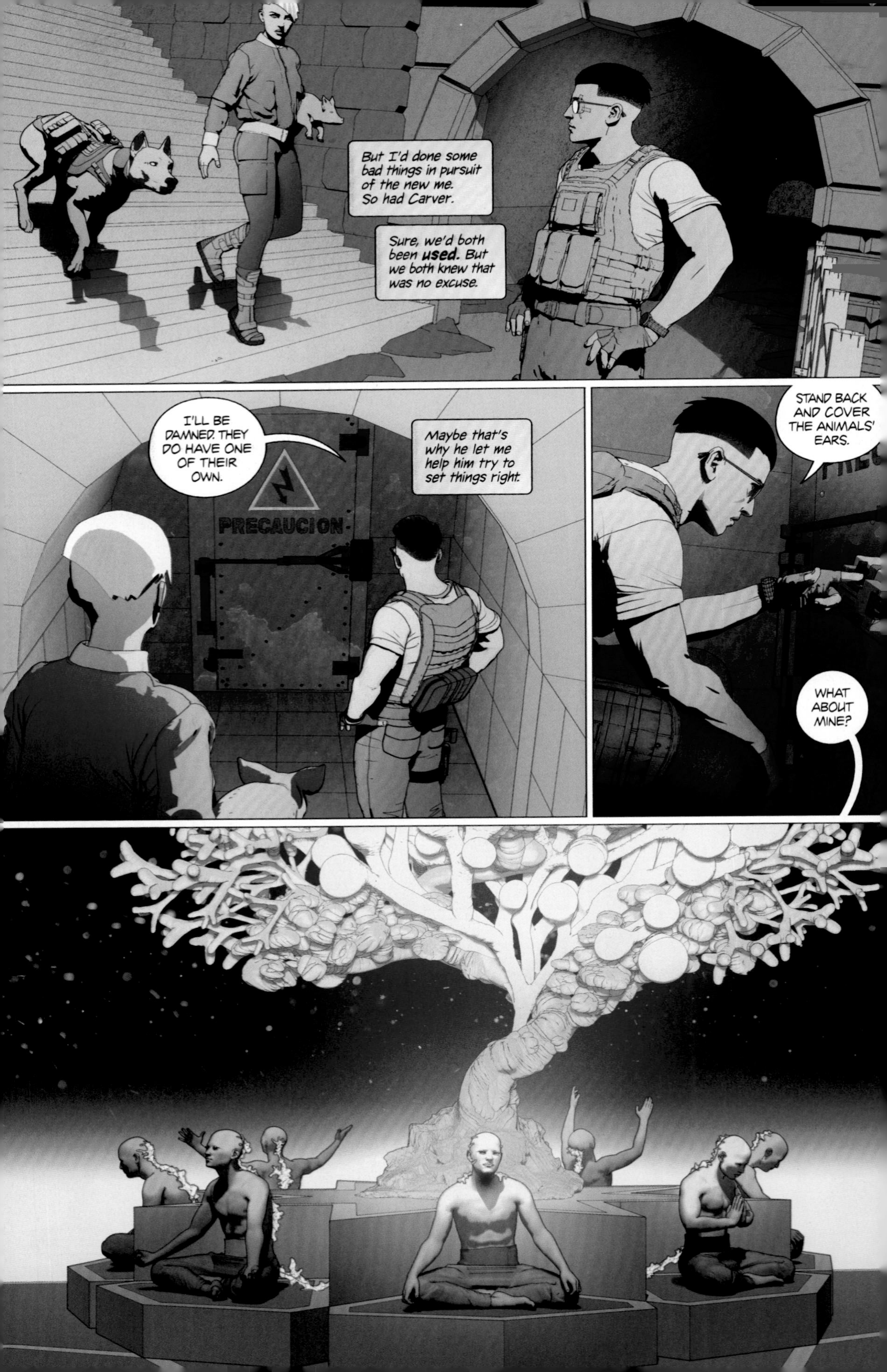

But I'd done some bad things in pursuit of the new me. So had Carver.
Sure, we'd both been **used.** But we both knew that was no excuse.
I'LL BE DAMNED. THEY DO HAVE ONE OF THEIR OWN.
Maybe that's why he let me help him try to set things right.
PRECAUCION
STAND BACK AND COVER THE ANIMALS' EARS.
WHAT ABOUT MINE?

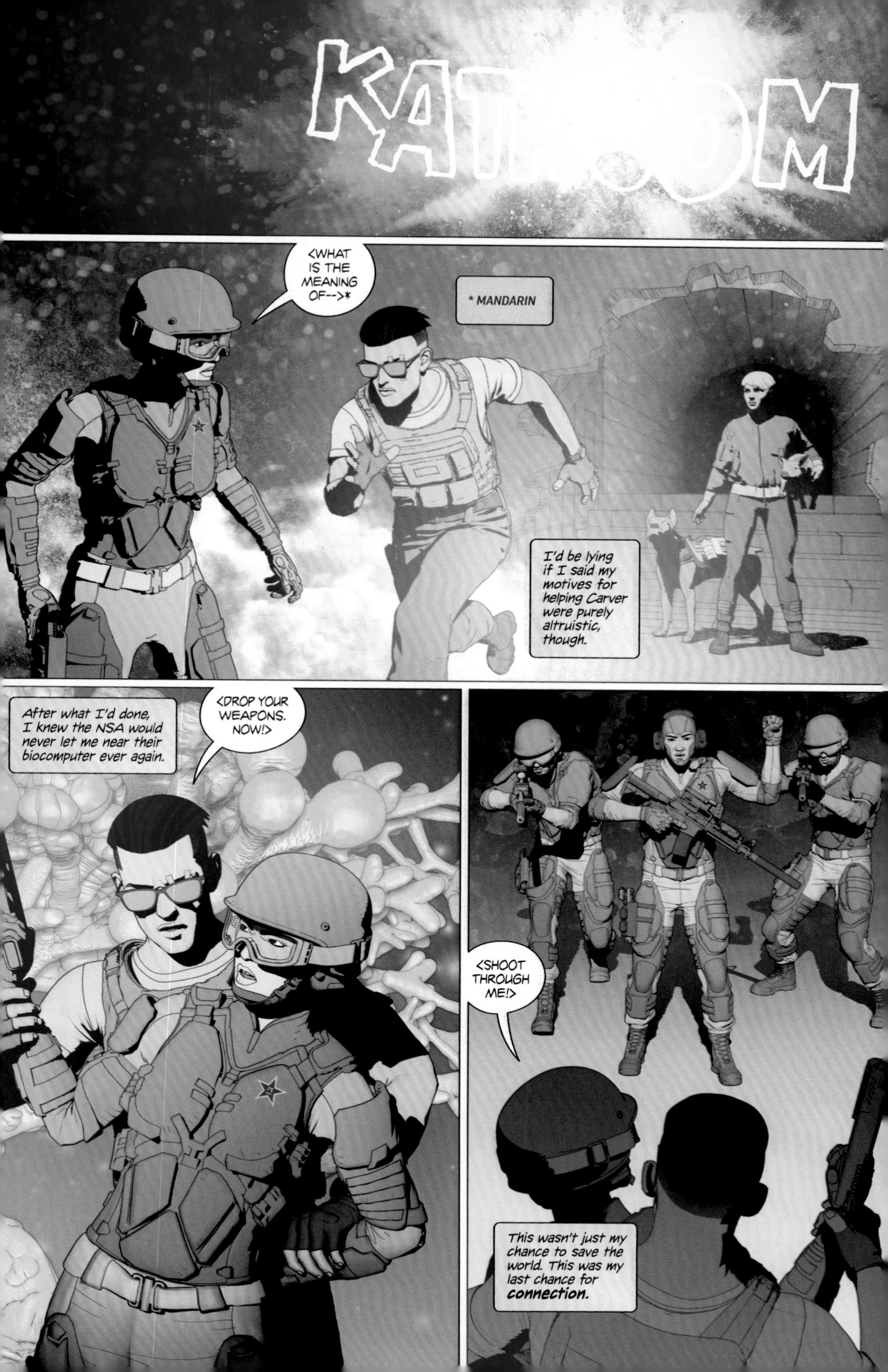
KATHOOM
<WHAT IS THE MEANING OF-->*
* MANDARIN
I'd be lying if I said my motives for helping Carver were purely altruistic, though.
After what I'd done, I knew the NSA would never let me near their biocomputer ever again.
<DROP YOUR WEAPONS. NOW!>
<SHOOT THROUGH ME!>
This wasn't just my chance to save the world. This was my last chance for **connection.**

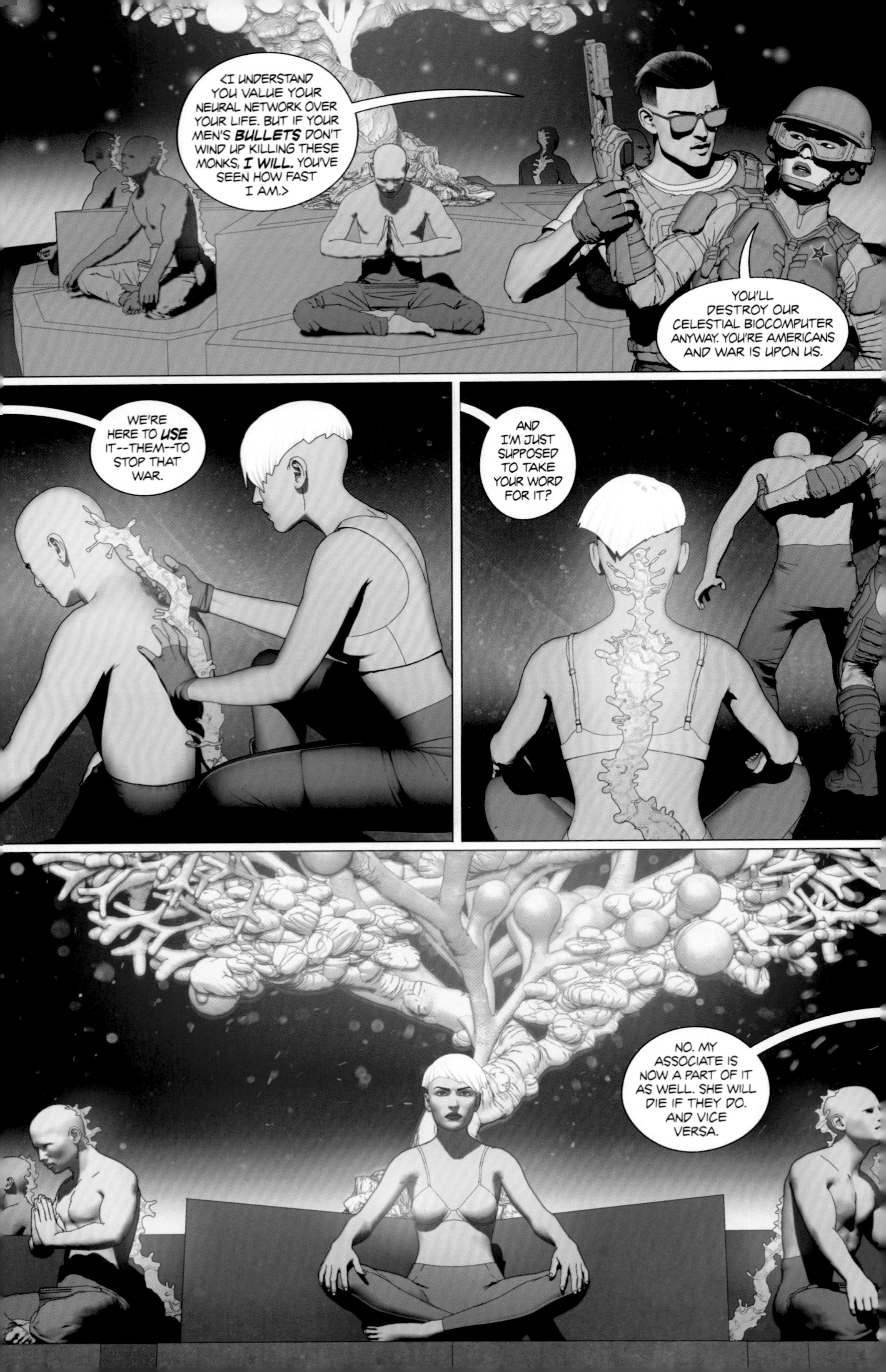
<I UNDERSTAND YOU VALUE YOUR NEURAL NETWORK OVER YOUR LIFE. BUT IF YOUR MEN'S BULLETS DON'T WIND UP KILLING THESE MONKS, I WILL. YOU'VE SEEN HOW FAST I AM.>
YOU'LL DESTROY OUR CELESTIAL BIOCOMPUTER ANYWAY. YOU'RE AMERICANS AND WAR IS UPON US.
WE'RE HERE TO USE IT--THEM--TO STOP THAT WAR.
AND I'M JUST SUPPOSED TO TAKE YOUR WORD FOR IT?
NO. MY ASSOCIATE IS NOW A PART OF IT AS WELL. SHE WILL DIE IF THEY DO. AND VICE VERSA.

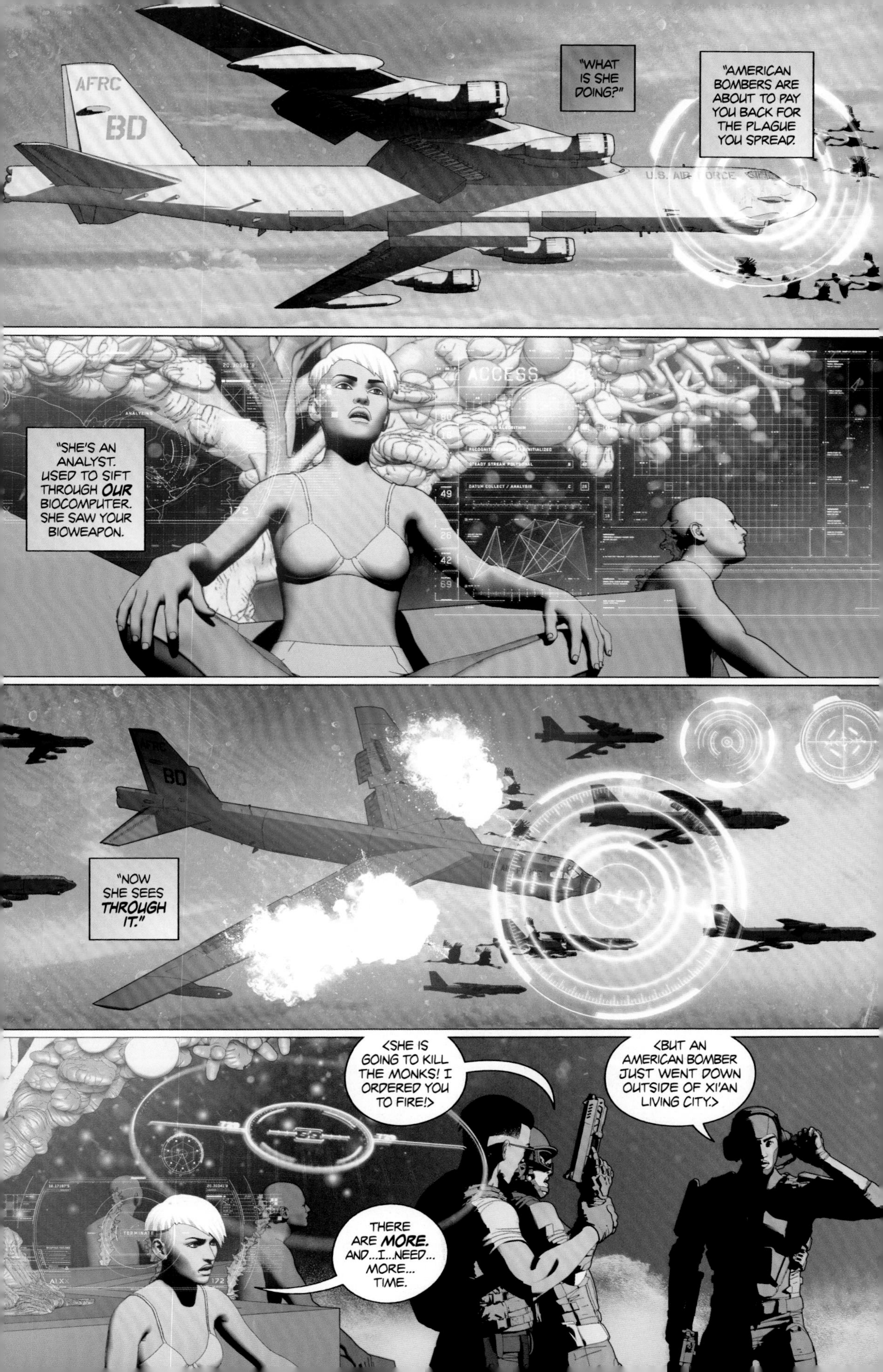
AFRC
BD
U.S. AIR FORCE
"WHAT IS SHE DOING?"
"AMERICAN BOMBERS ARE ABOUT TO PAY YOU BACK FOR THE PLAGUE YOU SPREAD.
ACCESS
"SHE'S AN ANALYST. USED TO SIFT THROUGH **OUR** BIOCOMPUTER. SHE SAW YOUR BIOWEAPON.
AFRC
BD
"NOW SHE SEES **THROUGH** IT."
<SHE IS GOING TO KILL THE MONKS! I ORDERED YOU TO FIRE!>
<BUT AN AMERICAN BOMBER JUST WENT DOWN OUTSIDE OF XI'AN LIVING CITY.>
THERE ARE **MORE.** AND...I...NEED... MORE... TIME.

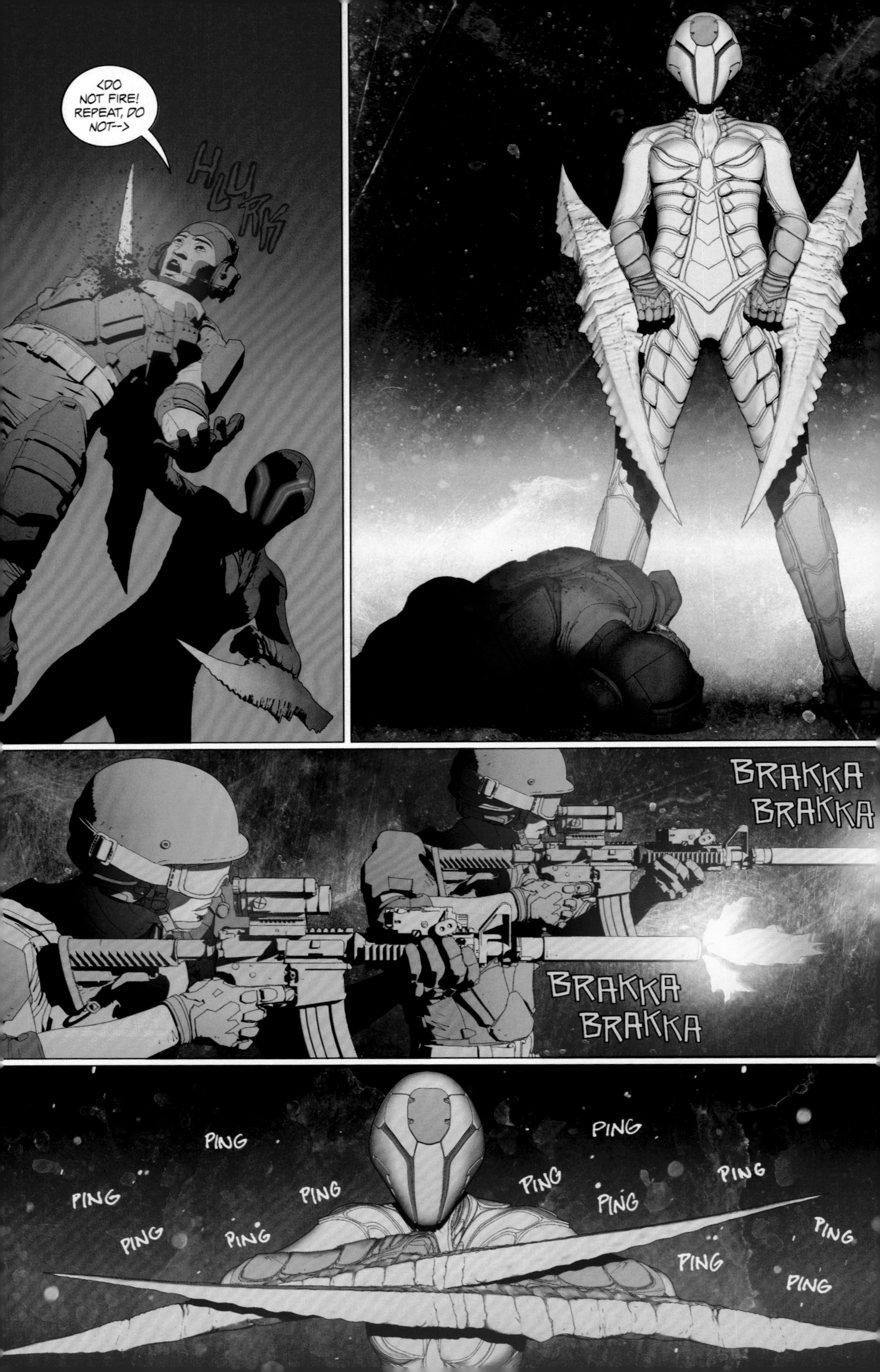
<DO NOT FIRE! REPEAT, DO NOT-->
HLURK
BRAKKA BRAKKA
BRAKKA BRAKKA
PING
PING
PING
PING
PING
PING
PING
PING
PING
PING
PING
PING

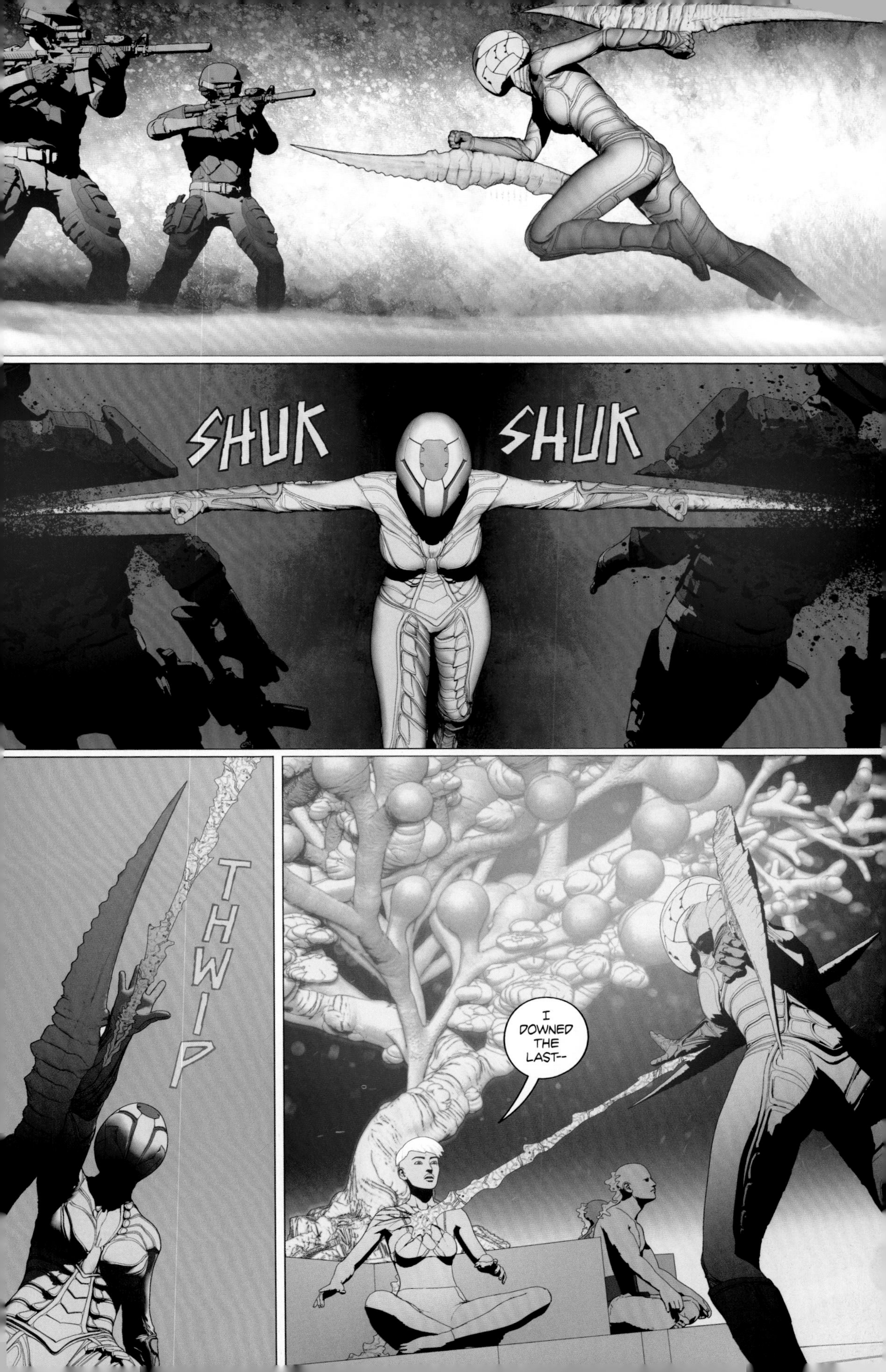
SHUK
SHUK
THWIP
I DOWNED THE LAST--

SZZZZTTT

NO. IT CAN'T BE.

SHUNK

Just as I was disconnected for the last time--

BRAKKA BRAKKA

KRISHH

KA-THINK

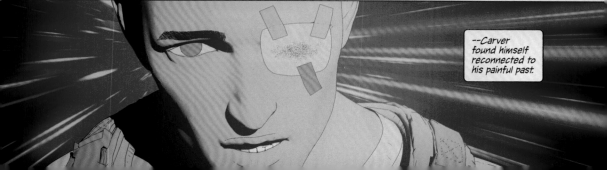

--Carver found himself reconnected to his painful past.

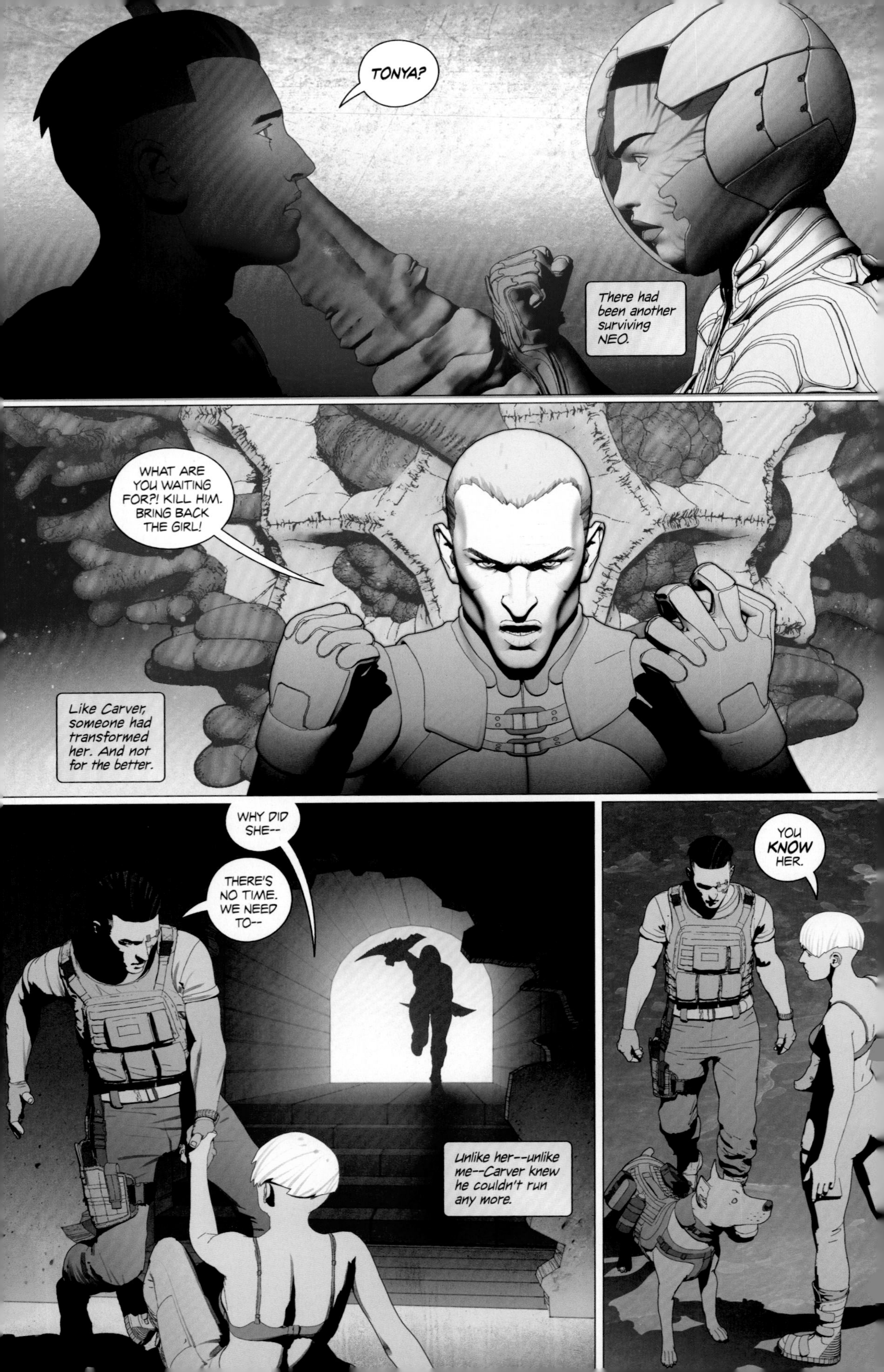
TONYA?
There had been another surviving NEO.
WHAT ARE YOU WAITING FOR?! KILL HIM. BRING BACK THE GIRL!
Like Carver, someone had transformed her. And not for the better.
WHY DID SHE--
THERE'S NO TIME. WE NEED TO--
Unlike her--unlike me--Carver knew he couldn't run any more.
YOU KNOW HER.

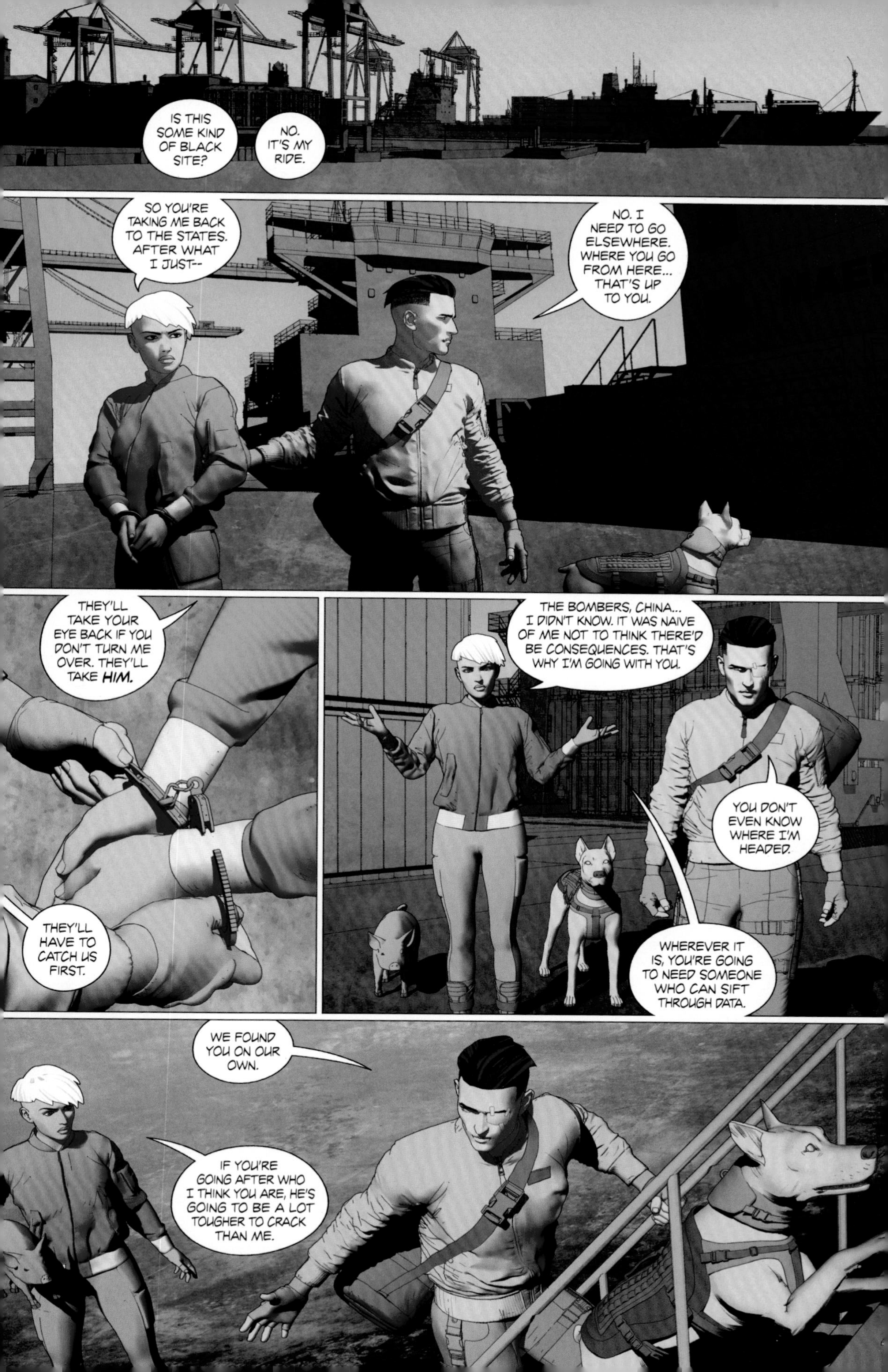
IS THIS SOME KIND OF BLACK SITE?
NO. IT'S MY RIDE.
SO YOU'RE TAKING ME BACK TO THE STATES. AFTER WHAT I JUST--
NO. I NEED TO GO ELSEWHERE. WHERE YOU GO FROM HERE... THAT'S UP TO YOU.
THEY'LL TAKE YOUR EYE BACK IF YOU DON'T TURN ME OVER. THEY'LL TAKE **HIM.**
THEY'LL HAVE TO CATCH US FIRST.
THE BOMBERS, CHINA... I DIDN'T KNOW. IT WAS NAIVE OF ME NOT TO THINK THERE'D BE CONSEQUENCES. THAT'S WHY I'M GOING WITH YOU.
YOU DON'T EVEN KNOW WHERE I'M HEADED.
WHEREVER IT IS, YOU'RE GOING TO NEED SOMEONE WHO CAN SIFT THROUGH DATA.
WE FOUND YOU ON OUR OWN.
IF YOU'RE GOING AFTER WHO I THINK YOU ARE, HE'S GOING TO BE A LOT TOUGHER TO CRACK THAN ME.

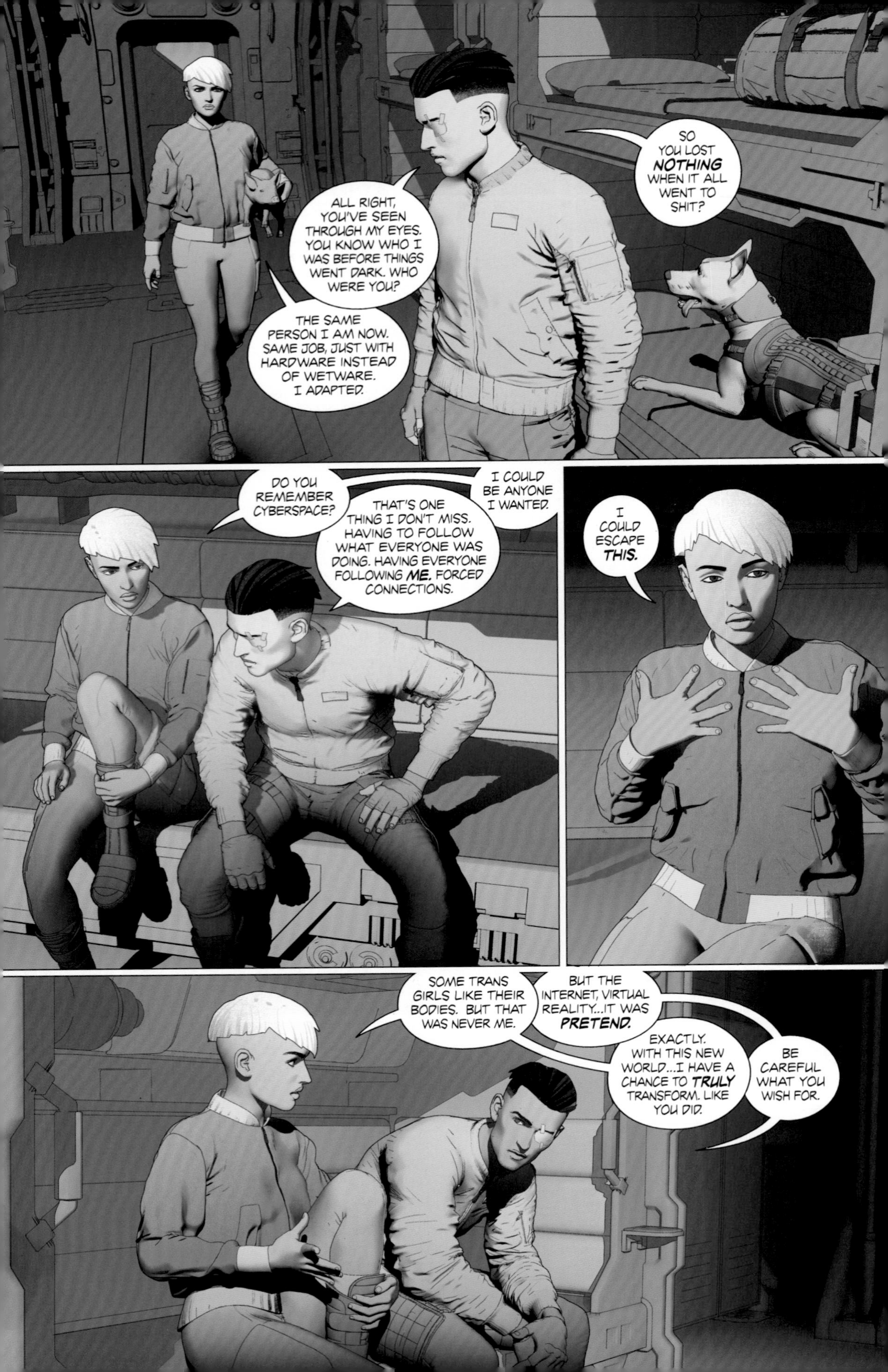
SO YOU LOST NOTHING WHEN IT ALL WENT TO SHIT?
ALL RIGHT, YOU'VE SEEN THROUGH MY EYES. YOU KNOW WHO I WAS BEFORE THINGS WENT DARK. WHO WERE YOU?
THE SAME PERSON I AM NOW. SAME JOB, JUST WITH HARDWARE INSTEAD OF WETWARE. I ADAPTED.
DO YOU REMEMBER CYBERSPACE?
I COULD BE ANYONE I WANTED.
THAT'S ONE THING I DON'T MISS. HAVING TO FOLLOW WHAT EVERYONE WAS DOING. HAVING EVERYONE FOLLOWING ME. FORCED CONNECTIONS.
I COULD ESCAPE THIS.
SOME TRANS GIRLS LIKE THEIR BODIES. BUT THAT WAS NEVER ME.
BUT THE INTERNET, VIRTUAL REALITY...IT WAS PRETEND.
EXACTLY. WITH THIS NEW WORLD...I HAVE A CHANCE TO TRULY TRANSFORM. LIKE YOU DID.
BE CAREFUL WHAT YOU WISH FOR.

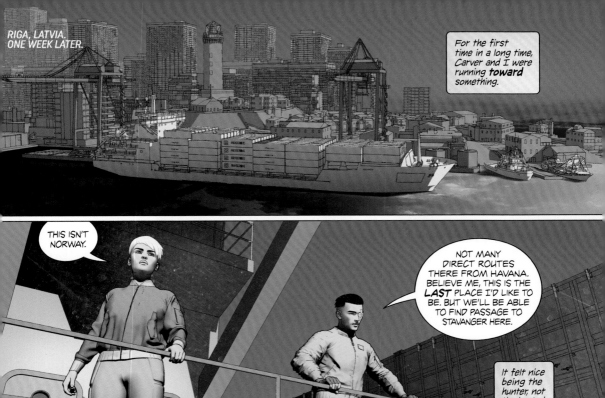

RIGA, LATVIA.
ONE WEEK LATER.

For the first time in a long time, Carver and I were running **toward** something.

THIS ISN'T NORWAY.

NOT MANY DIRECT ROUTES THERE FROM HAVANA. BELIEVE ME, THIS IS THE **LAST** PLACE I'D LIKE TO BE. BUT WE'LL BE ABLE TO FIND PASSAGE TO STAVANGER HERE.

It felt nice being the hunter, not the hunted.

I don't imagine that role reversal felt good to Carver.

WHAT IS IT, BOY?

GRRRR

OH, SHIT.

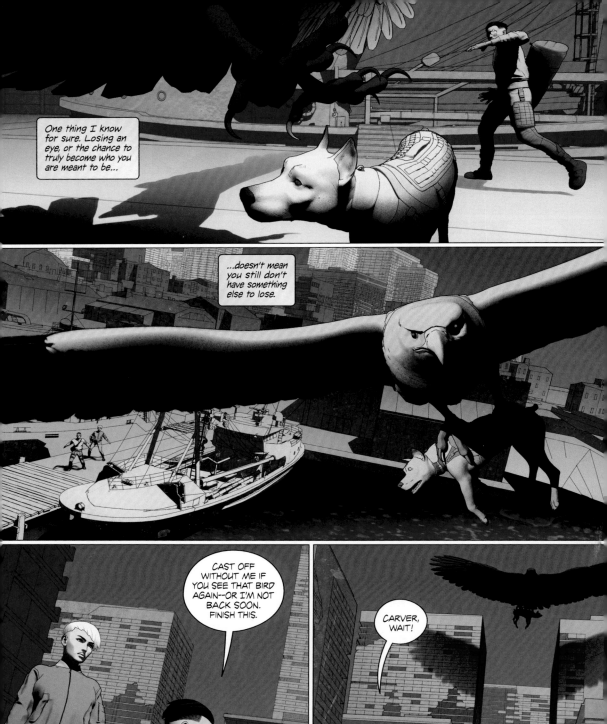

One thing I know for sure. Losing an eye, or the chance to truly become who you are meant to be...

...doesn't mean you still don't have something else to lose.

CAST OFF WITHOUT ME IF YOU SEE THAT BIRD AGAIN--OR I'M NOT BACK SOON. FINISH THIS.

CARVER, WAIT!

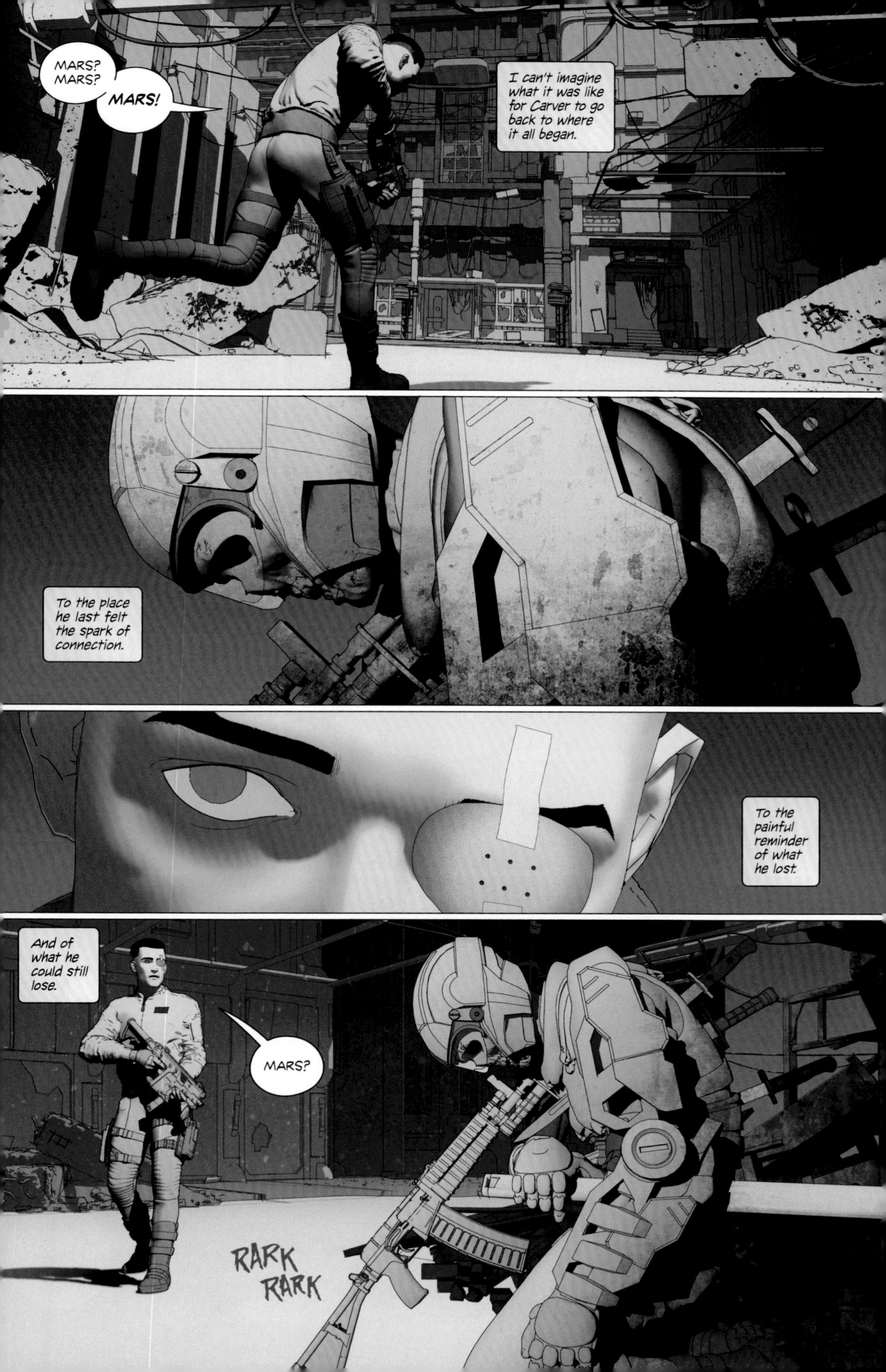
MARS? MARS?
MARS!
I can't imagine what it was like for Carver to go back to where it all began.
To the place he last felt the spark of connection.
To the painful reminder of what he lost.
And of what he could still lose.
MARS?
RARK RARK

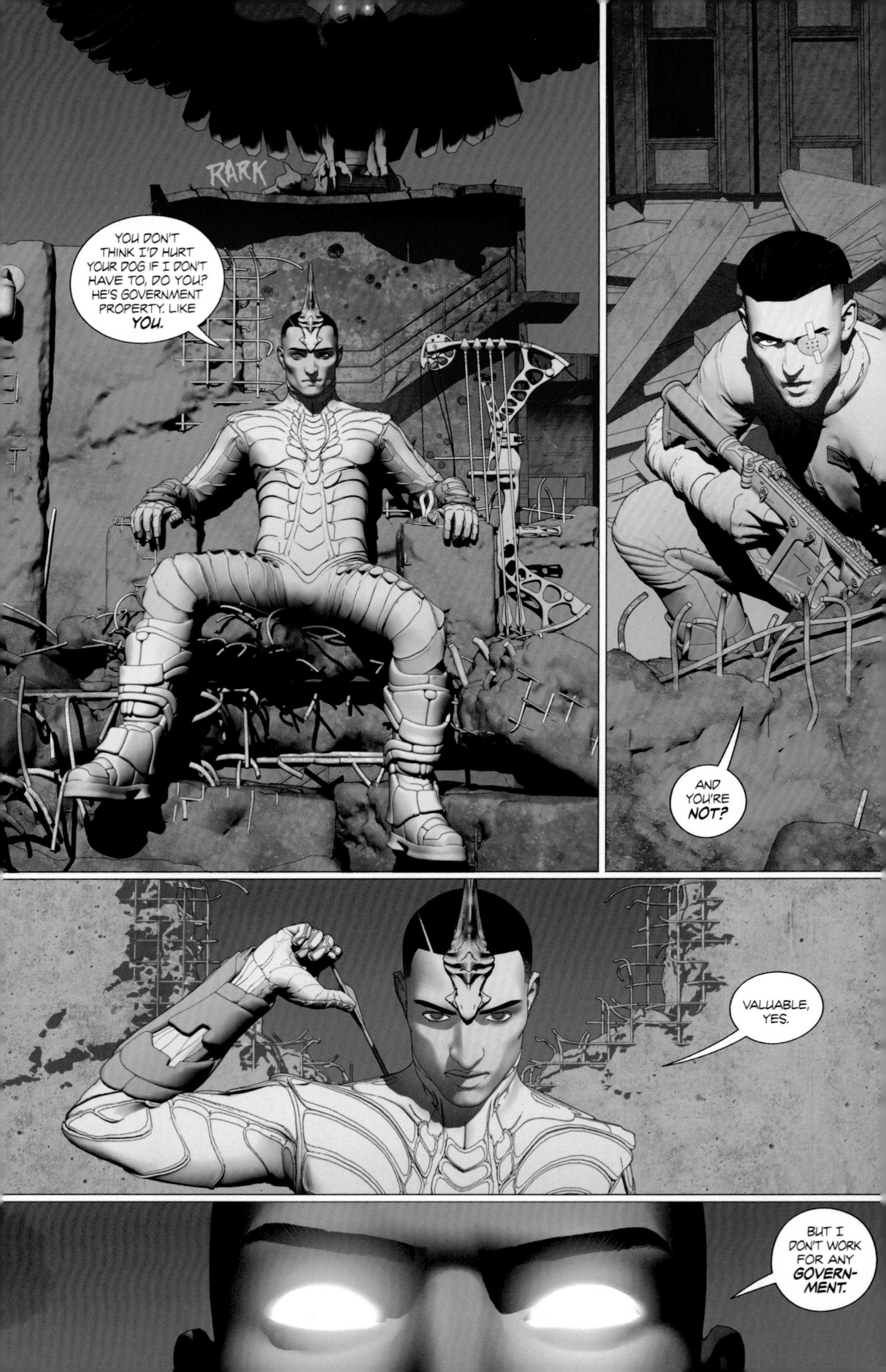
RARK
YOU DON'T THINK I'D HURT YOUR DOG IF I DON'T HAVE TO, DO YOU? HE'S GOVERNMENT PROPERTY. LIKE **YOU.**
AND YOU'RE **NOT?**
VALUABLE, YES.
BUT I DON'T WORK FOR ANY **GOVERN-MENT.**

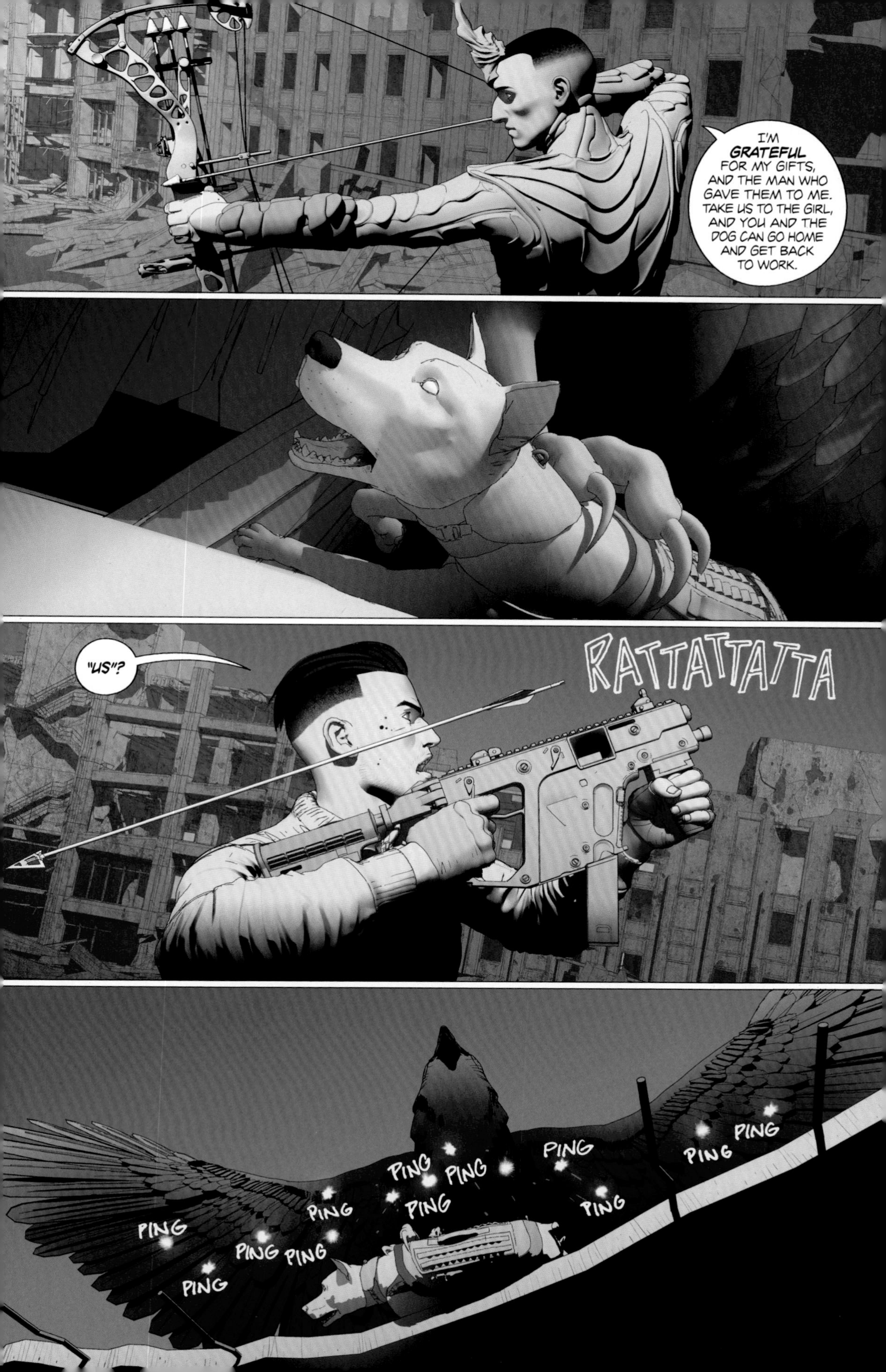
I'M GRATEFUL FOR MY GIFTS, AND THE MAN WHO GAVE THEM TO ME. TAKE US TO THE GIRL, AND YOU AND THE DOG CAN GO HOME AND GET BACK TO WORK.
"US"?
RATTATTATTA
PING
PING
PING
PING
PING
PING
PING
PING
PING
PING
PING
PING
PING

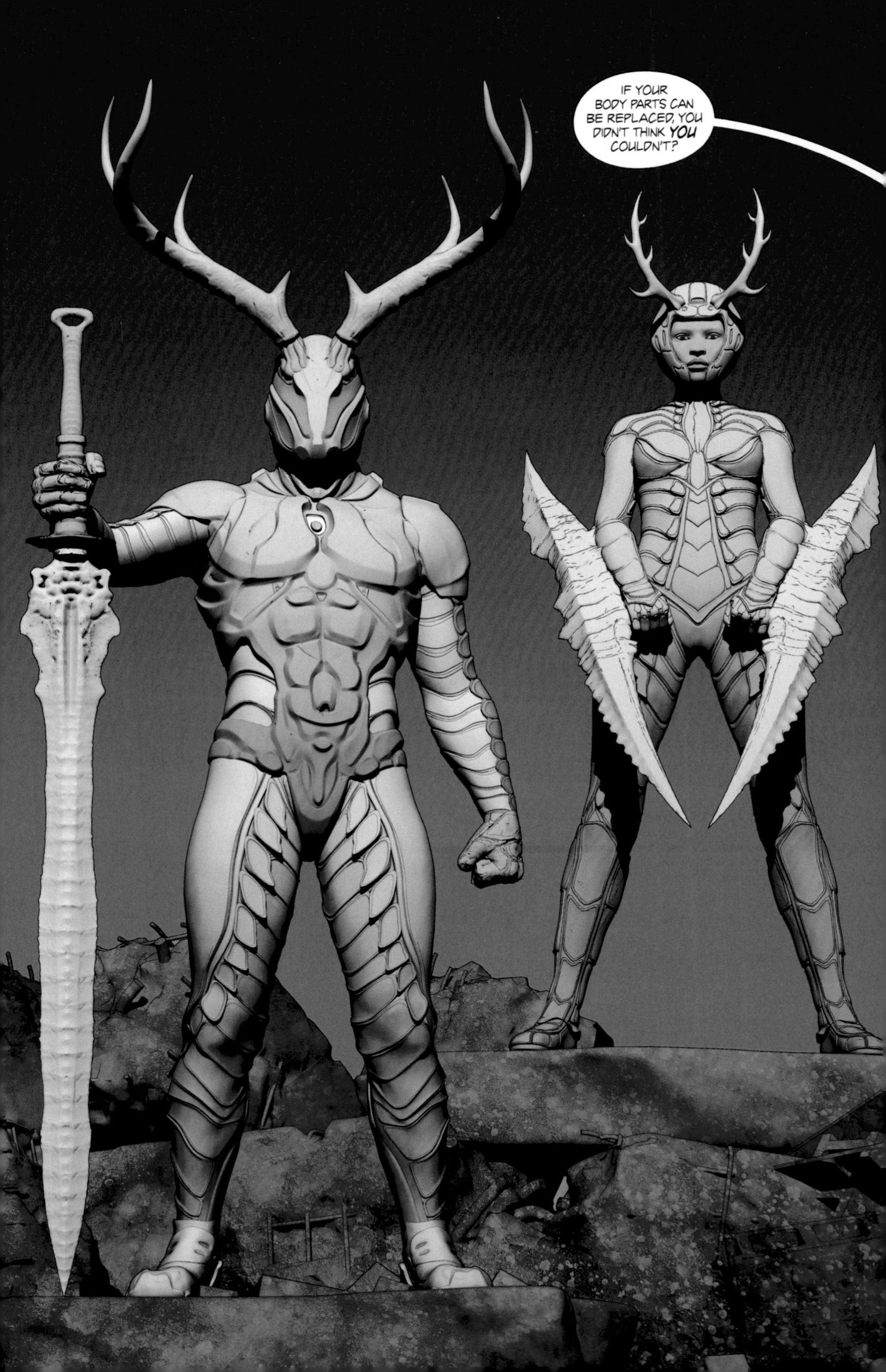
IF YOUR BODY PARTS CAN BE REPLACED, YOU DIDN'T THINK YOU COULDN'T?

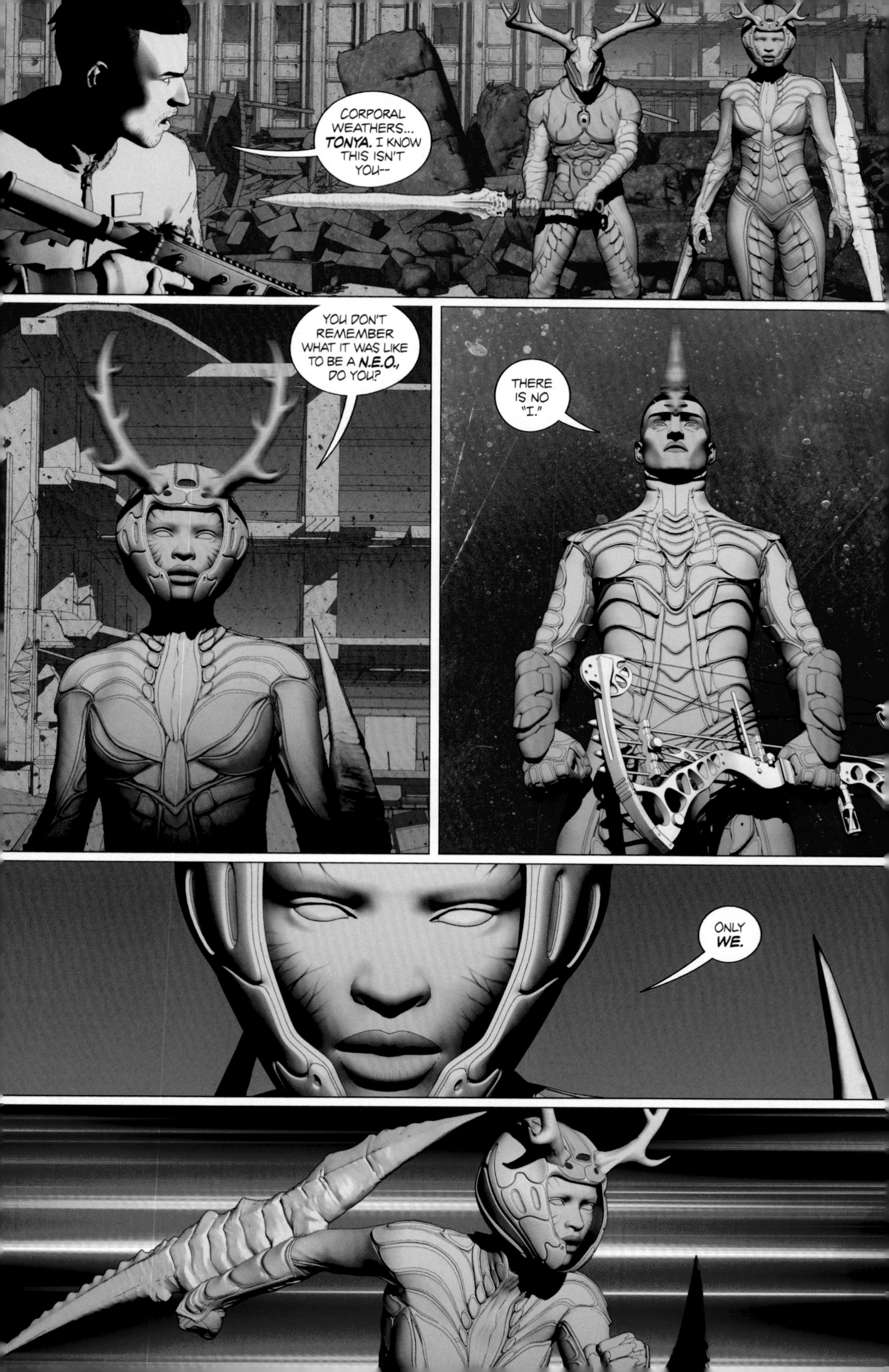
CORPORAL WEATHERS... TONYA. I KNOW THIS ISN'T YOU--
YOU DON'T REMEMBER WHAT IT WAS LIKE TO BE A N.E.O., DO YOU?
THERE IS NO "I."
ONLY WE.

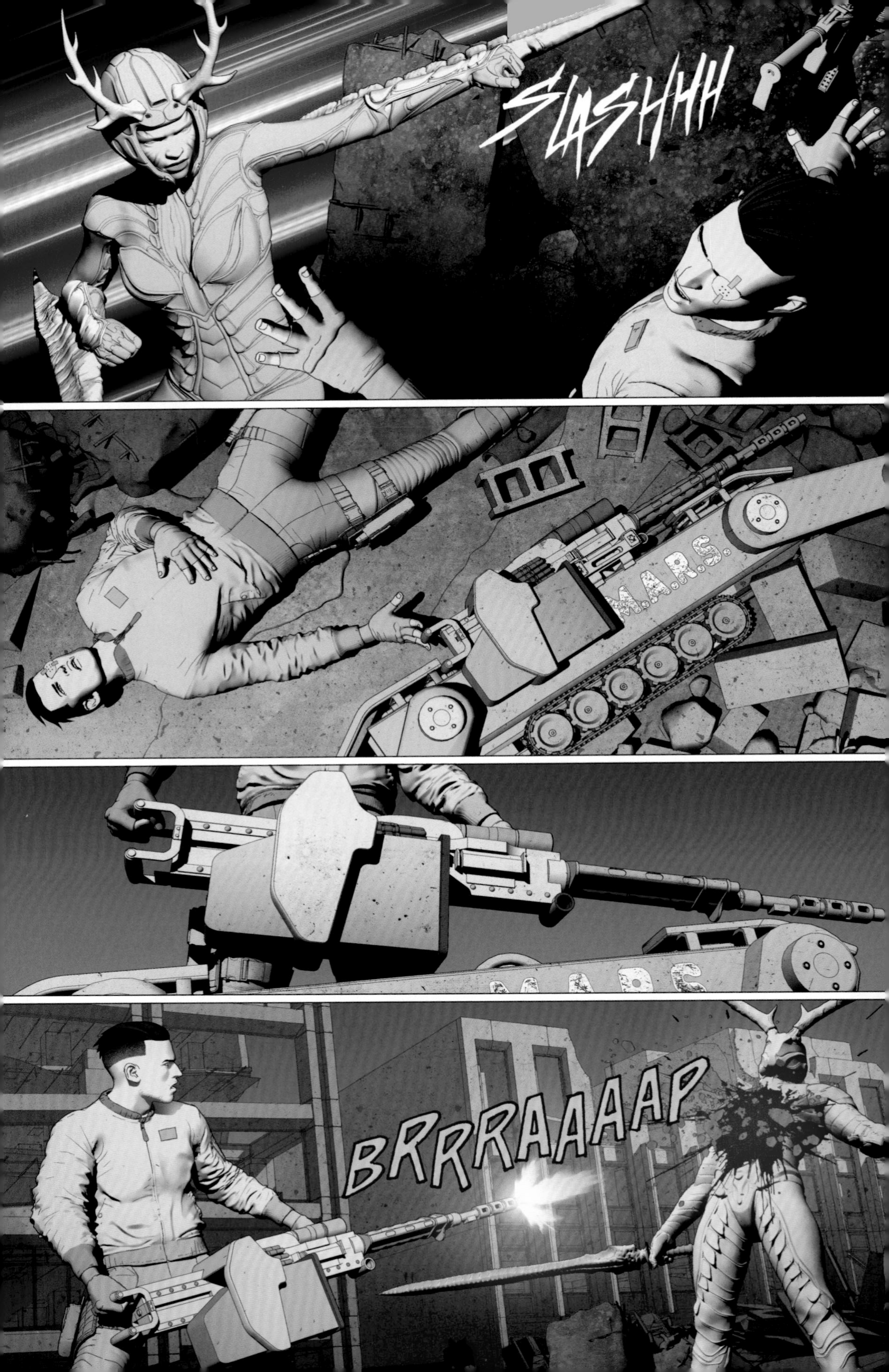
SLASHHH
M.A.R.S.
BRRRAAAAP

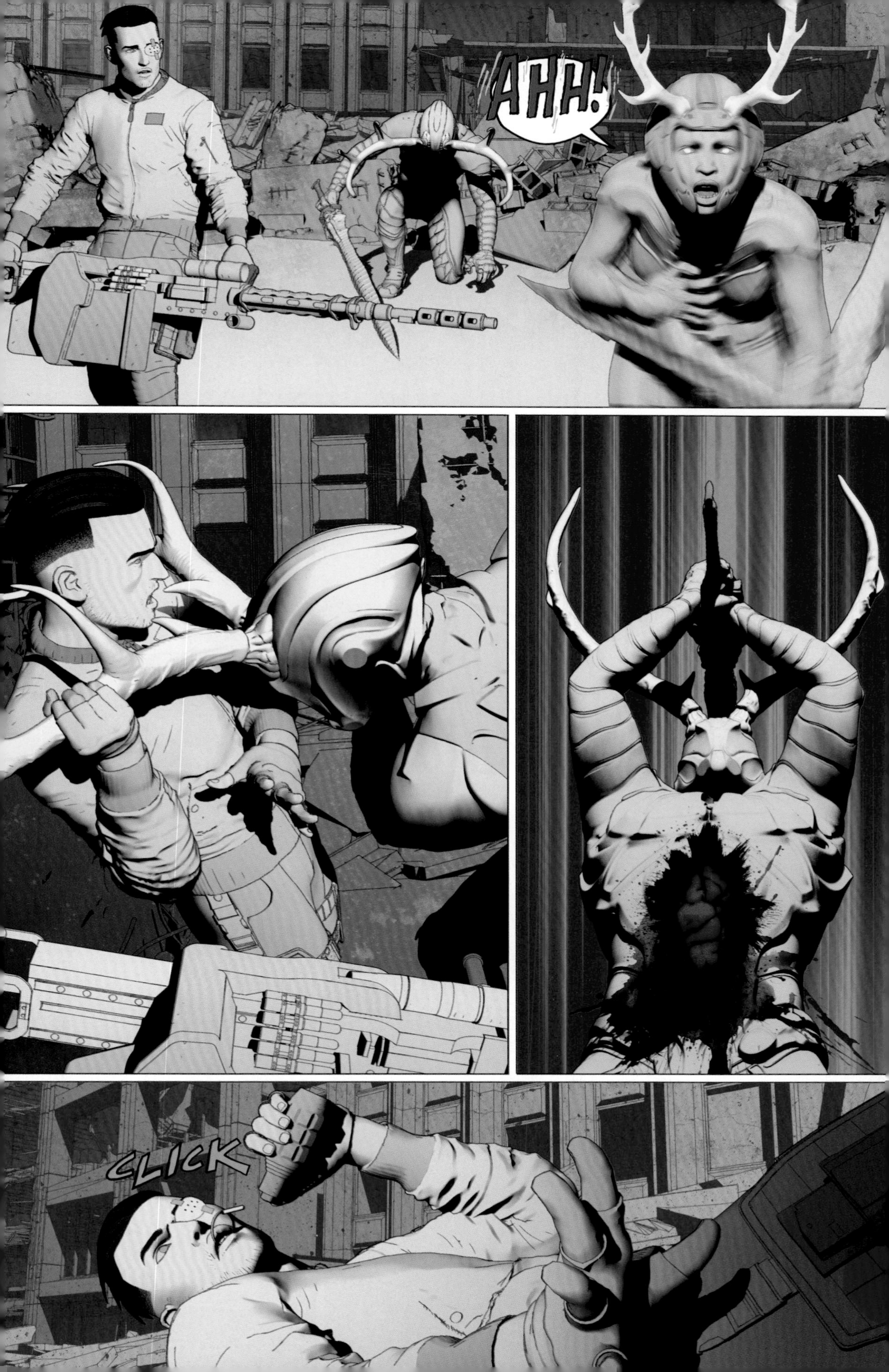
AHH!
CLICK

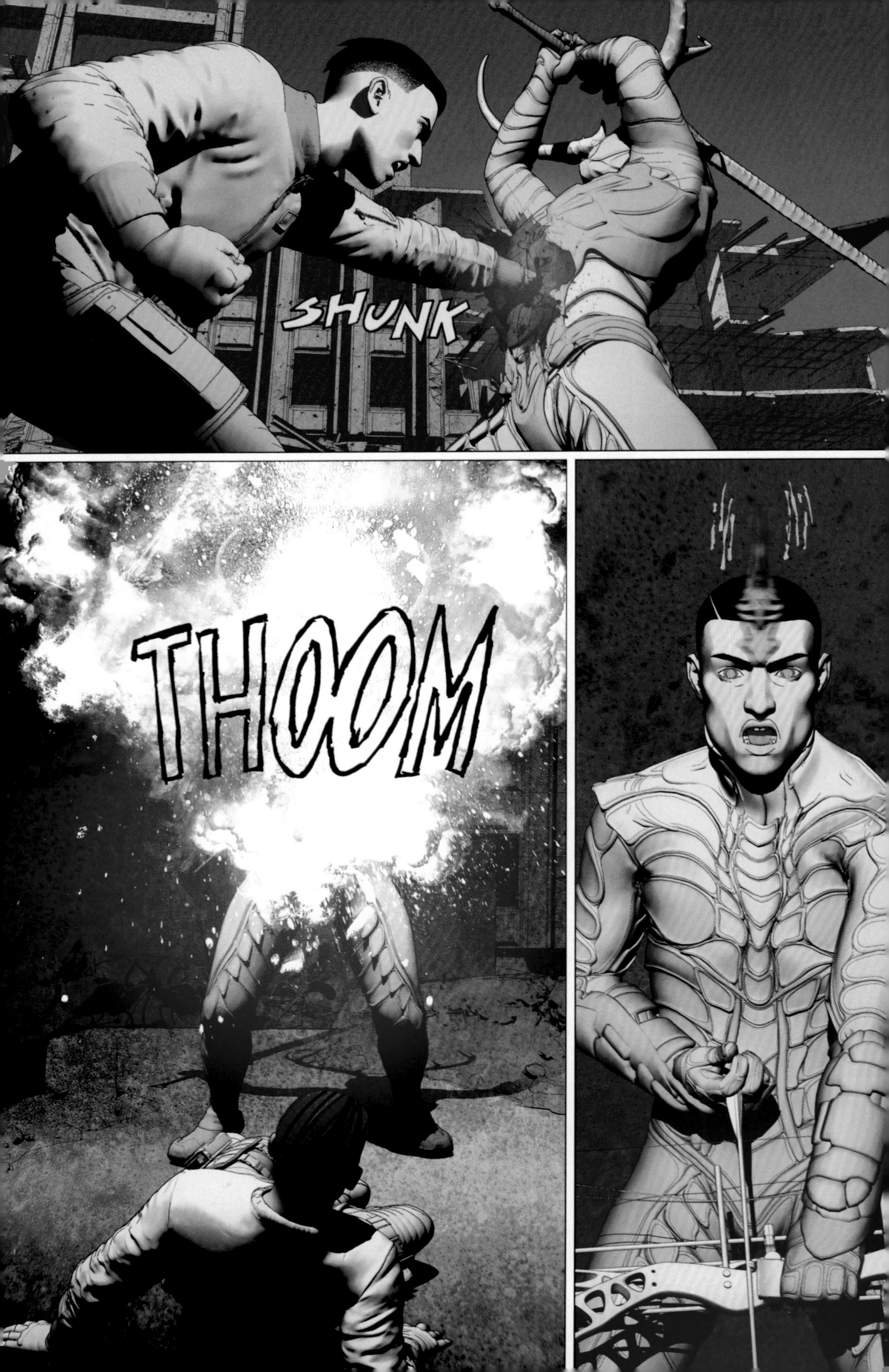
SHUNK
THOOM

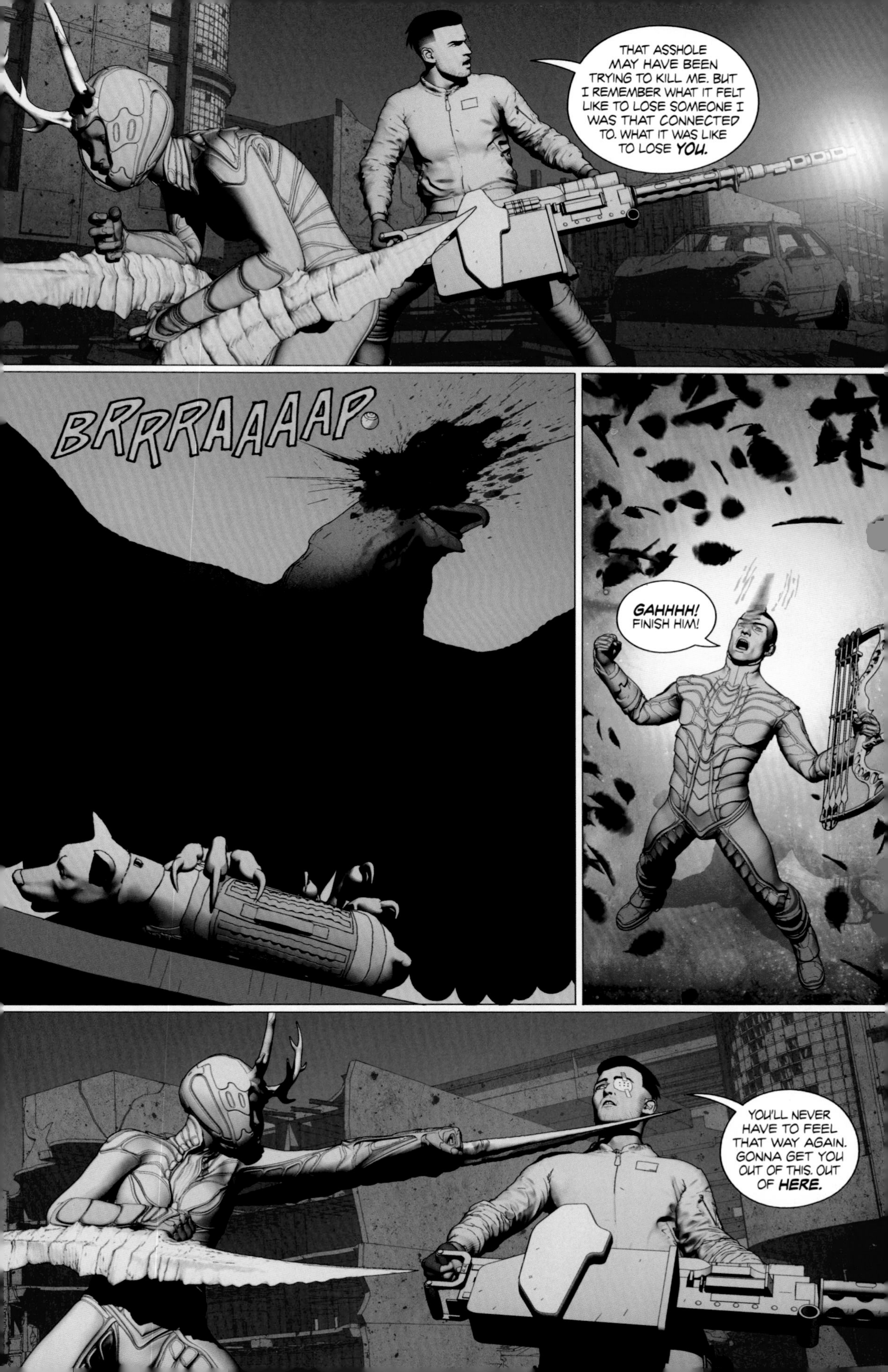
THAT ASSHOLE MAY HAVE BEEN TRYING TO KILL ME. BUT I REMEMBER WHAT IT FELT LIKE TO LOSE SOMEONE I WAS THAT CONNECTED TO. WHAT IT WAS LIKE TO LOSE **YOU.**
BRRRAAAAP
GAHHHH! FINISH HIM!
YOU'LL NEVER HAVE TO FEEL THAT WAY AGAIN. GONNA GET YOU OUT OF THIS. OUT OF **HERE.**

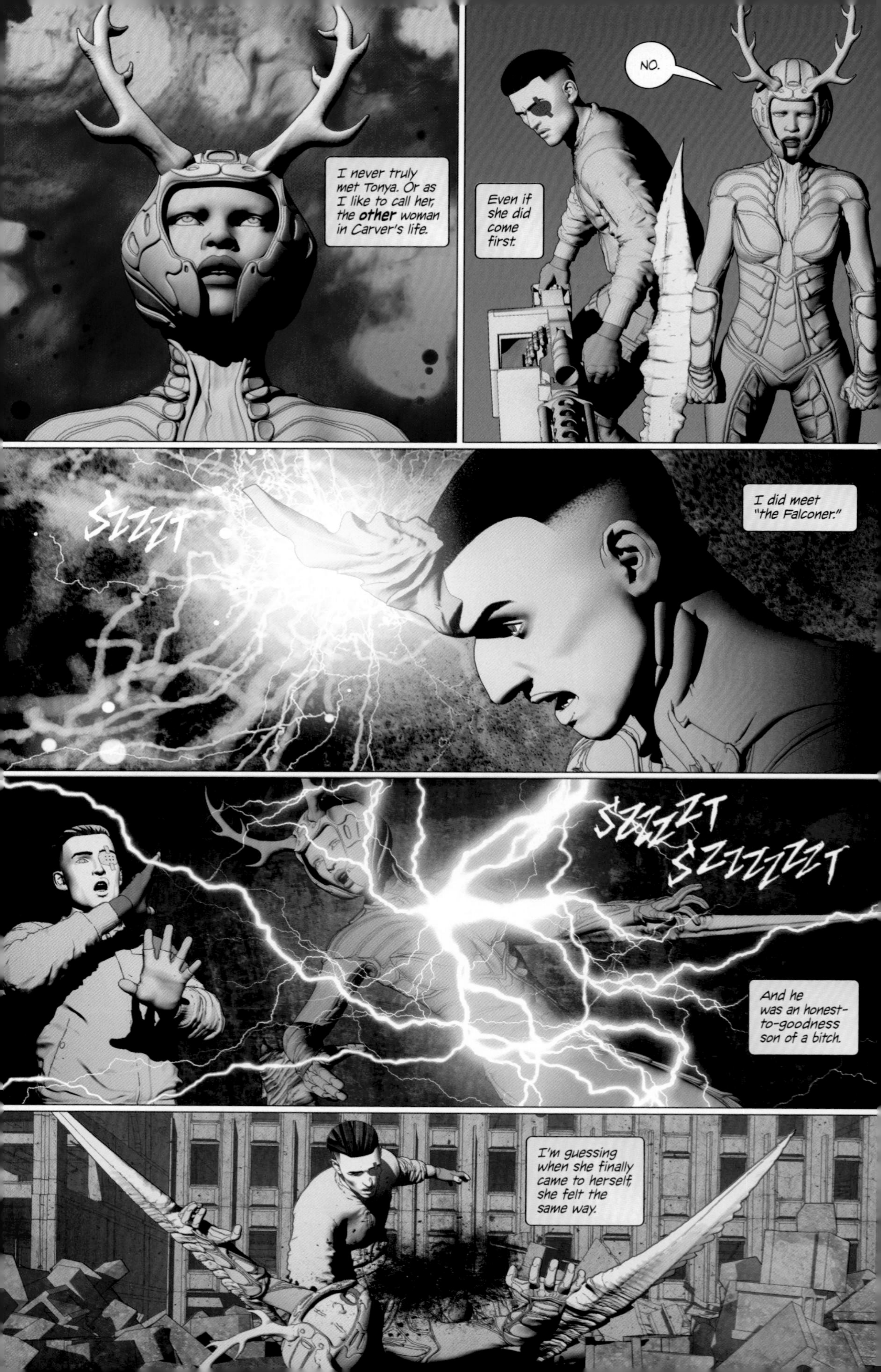
I never truly met Tonya. Or as I like to call her, the **other** woman in Carver's life.
NO.
Even if she did come first.
SZZZT
I did meet "the Falconer."
SZZZZT
SZZZZZZZT
And he was an honest-to-goodness son of a bitch.
I'm guessing when she finally came to herself, she felt the same way.

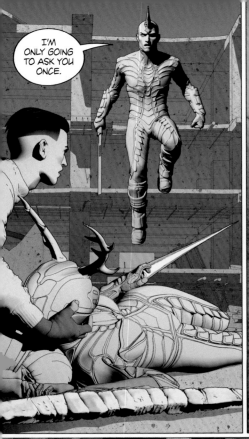

I'M ONLY GOING TO ASK YOU ONCE.

WHERE. IS. THE. GIRL?

RIGHT. FUCKING. HERE!

SHNKK

THRIP

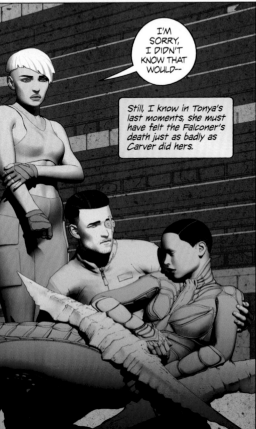

I'M SORRY, I DIDN'T KNOW THAT WOULD--

Still, I know in Tonya's last moments, she must have felt the Falconer's death just as badly as Carver did hers.

YOU ENDED HER SUFFERING. IF YOU'RE UP FOR IT, IT'S TIME TO MAKE SURE NO ONE ELSE HAS TO.

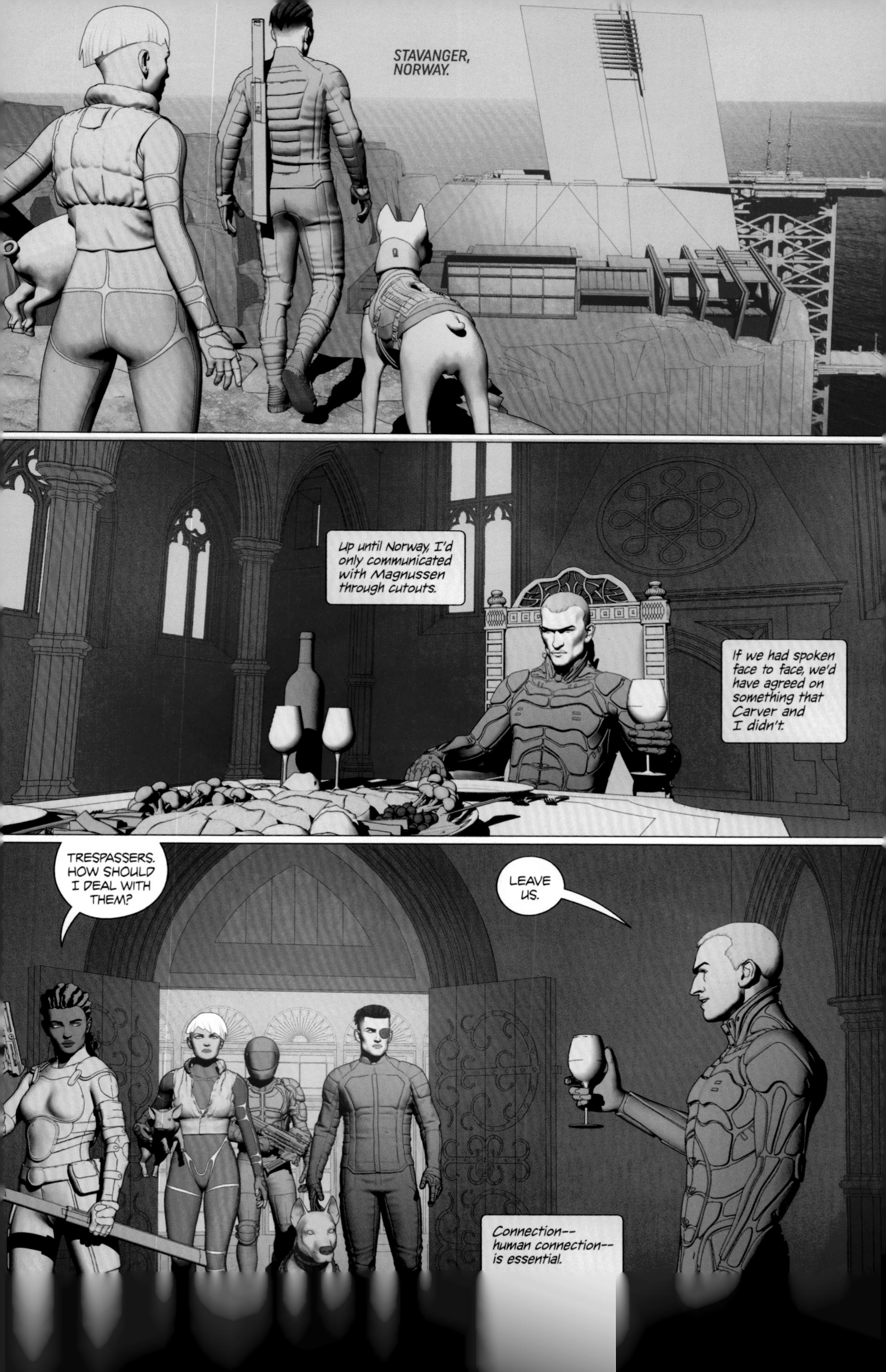
STAVANGER, NORWAY.
Up until Norway, I'd only communicated with Magnussen through cutouts.
If we had spoken face to face, we'd have agreed on something that Carver and I didn't.
TRESPASSERS. HOW SHOULD I DEAL WITH THEM?
LEAVE US.
Connection-- human connection-- is essential.

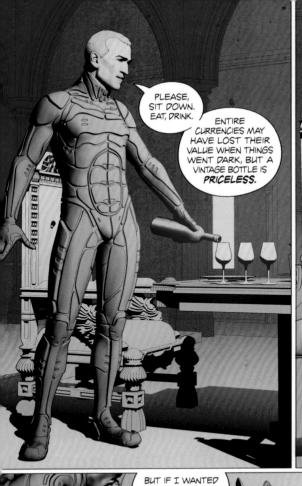

PLEASE, SIT DOWN. EAT, DRINK.

ENTIRE CURRENCIES MAY HAVE LOST THEIR VALUE WHEN THINGS WENT DARK, BUT A VINTAGE BOTTLE IS *PRICELESS.*

YOU WON'T FIND ANY POISON. MUST I PROVE IT? I'LL DRINK FIRST.

Sniff sniff

BUT IF I WANTED YOU DEAD, I COULD HAVE HAD YOU SHOT AT THE GATE.

WILL YOU AT LEAST ALLOW ME TO FEED THESE POOR CREATURES? THEY LOOK FAMISHED.

QUITE RIGHT. *BIG BROTHER* IS MORE RESILIENT THAN SOCIETY ITSELF. TRYING TO STOP THEM IS LIKE TRYING TO STOP *PROGRESS.*

NATURE-- HUMAN OR OTHERWISE-- ALWAYS FINDS A WAY.

WHAT DID YOU HAVE CAMILLE INTRODUCE INTO THE BIOCOMPUTER AT *BUMBLEHIVE?* A VIRUS? THE N.S.A.'S UTAH DATA CENTER IS JUST ONE OF *MANY.*

IF YOU WANTED TO DESTROY THE DATA, TO STOP ITS COLLECTION... YOU'VE FAILED.

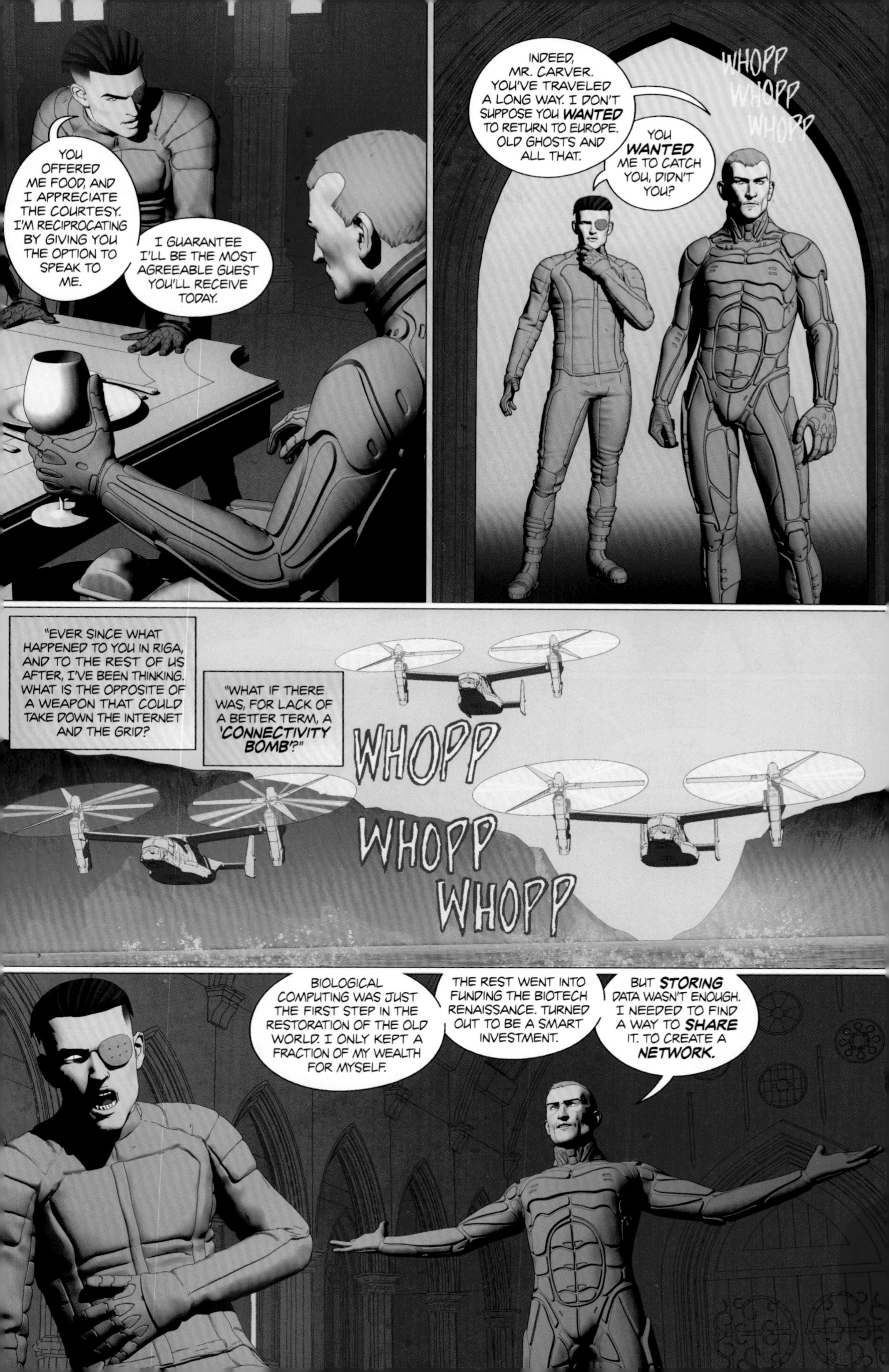
YOU OFFERED ME FOOD, AND I APPRECIATE THE COURTESY. I'M RECIPROCATING BY GIVING YOU THE OPTION TO SPEAK TO ME.
I GUARANTEE I'LL BE THE MOST AGREEABLE GUEST YOU'LL RECEIVE TODAY.
INDEED, MR. CARVER. YOU'VE TRAVELED A LONG WAY. I DON'T SUPPOSE YOU WANTED TO RETURN TO EUROPE. OLD GHOSTS AND ALL THAT.
YOU WANTED ME TO CATCH YOU, DIDN'T YOU?
WHOPP WHOPP WHOPP
"EVER SINCE WHAT HAPPENED TO YOU IN RIGA, AND TO THE REST OF US AFTER, I'VE BEEN THINKING. WHAT IS THE OPPOSITE OF A WEAPON THAT COULD TAKE DOWN THE INTERNET AND THE GRID?
"WHAT IF THERE WAS, FOR LACK OF A BETTER TERM, A 'CONNECTIVITY BOMB'?"
WHOPP WHOPP WHOPP
BIOLOGICAL COMPUTING WAS JUST THE FIRST STEP IN THE RESTORATION OF THE OLD WORLD. I ONLY KEPT A FRACTION OF MY WEALTH FOR MYSELF.
THE REST WENT INTO FUNDING THE BIOTECH RENAISSANCE. TURNED OUT TO BE A SMART INVESTMENT.
BUT STORING DATA WASN'T ENOUGH. I NEEDED TO FIND A WAY TO SHARE IT. TO CREATE A NETWORK.

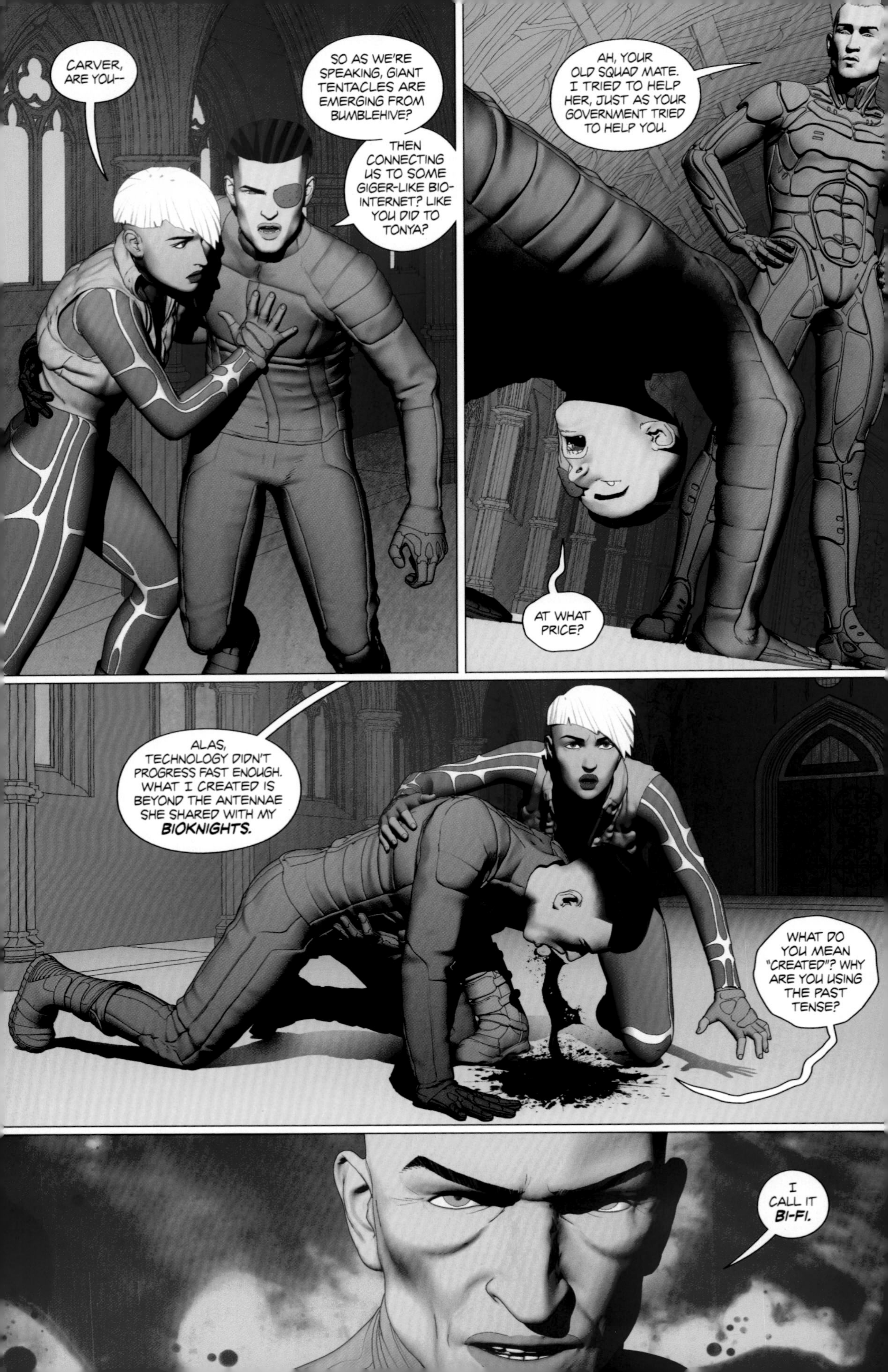
CARVER, ARE YOU--
SO AS WE'RE SPEAKING, GIANT TENTACLES ARE EMERGING FROM BUMBLEHIVE?
THEN CONNECTING US TO SOME GIGER-LIKE BIO-INTERNET? LIKE YOU DID TO TONYA?
AH, YOUR OLD SQUAD MATE. I TRIED TO HELP HER, JUST AS YOUR GOVERNMENT TRIED TO HELP YOU.
AT WHAT PRICE?
ALAS, TECHNOLOGY DIDN'T PROGRESS FAST ENOUGH. WHAT I CREATED IS BEYOND THE ANTENNAE SHE SHARED WITH MY BIOKNIGHTS.
WHAT DO YOU MEAN "CREATED"? WHY ARE YOU USING THE PAST TENSE?
I CALL IT BI-FI.

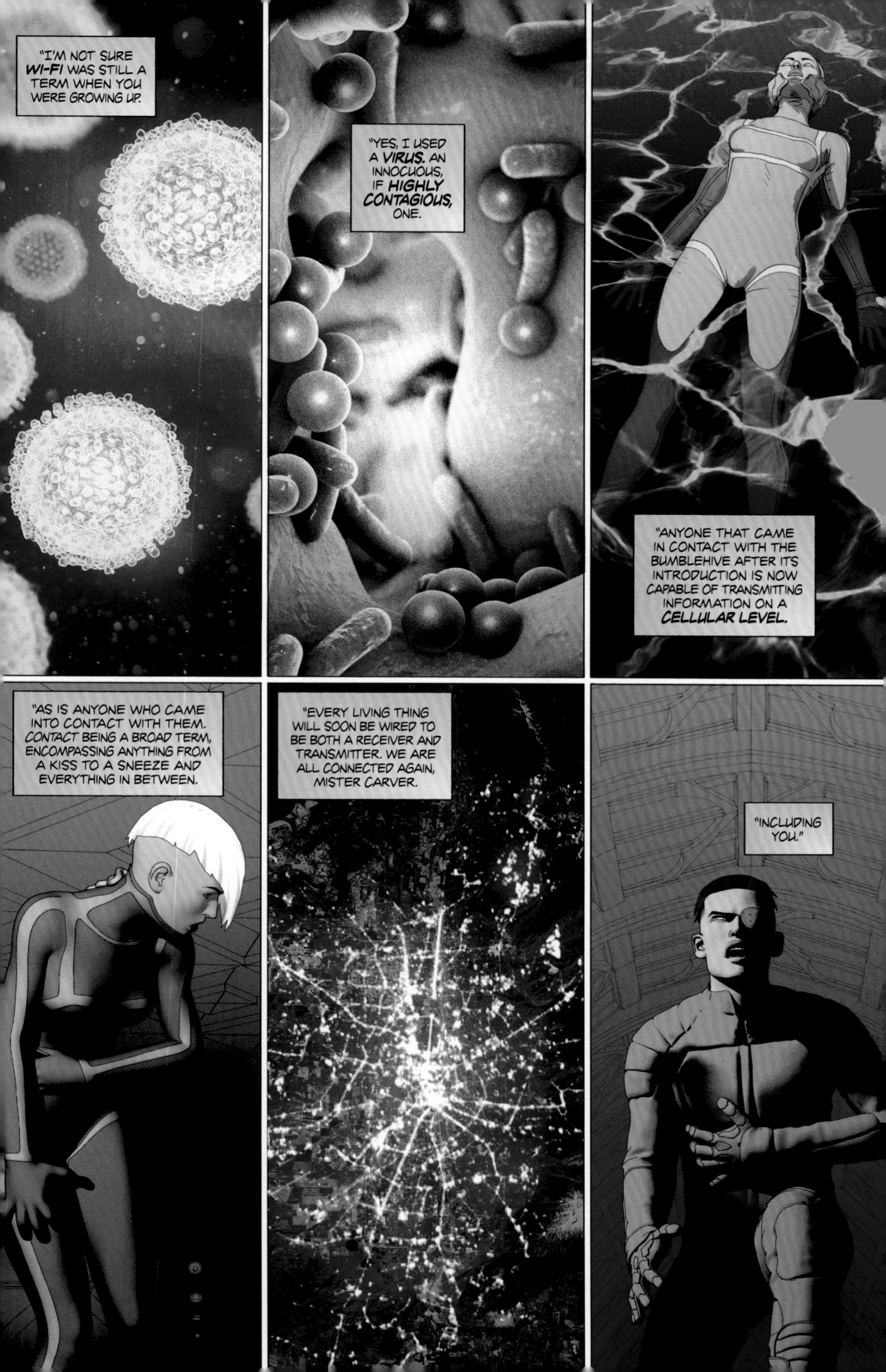
"I'M NOT SURE WI-FI WAS STILL A TERM WHEN YOU WERE GROWING UP.
"YES, I USED A VIRUS. AN INNOCUOUS, IF HIGHLY CONTAGIOUS, ONE.
"ANYONE THAT CAME IN CONTACT WITH THE BUMBLEHIVE AFTER ITS INTRODUCTION IS NOW CAPABLE OF TRANSMITTING INFORMATION ON A CELLULAR LEVEL.
"AS IS ANYONE WHO CAME INTO CONTACT WITH THEM. CONTACT BEING A BROAD TERM, ENCOMPASSING ANYTHING FROM A KISS TO A SNEEZE AND EVERYTHING IN BETWEEN.
"EVERY LIVING THING WILL SOON BE WIRED TO BE BOTH A RECEIVER AND TRANSMITTER. WE ARE ALL CONNECTED AGAIN, MISTER CARVER.
"INCLUDING YOU."

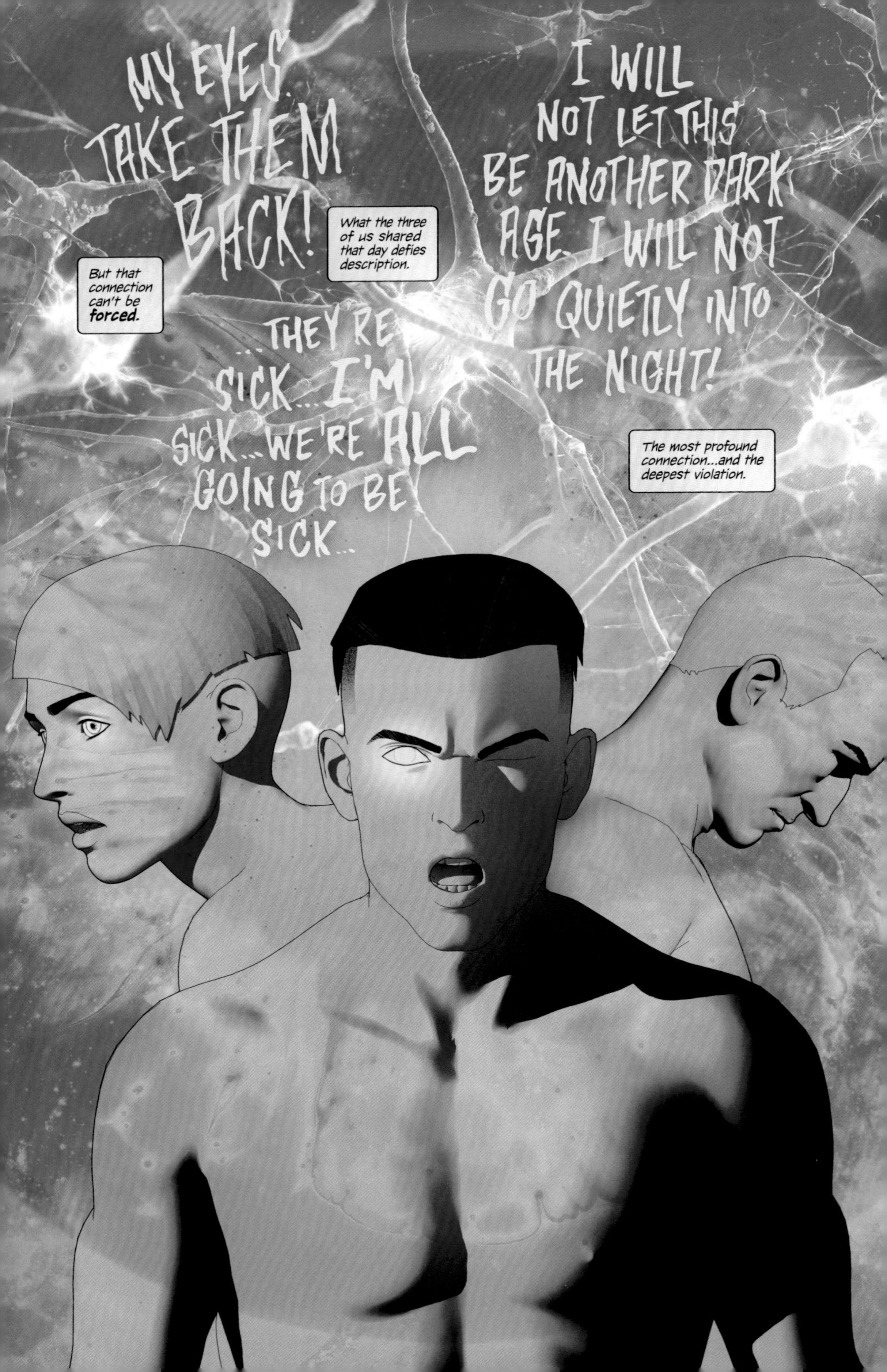
MY EYES. TAKE THEM BACK!
But that connection can't be **forced**.
What the three of us shared that day defies description.
...THEY'RE SICK... I'M SICK... WE'RE ALL GOING TO BE SICK...
I WILL NOT LET THIS BE ANOTHER DARK AGE. I WILL NOT GO QUIETLY INTO THE NIGHT!
The most profound connection...and the deepest violation.

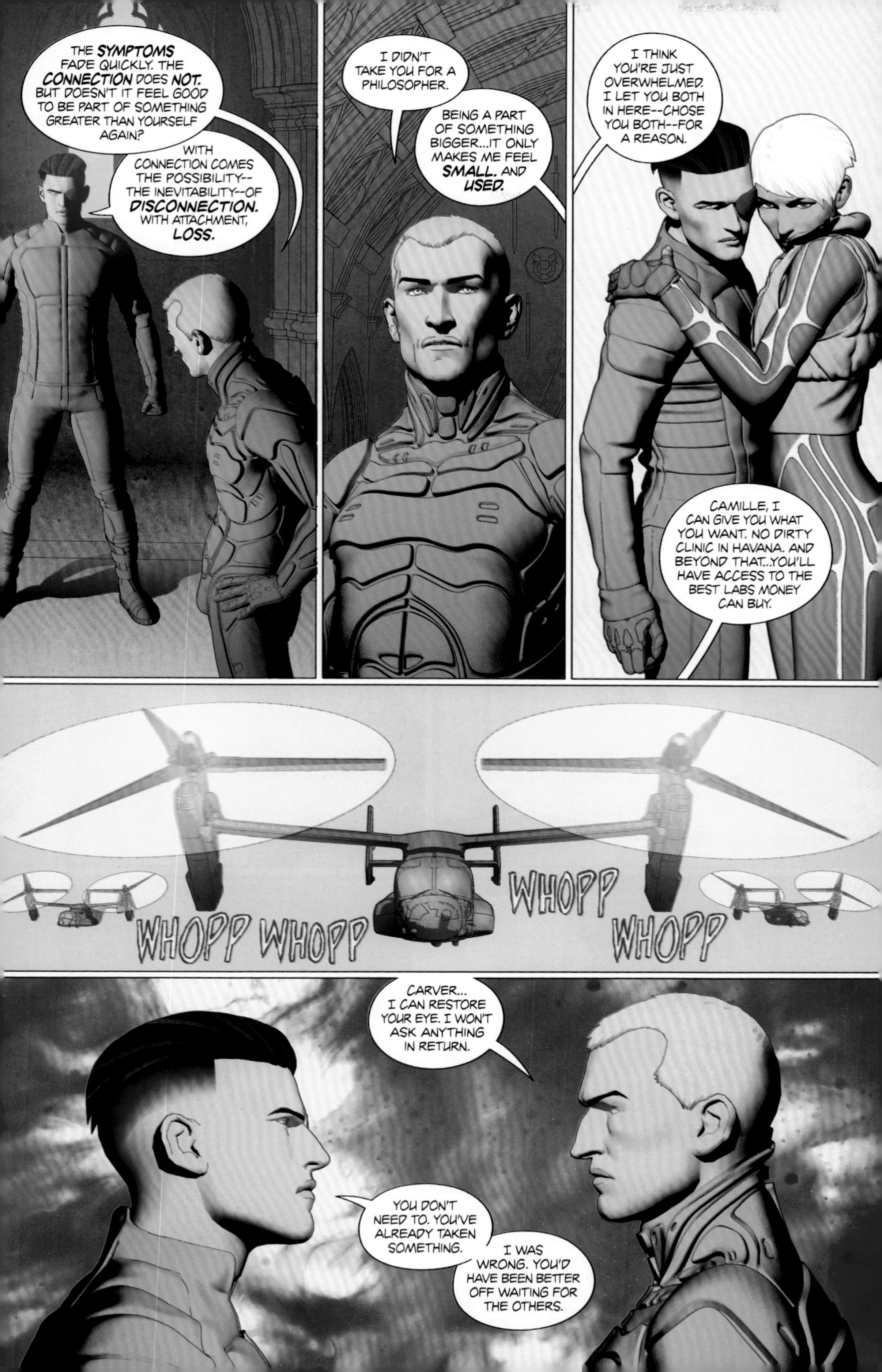
THE SYMPTOMS FADE QUICKLY. THE CONNECTION DOES NOT. BUT DOESN'T IT FEEL GOOD TO BE PART OF SOMETHING GREATER THAN YOURSELF AGAIN?
WITH CONNECTION COMES THE POSSIBILITY-- THE INEVITABILITY--OF DISCONNECTION. WITH ATTACHMENT, LOSS.
I DIDN'T TAKE YOU FOR A PHILOSOPHER.
BEING A PART OF SOMETHING BIGGER...IT ONLY MAKES ME FEEL SMALL. AND USED.
I THINK YOU'RE JUST OVERWHELMED. I LET YOU BOTH IN HERE--CHOSE YOU BOTH--FOR A REASON.
CAMILLE, I CAN GIVE YOU WHAT YOU WANT. NO DIRTY CLINIC IN HAVANA. AND BEYOND THAT...YOU'LL HAVE ACCESS TO THE BEST LABS MONEY CAN BUY.
WHOPP WHOPP
WHOPP WHOPP
CARVER... I CAN RESTORE YOUR EYE. I WON'T ASK ANYTHING IN RETURN.
YOU DON'T NEED TO. YOU'VE ALREADY TAKEN SOMETHING.
I WAS WRONG. YOU'D HAVE BEEN BETTER OFF WAITING FOR THE OTHERS.

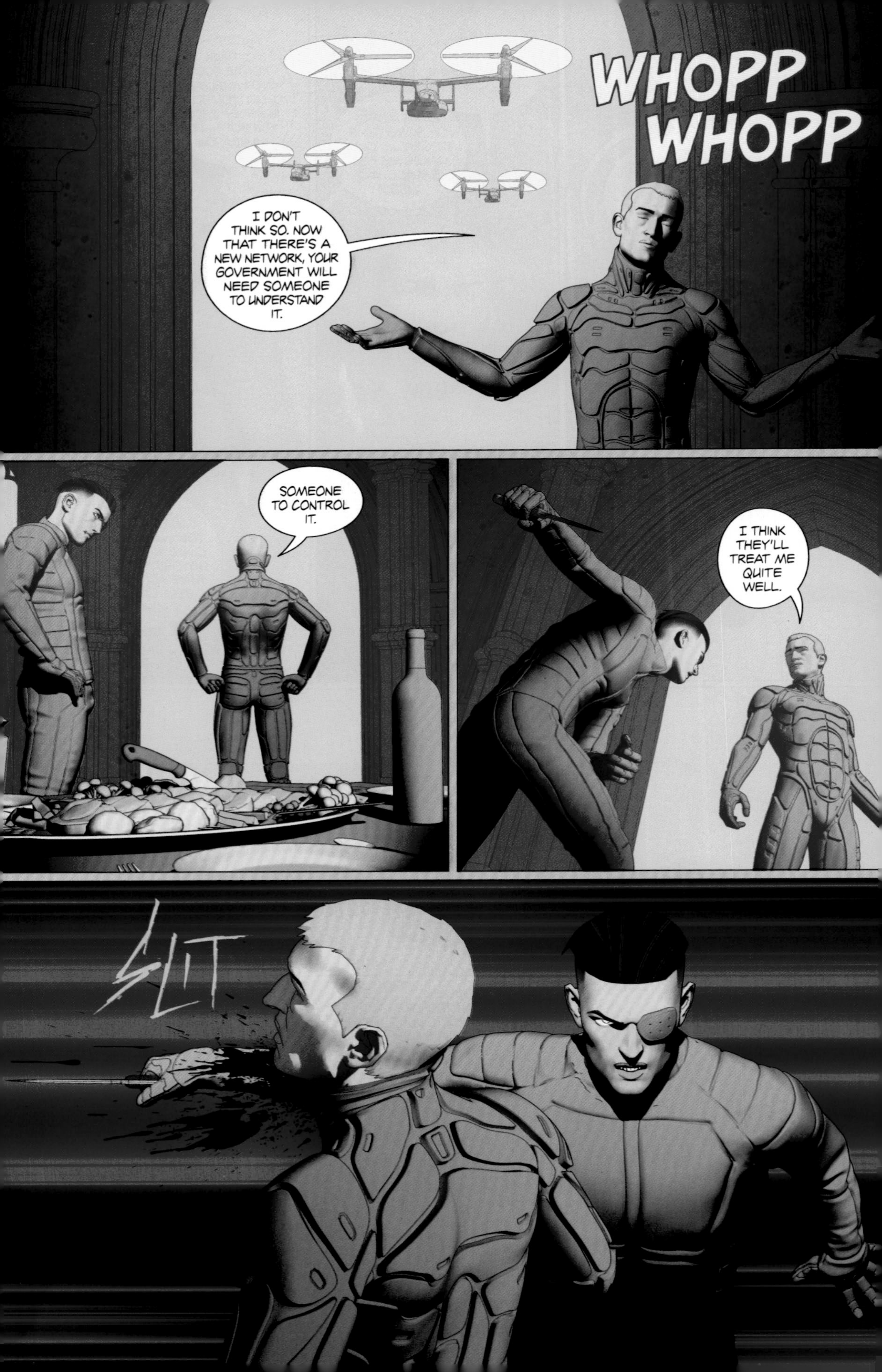
WHOPP WHOPP
I DON'T THINK SO. NOW THAT THERE'S A NEW NETWORK, YOUR GOVERNMENT WILL NEED SOMEONE TO UNDERSTAND IT.
SOMEONE TO CONTROL IT.
I THINK THEY'LL TREAT ME QUITE WELL.
SLIT

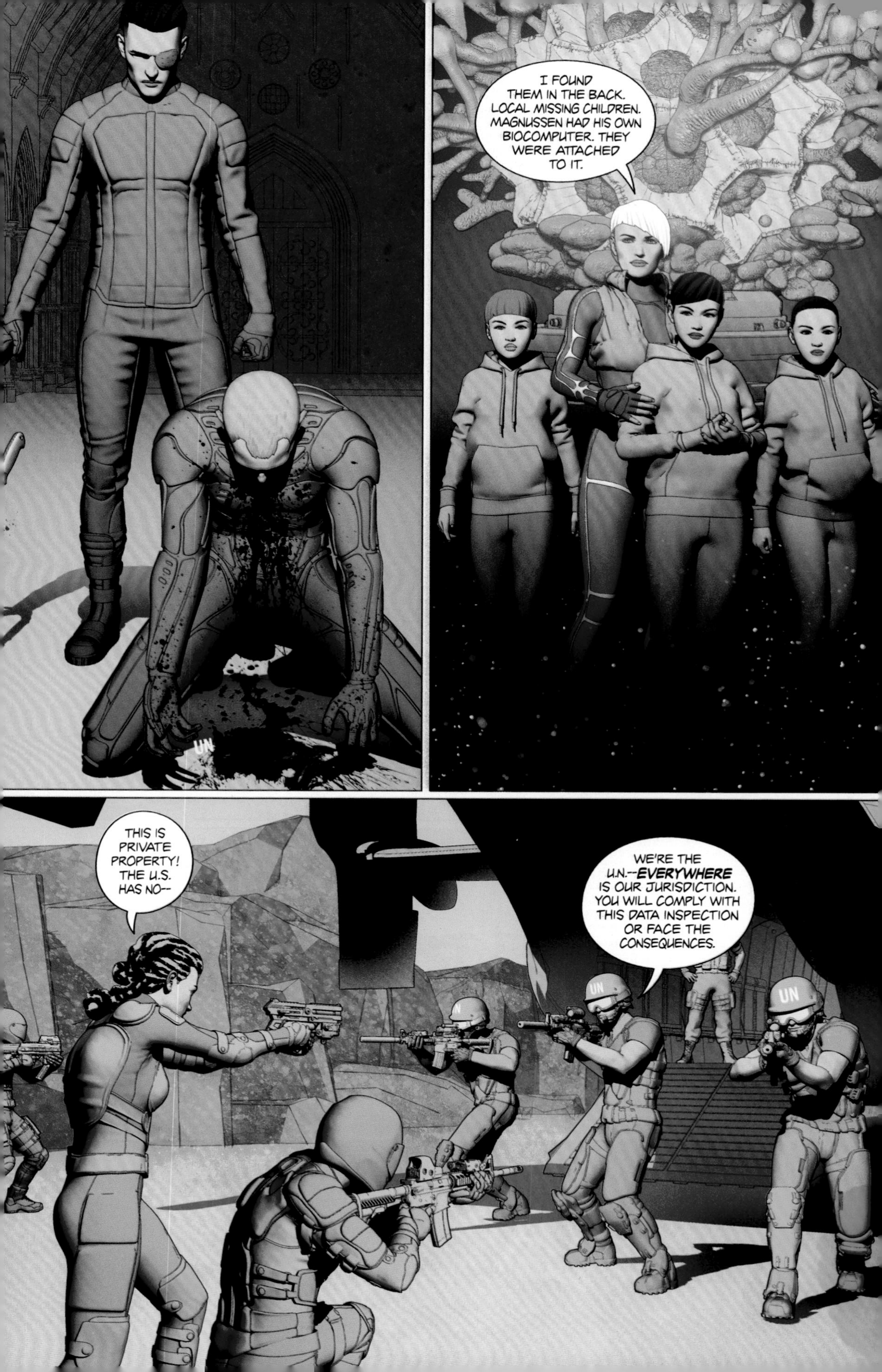
I FOUND THEM IN THE BACK. LOCAL MISSING CHILDREN. MAGNUSSEN HAD HIS OWN BIOCOMPUTER. THEY WERE ATTACHED TO IT.
THIS IS PRIVATE PROPERTY! THE U.S. HAS NO--
WE'RE THE U.N.--**EVERYWHERE** IS OUR JURISDICTION. YOU WILL COMPLY WITH THIS DATA INSPECTION OR FACE THE CONSEQUENCES.

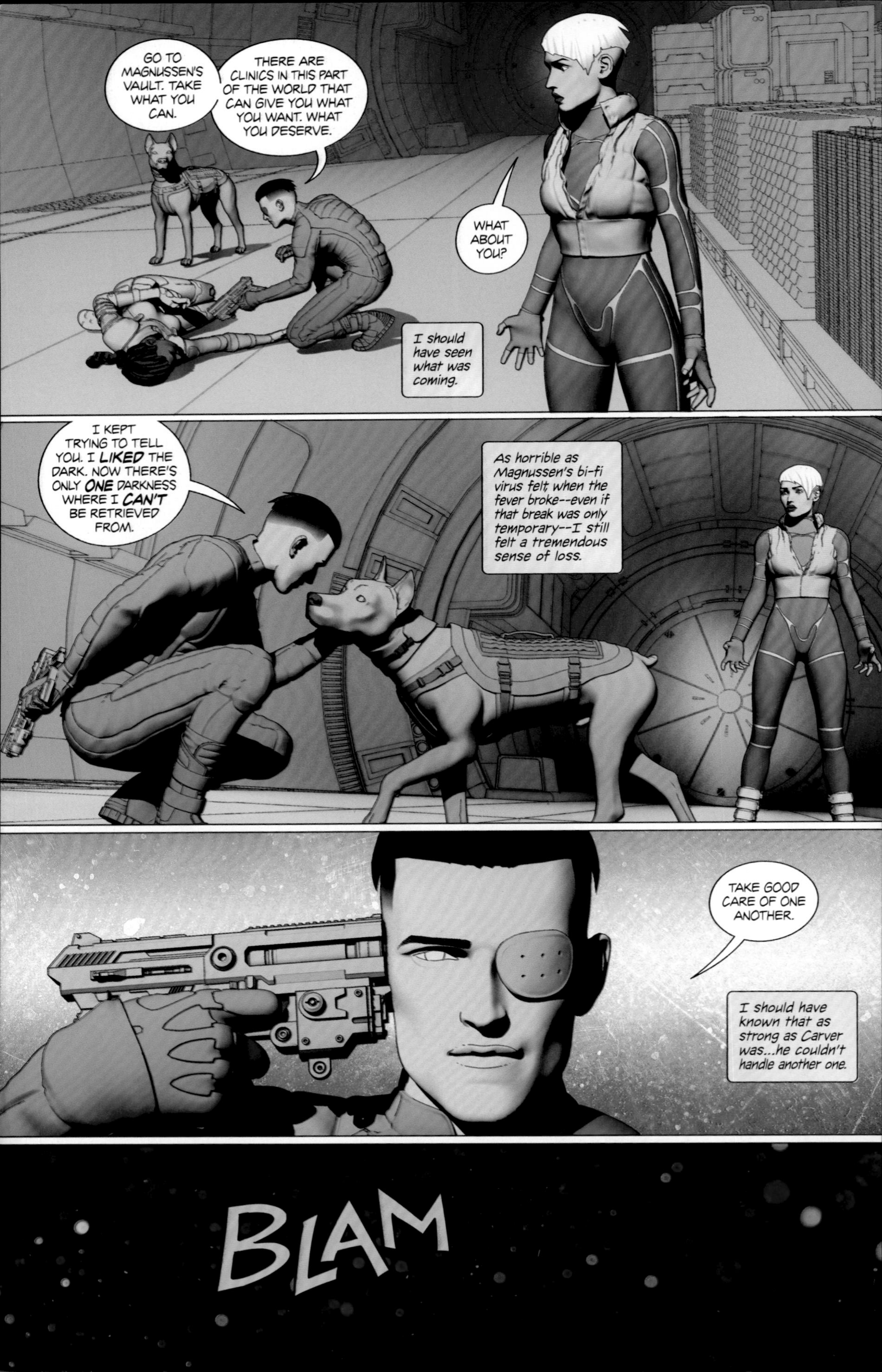
GO TO MAGNUSSEN'S VAULT. TAKE WHAT YOU CAN.
THERE ARE CLINICS IN THIS PART OF THE WORLD THAT CAN GIVE YOU WHAT YOU WANT. WHAT YOU DESERVE.
WHAT ABOUT YOU?
I should have seen what was coming.
I KEPT TRYING TO TELL YOU. I LIKED THE DARK. NOW THERE'S ONLY ONE DARKNESS WHERE I CAN'T BE RETRIEVED FROM.
As horrible as Magnussen's bi-fi virus felt, when the fever broke--even if that break was only temporary--I still felt a tremendous sense of loss.
TAKE GOOD CARE OF ONE ANOTHER.
I should have known that as strong as Carver was...he couldn't handle another one.
BLAM

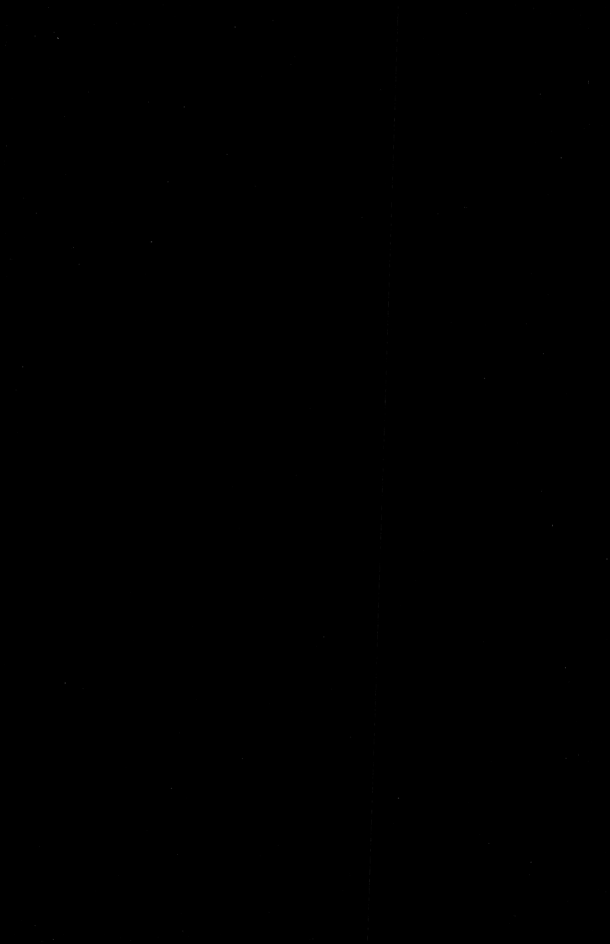

ONE YEAR LATER.

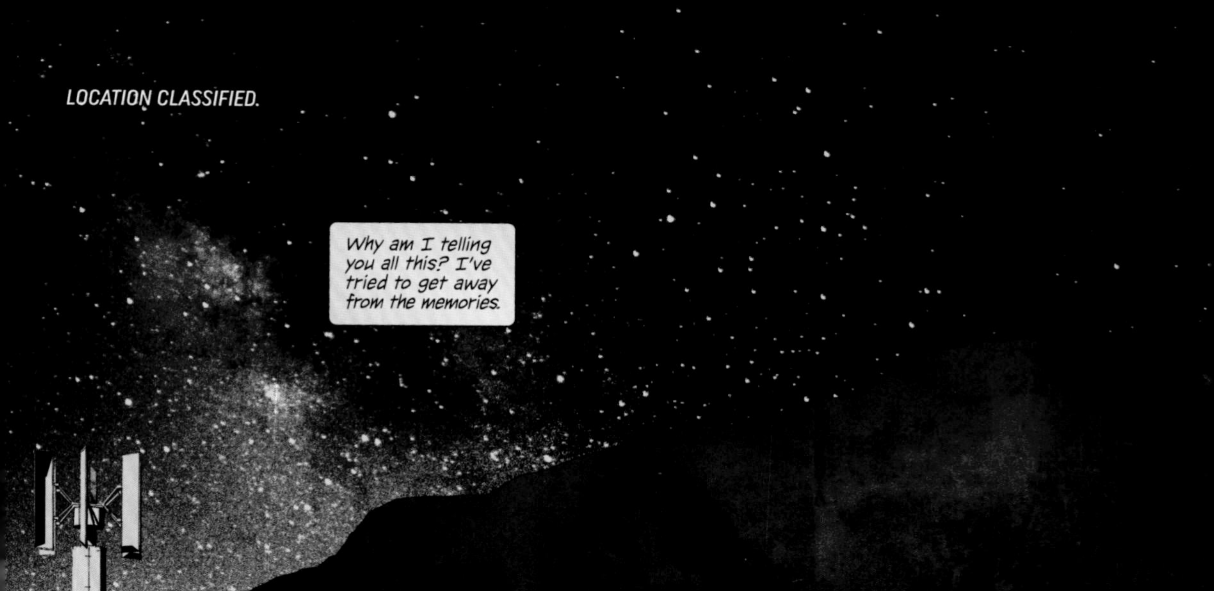
LOCATION CLASSIFIED.
Why am I telling you all this? I've tried to get away from the memories.

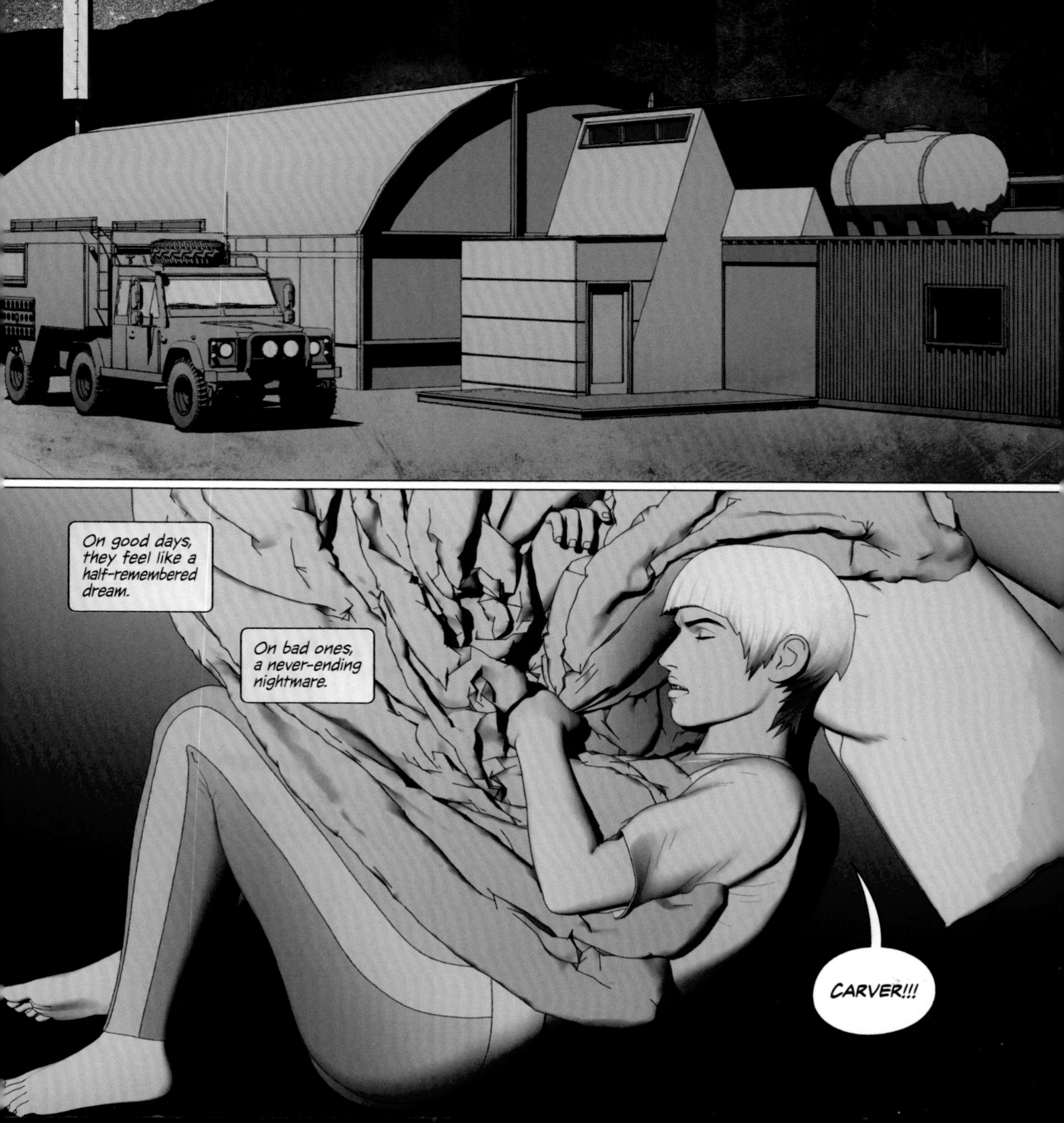
On good days, they feel like a half-remembered dream.
On bad ones, a never-ending nightmare.
CARVER!!!

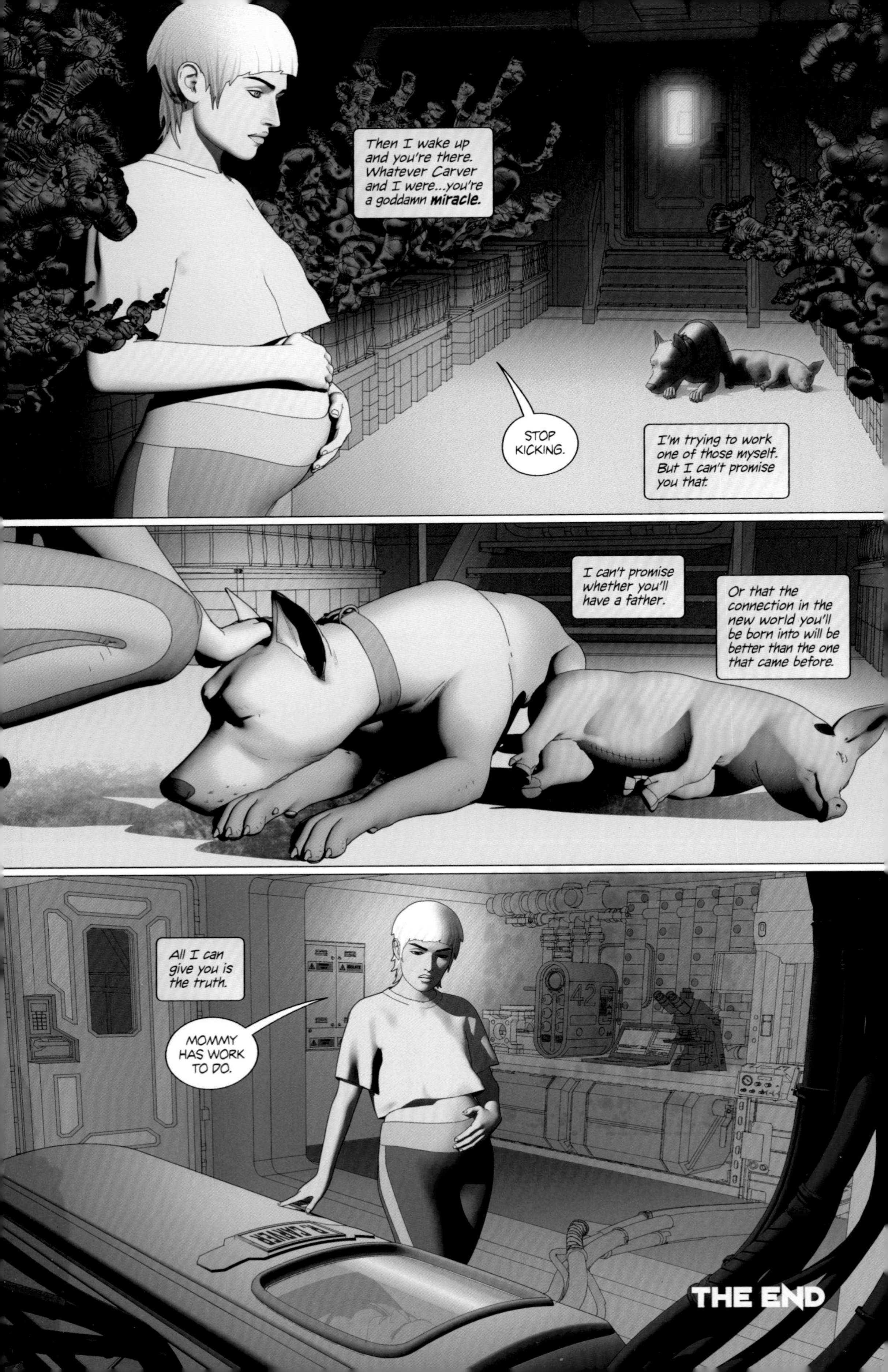
Then I wake up and you're there. Whatever Carver and I were...you're a goddamn **miracle.**
STOP KICKING.
I'm trying to work one of those myself. But I can't promise you that.
I can't promise whether you'll have a father.
Or that the connection in the new world you'll be born into will be better than the one that came before.
All I can give you is the truth.
MOMMY HAS WORK TO DO.
THE END